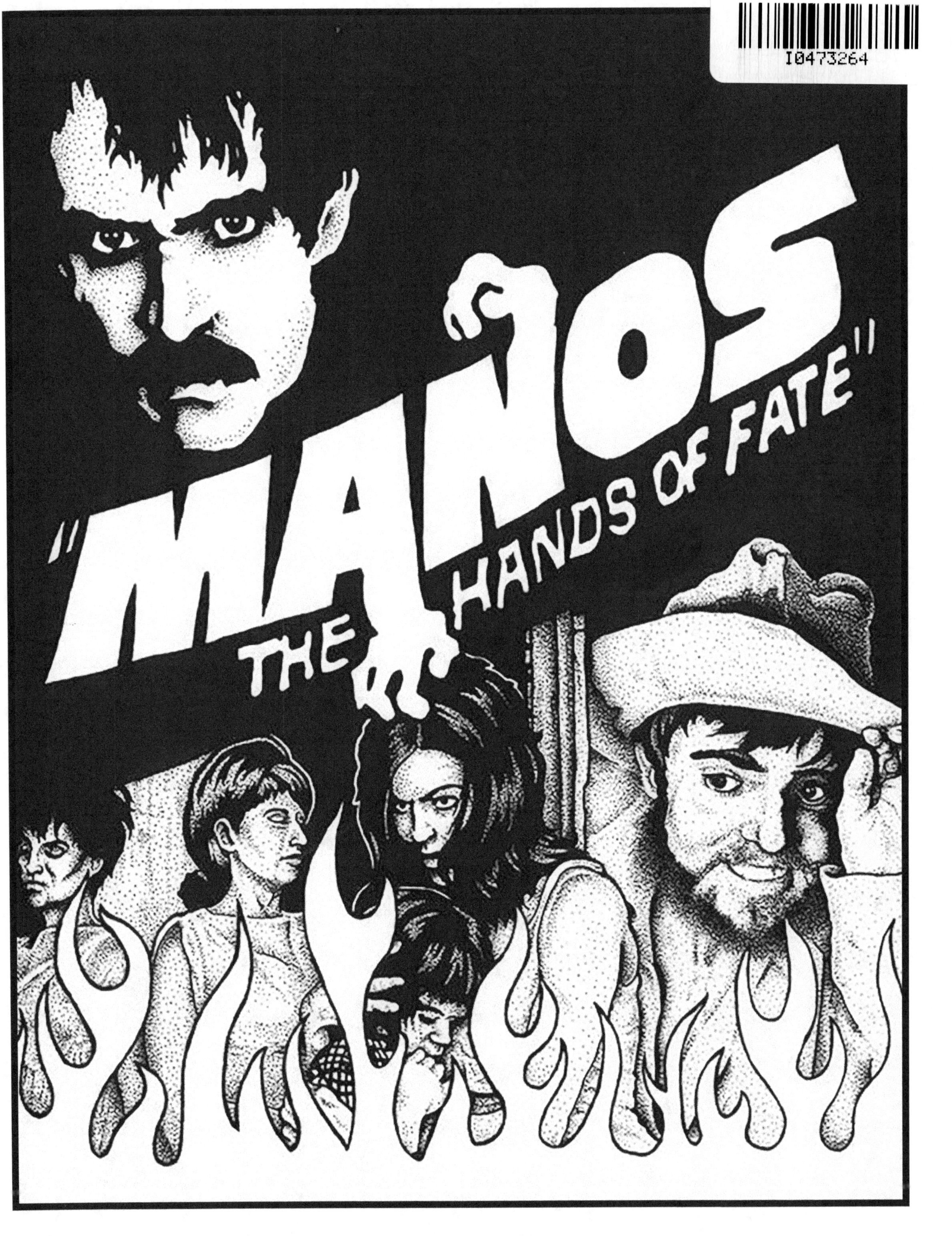

MANOS THE HANDS OF FATE: THE COLORING BOOK

HORRID COLORING BOOKS VOL 3

WRITTEN AND COMPILED BY
JORDAN R. COLTON

COVER ART BY
PATRICK KENDALL

Copyright © 2016 Apparition Studios
All rights reserved.
ISBN: 0692667113
ISBN-13: 978-0692667118

DEDICATION

THIS IS DEDICATED TO ALL OF THE GENIUSES AT MYSTERY SCIENCE THEATER 3000! THANK YOU FOR TEACHING US TO FIND THE GOOD IN THE VERY, VERY, VERY, VERY BAD!

```
D  N  E  S  G  D  O  H  L  E  O  J  F  T  H
Y  Q  T  P  H  U  A  T  G  T  W  R  K  E  A
Z  H  A  R  V  G  L  V  F  Z  A  Z  A  B  R
G  H  P  Y  A  X  U  J  Y  N  L  V  Q  R  O
C  K  T  R  Q  C  A  D  K  K  I  D  G  O  L
T  N  N  U  U  M  E  C  L  O  M  G  W  C  D
G  J  S  H  Q  M  O  B  P  G  H  F  O  L  P
O  F  B  C  T  N  N  J  E  X  H  P  W  L  W
J  A  C  L  N  W  I  I  D  A  V  I  L  I  A
Q  Y  I  I  Q  S  Z  O  V  W  U  F  Y  B  R
M  Z  F  O  G  C  Y  P  S  E  E  L  L  B  R
U  F  S  S  Y  B  I  T  I  U  K  N  I  I  E
M  I  C  H  A  E  L  N  E  L  S  O  N  E  N
L  B  K  Y  U  T  M  K  S  H  Z  Y  J  B  U
Y  O  J  O  E  S  I  N  X  Z  I  I  F  F  Q
```

BILL CORBET   FRANK CONNIFF   MICHAEL NELSON
JOEL HODGSEN   KEVIN MURPHY   HAROLD WARREN
TRACE BEAULIEU

JORDAN COLTON PRESENTS

A HORRID COLORING BOOK

"MANOS"

The Hands of Fate

Cast of Characters Scramble
Unscramble the cast and their characters!

1. moT meNyna Teh taMesr

   _____

2. hJon eRyosldn oorTg

   _____

3. Daein odnleAs reMartga

   _____

4. Hardlo P. Waernr Maeilch

   _____

5. cayJke nmaeNy yebbD

   _____

6. Staepnieh ilNenso ifeW

   _____

7. ehryrS Pcoortr ifeW

   _____

8. iobnR Redd feWi

   _____

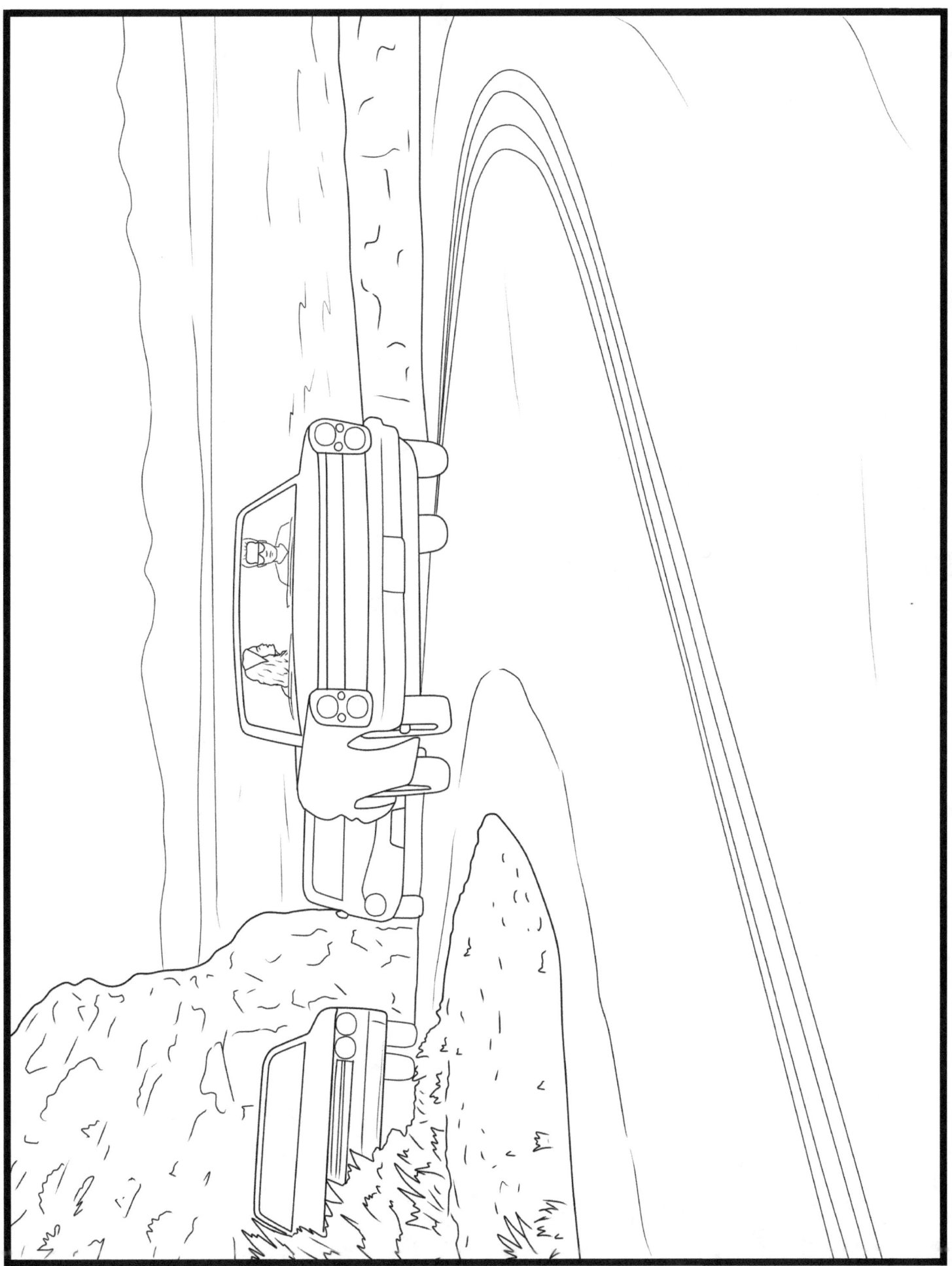

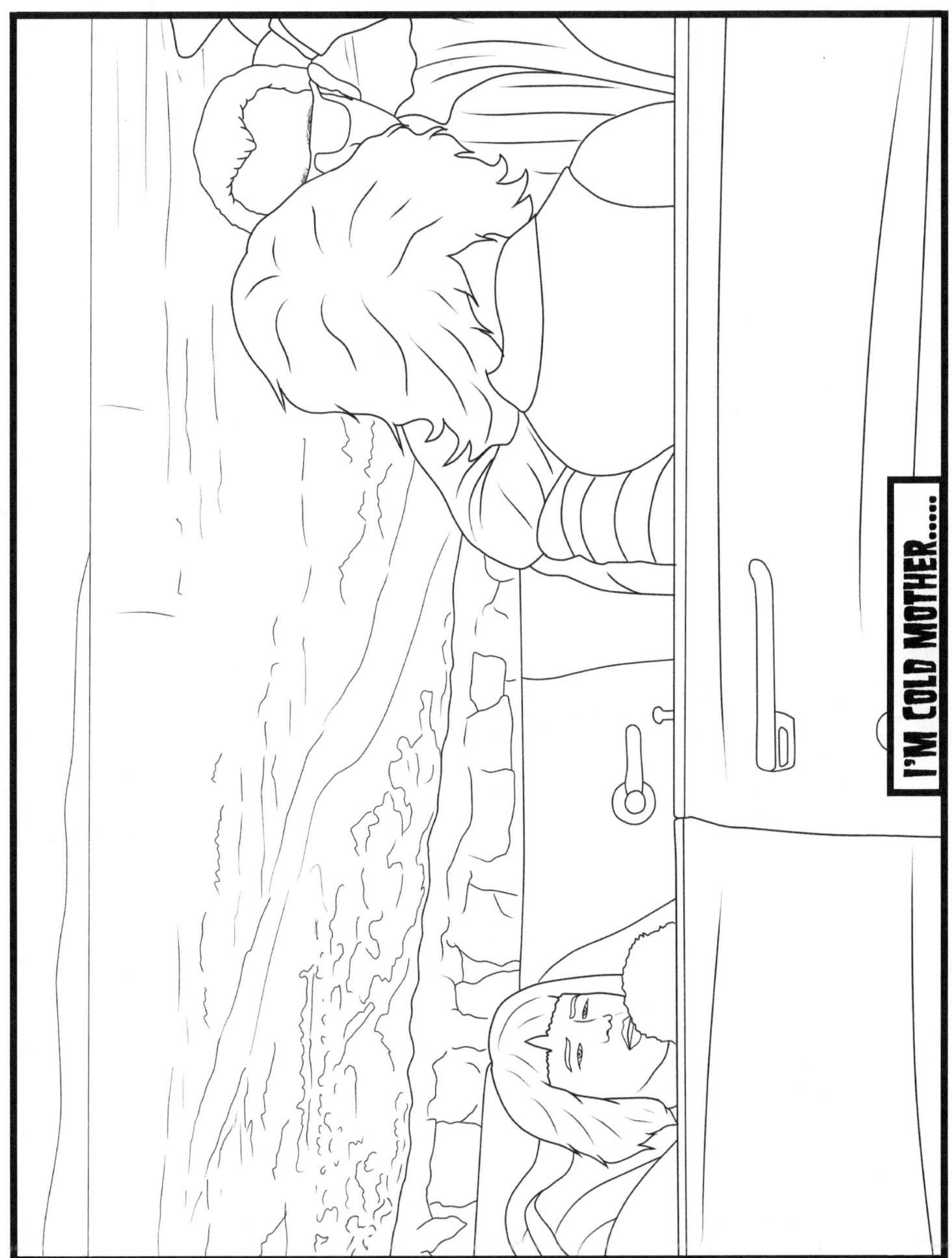

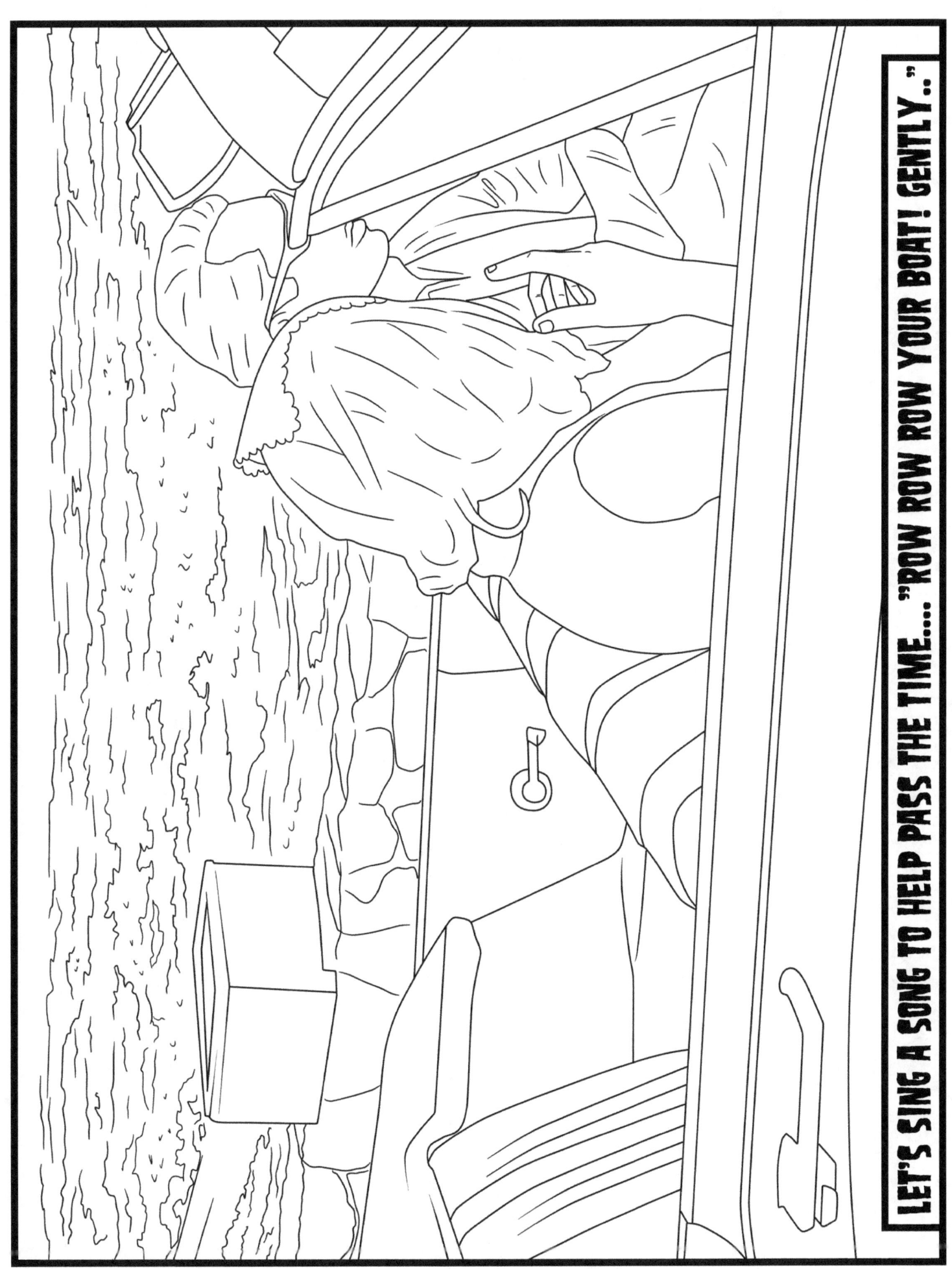

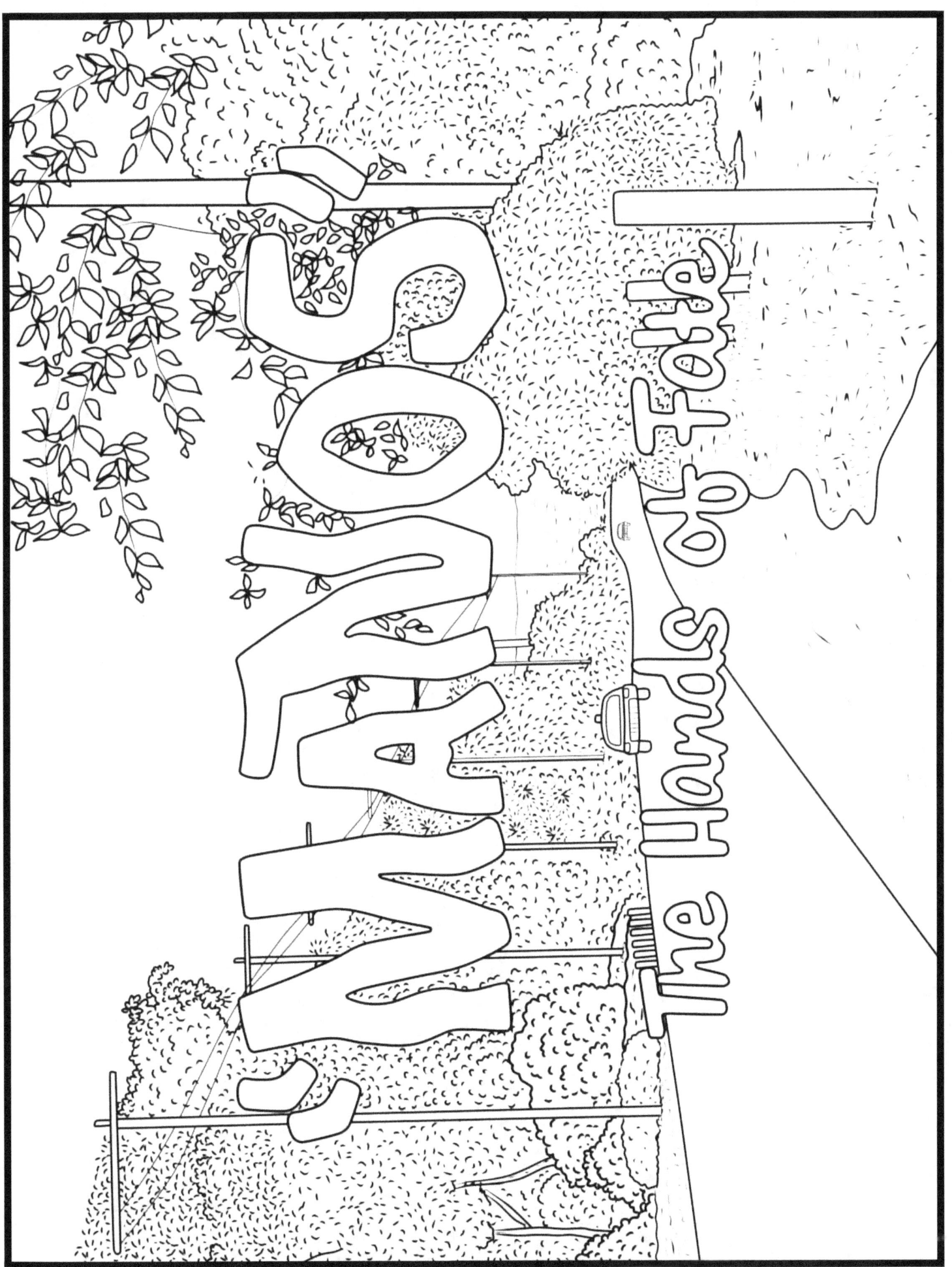

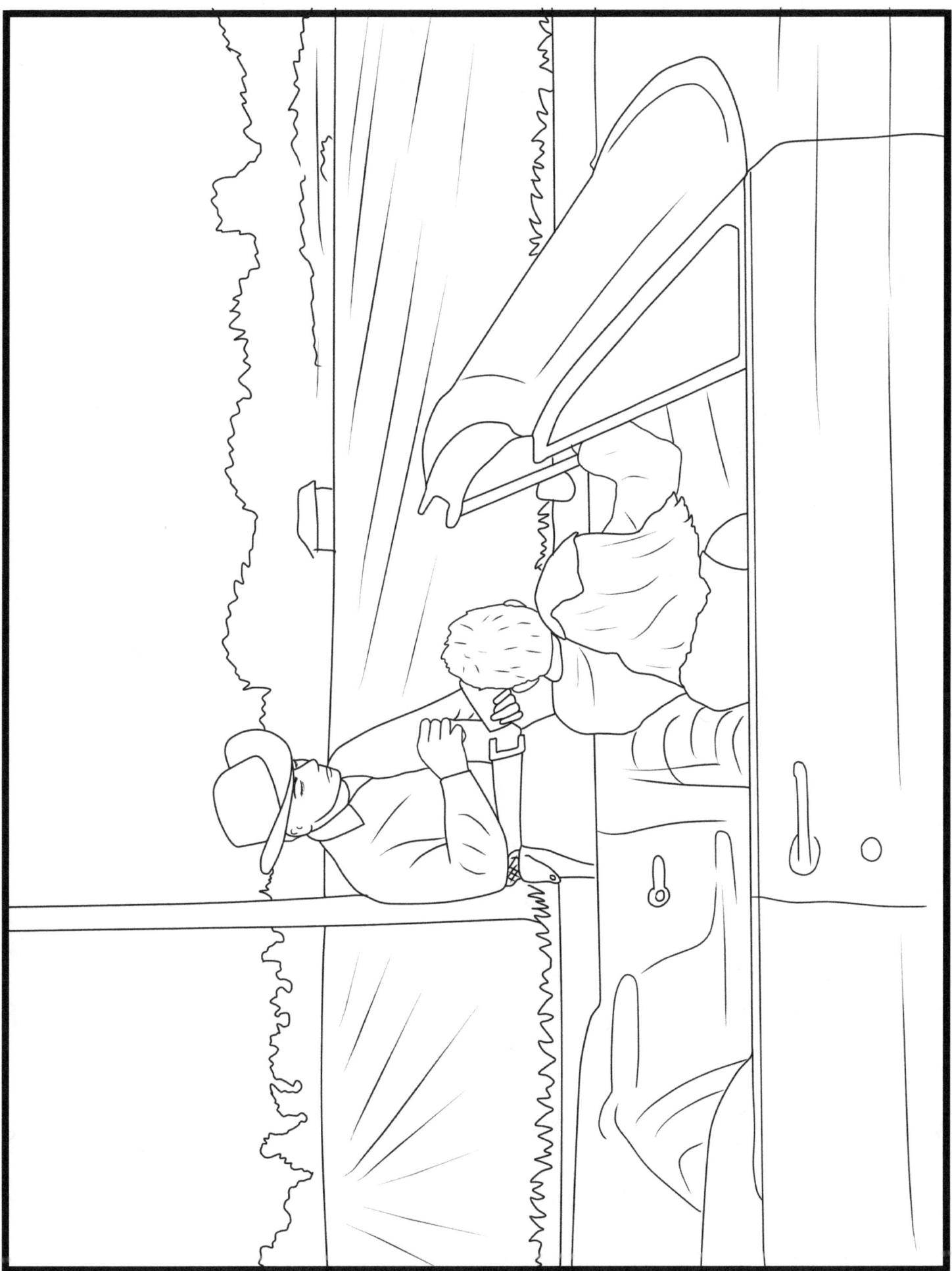

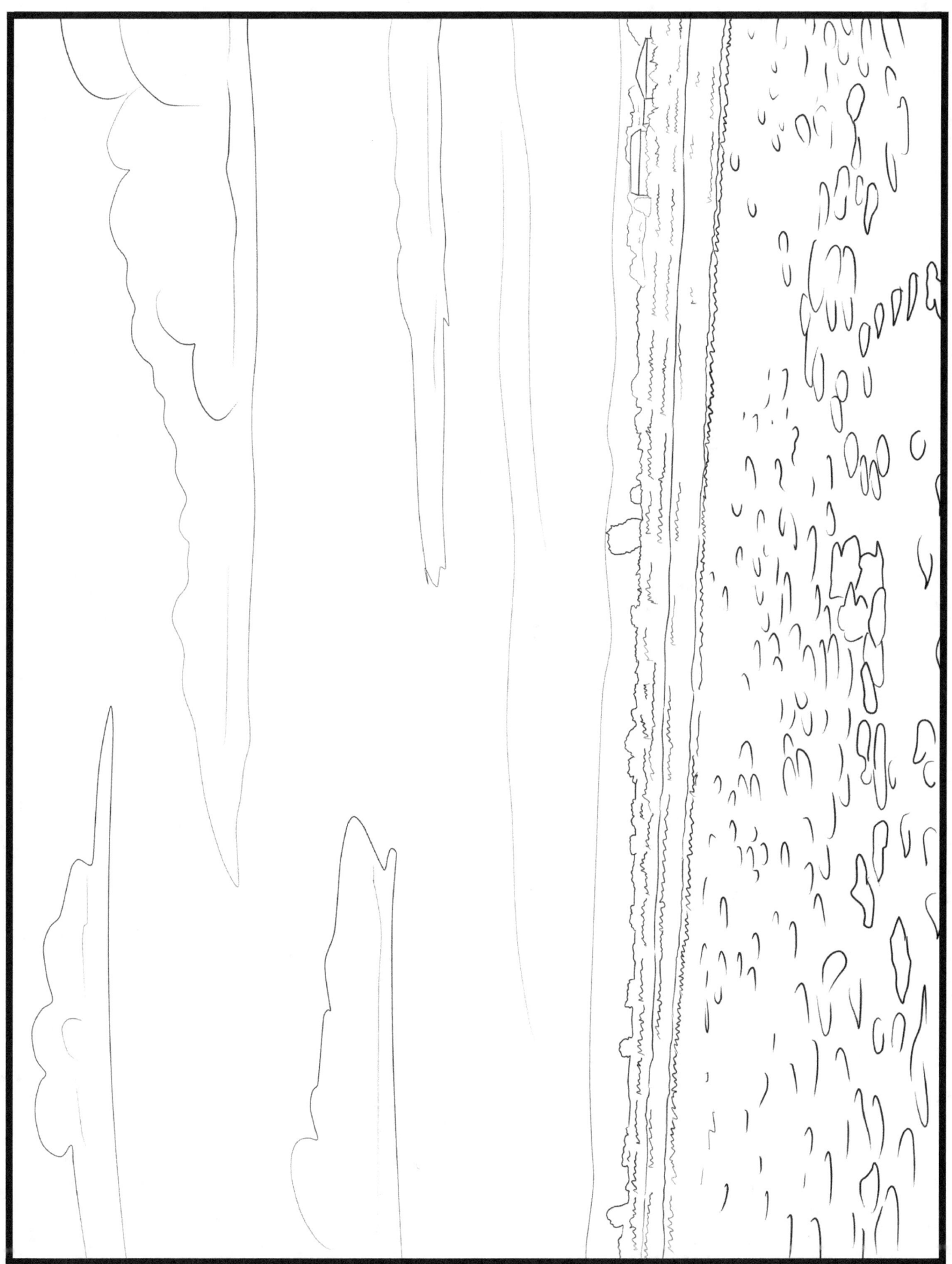

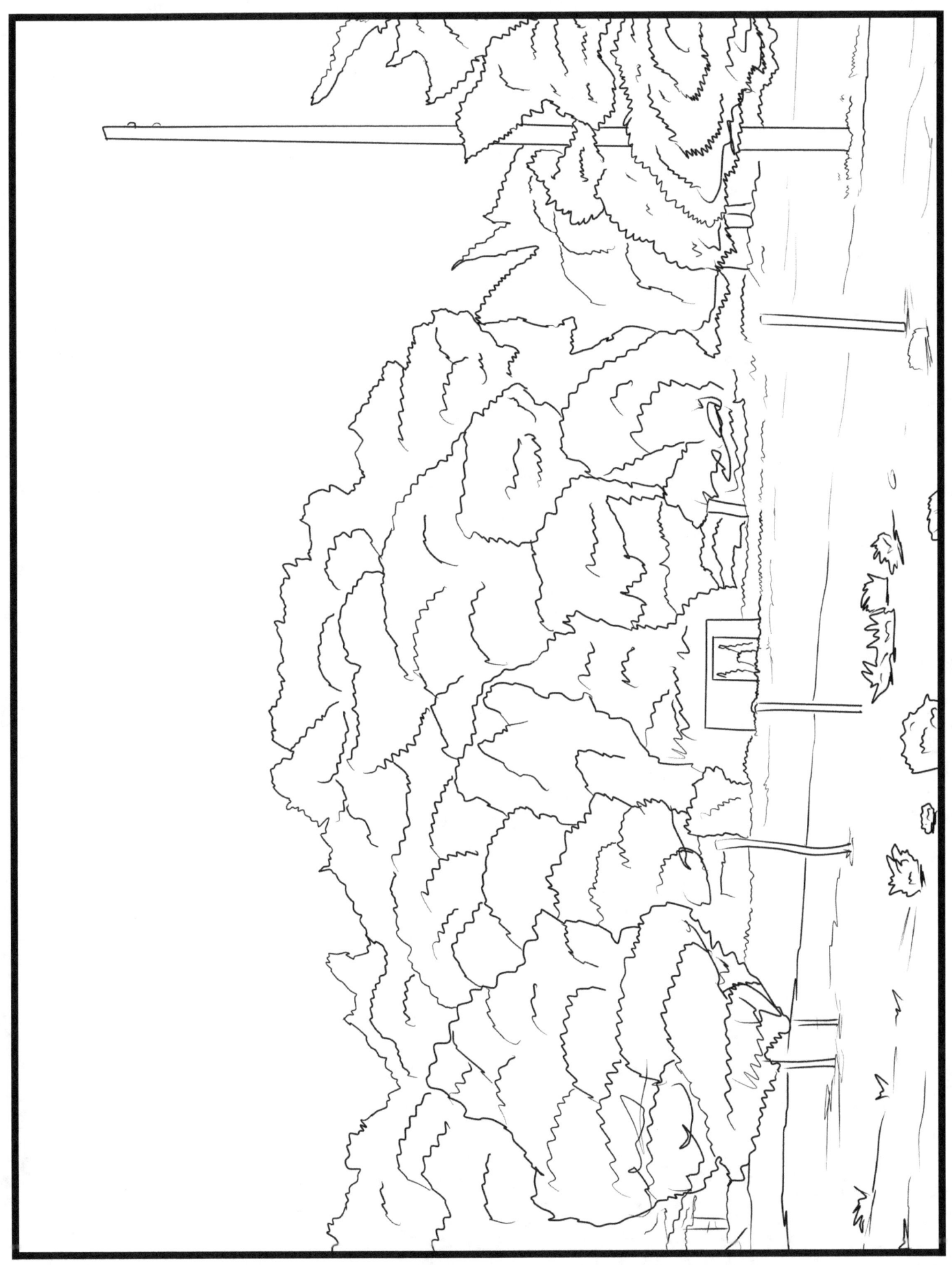

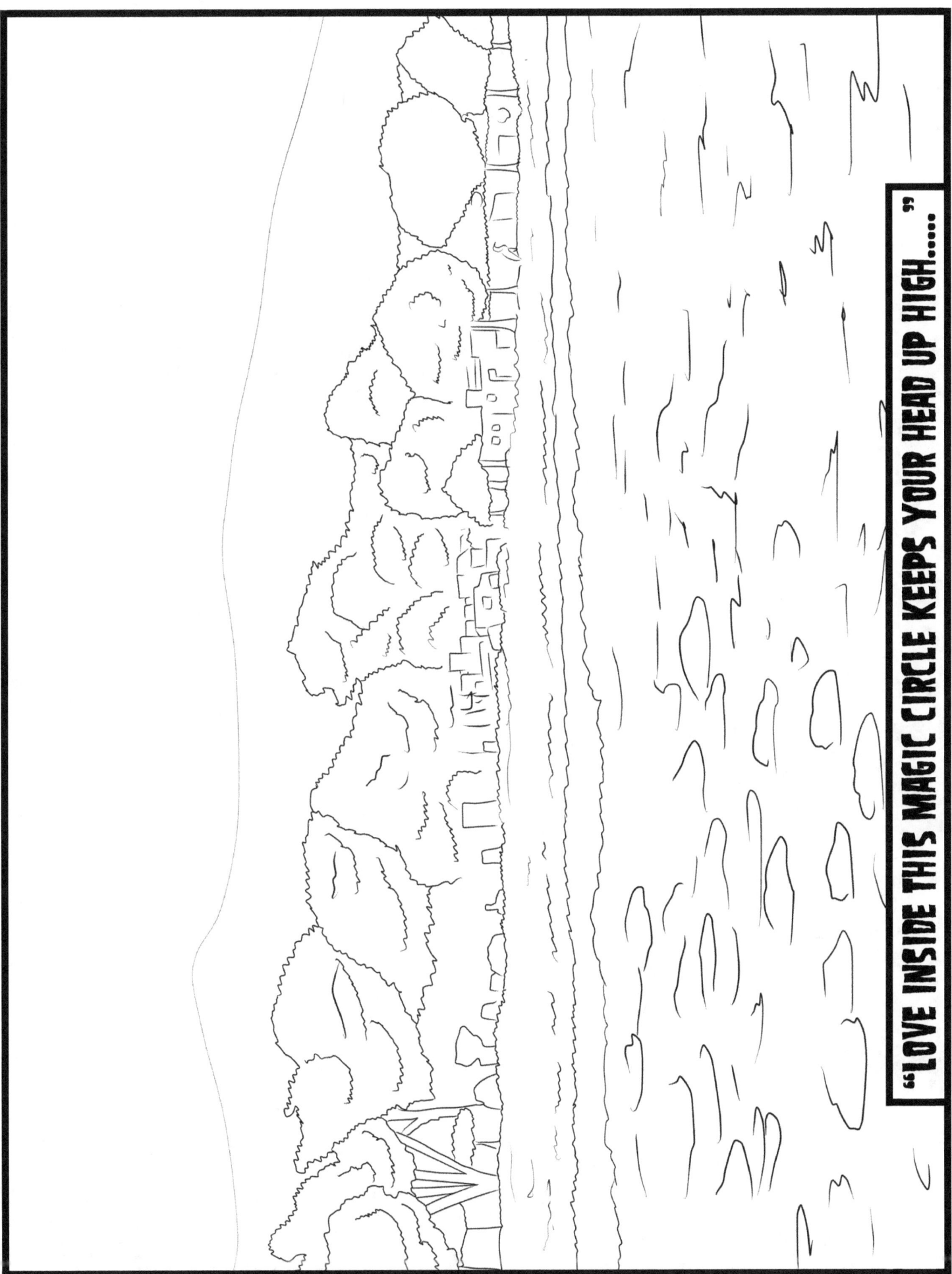

"LOVE INSIDE THIS MAGIC CIRCLE KEEPS YOUR HEAD UP HIGH....."

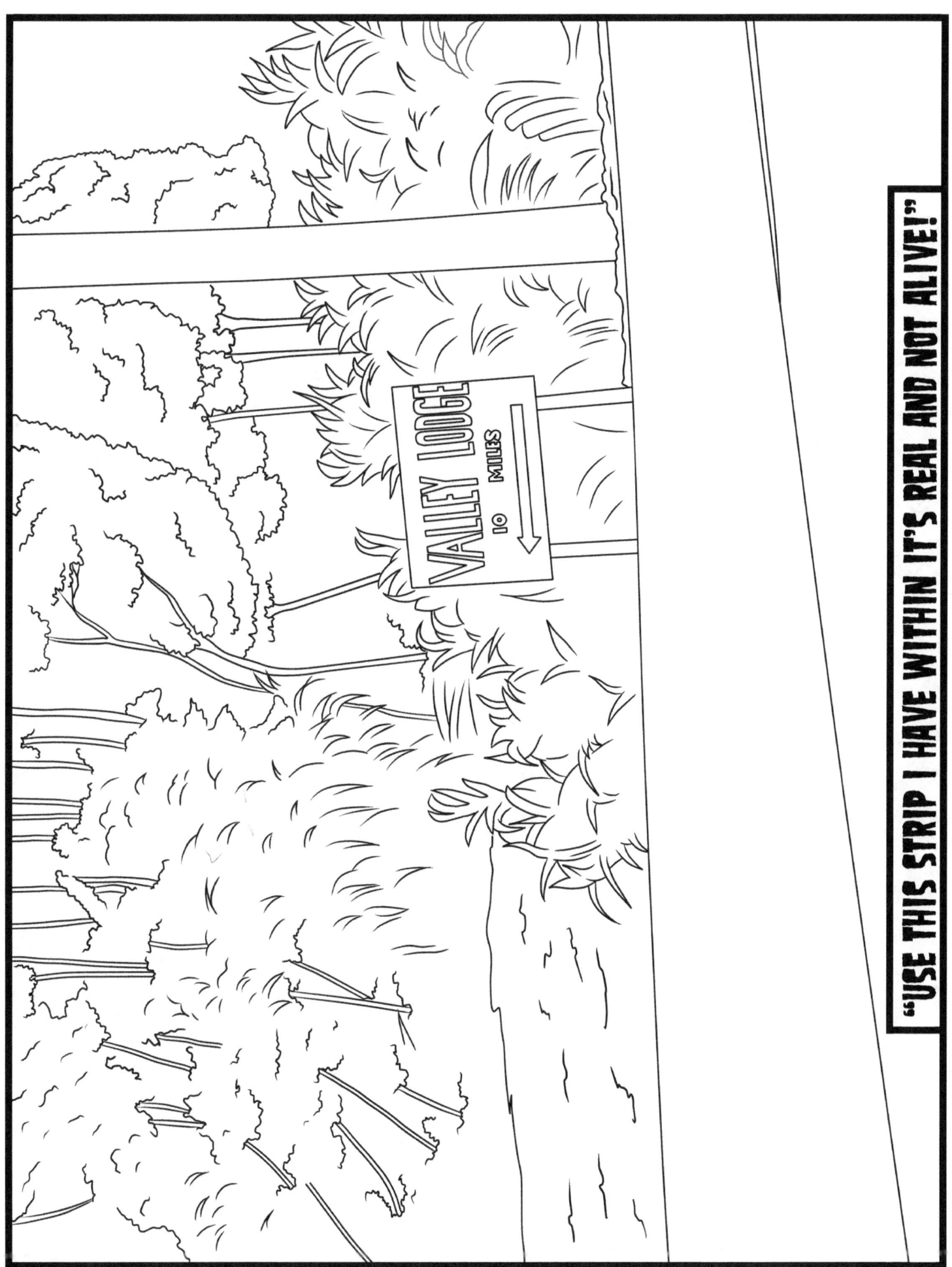

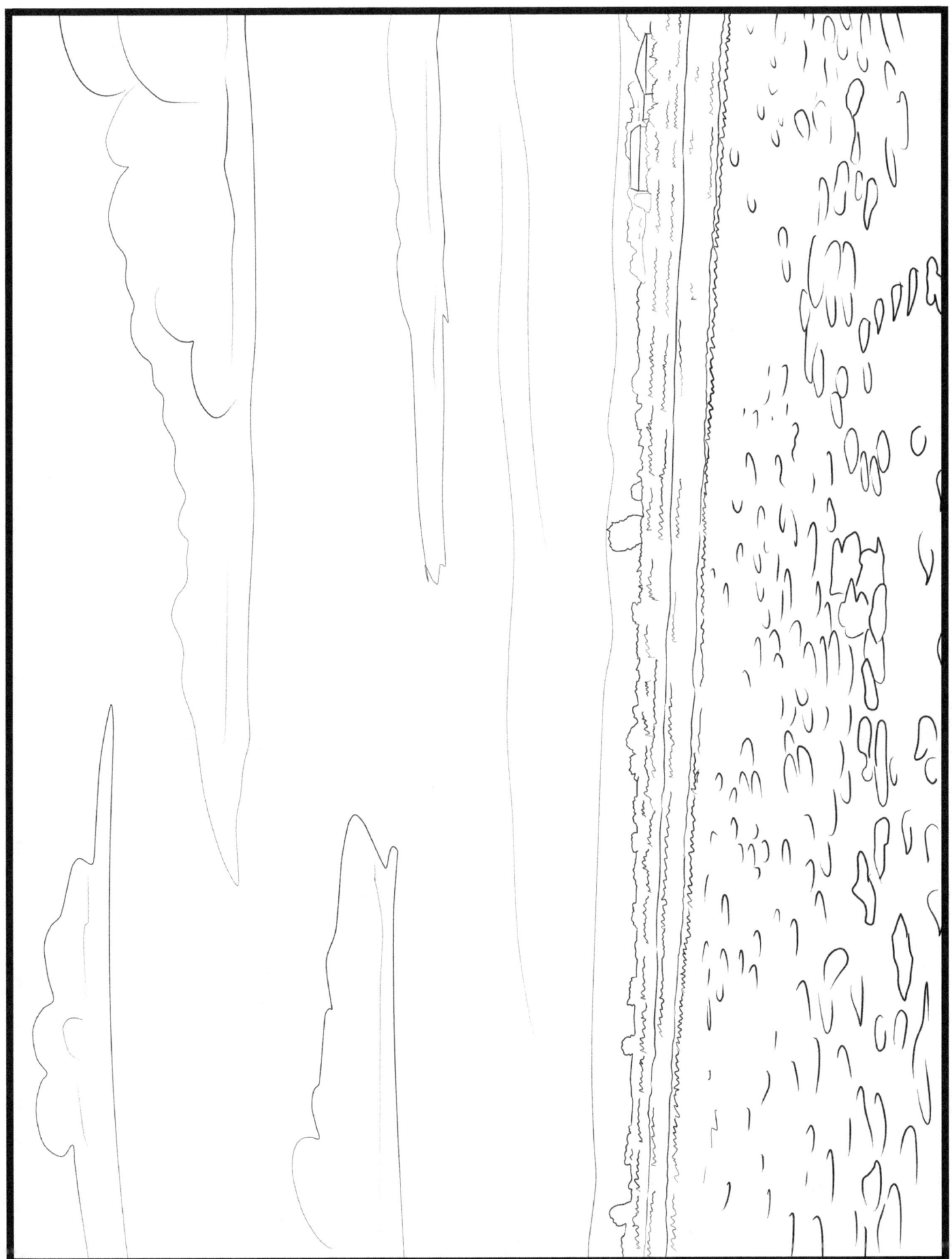

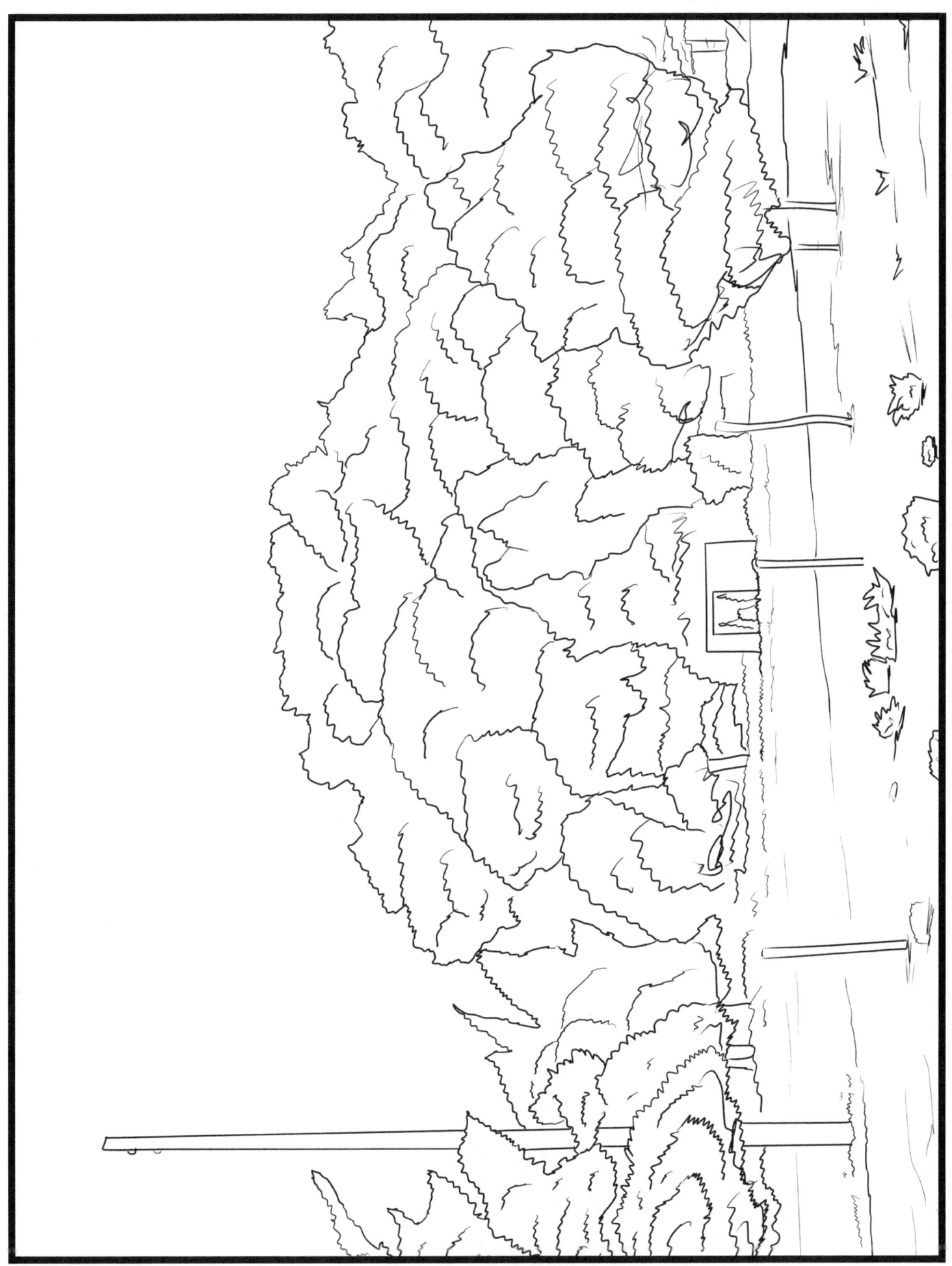

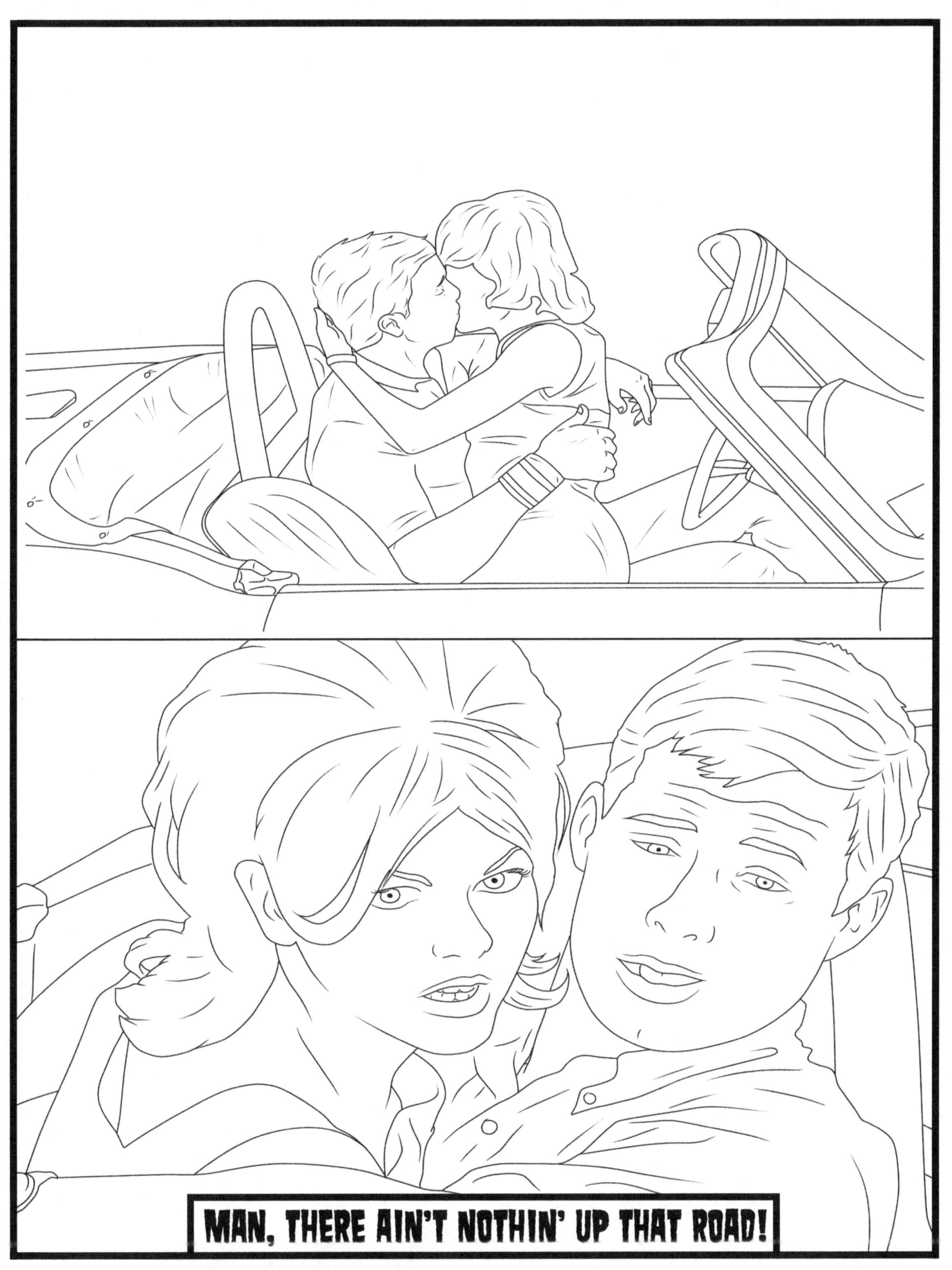

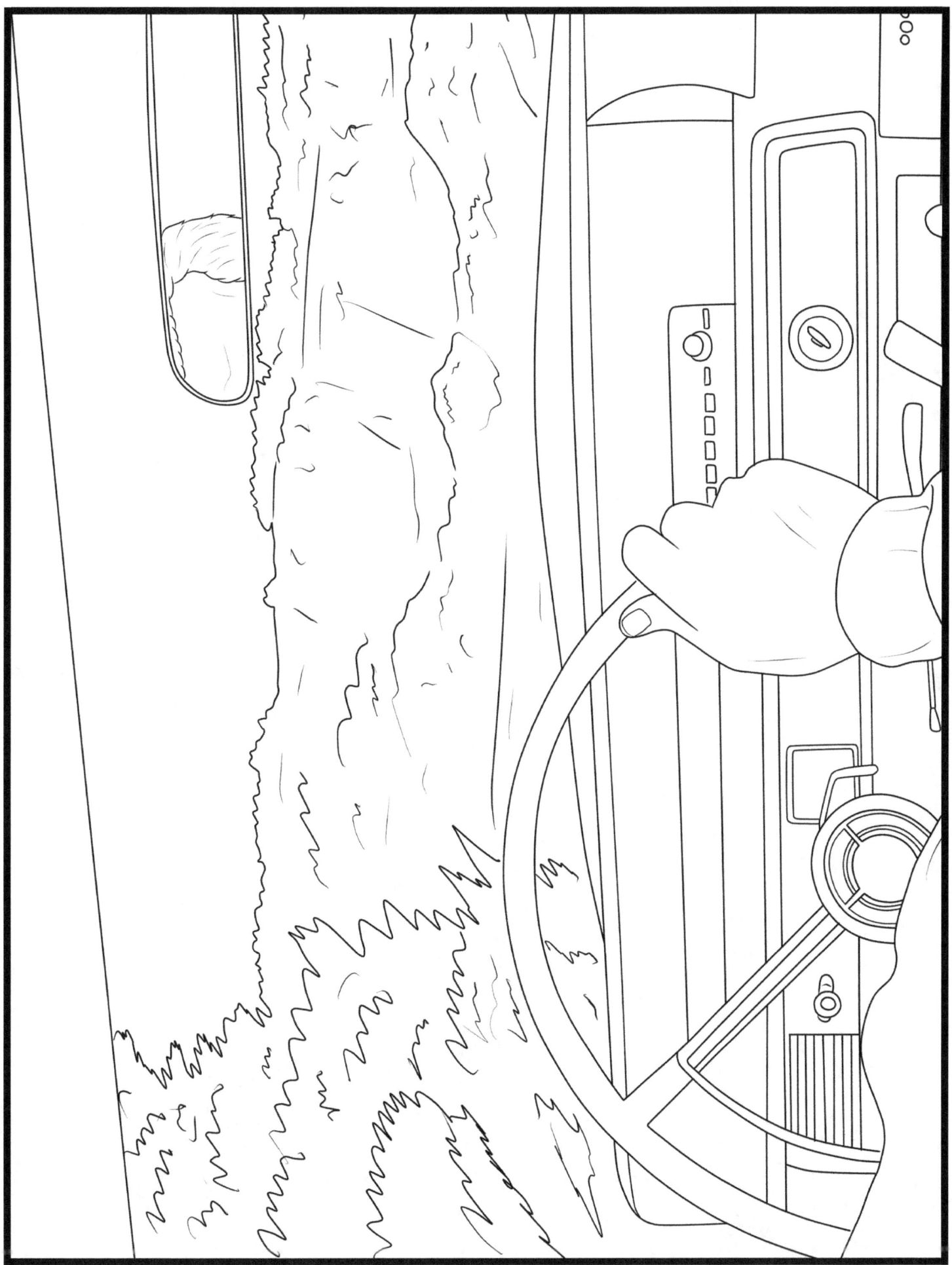

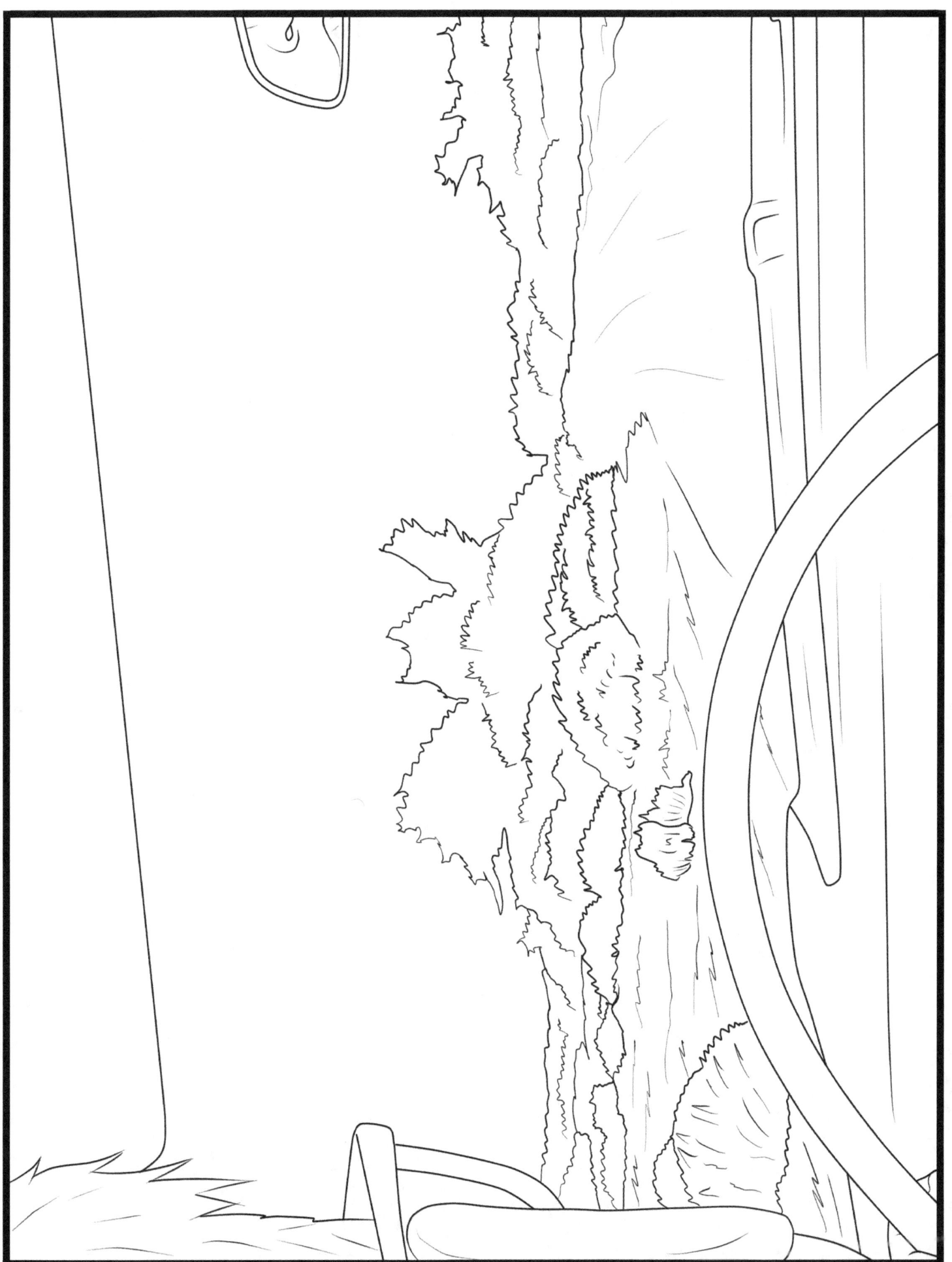

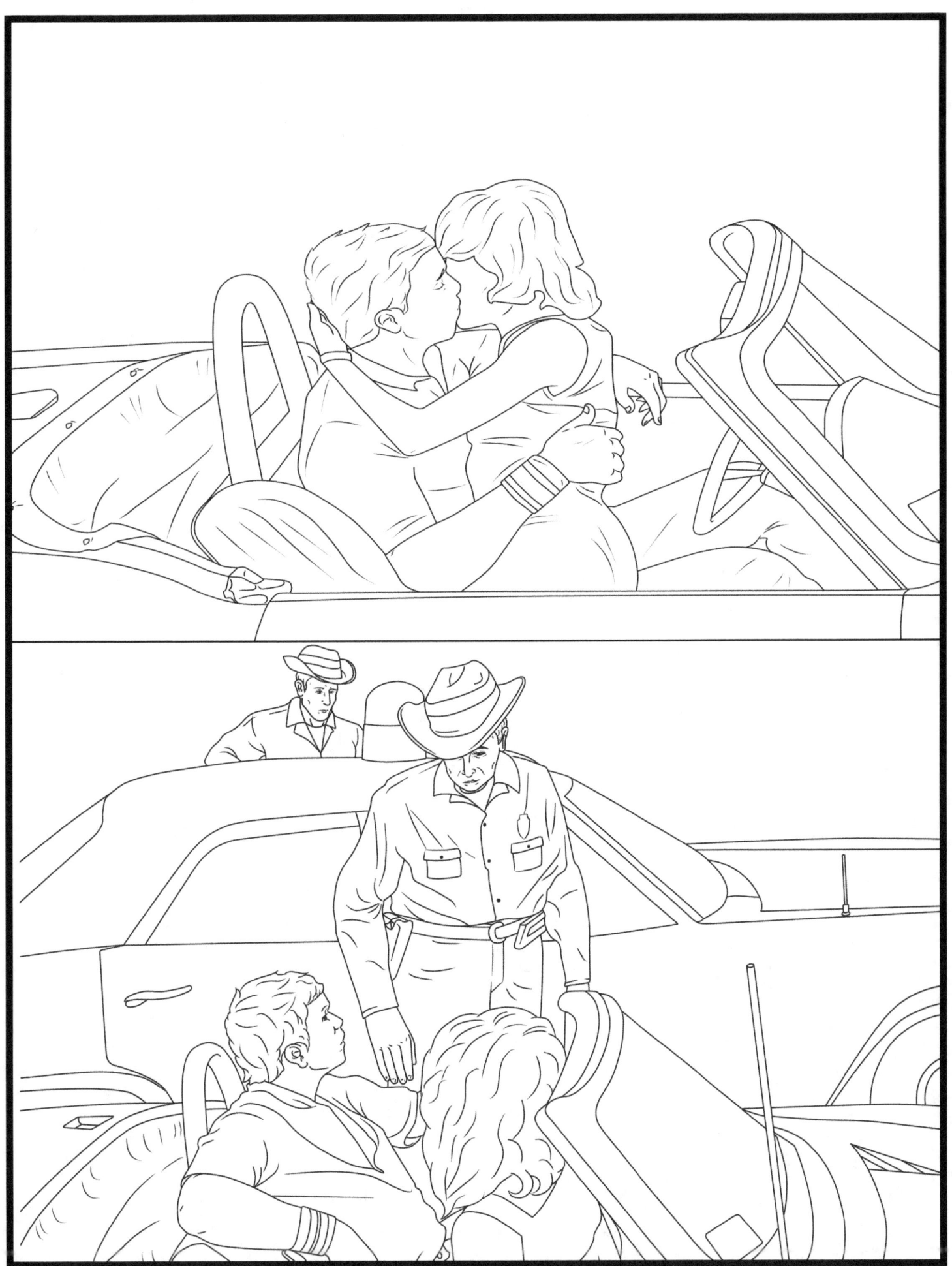

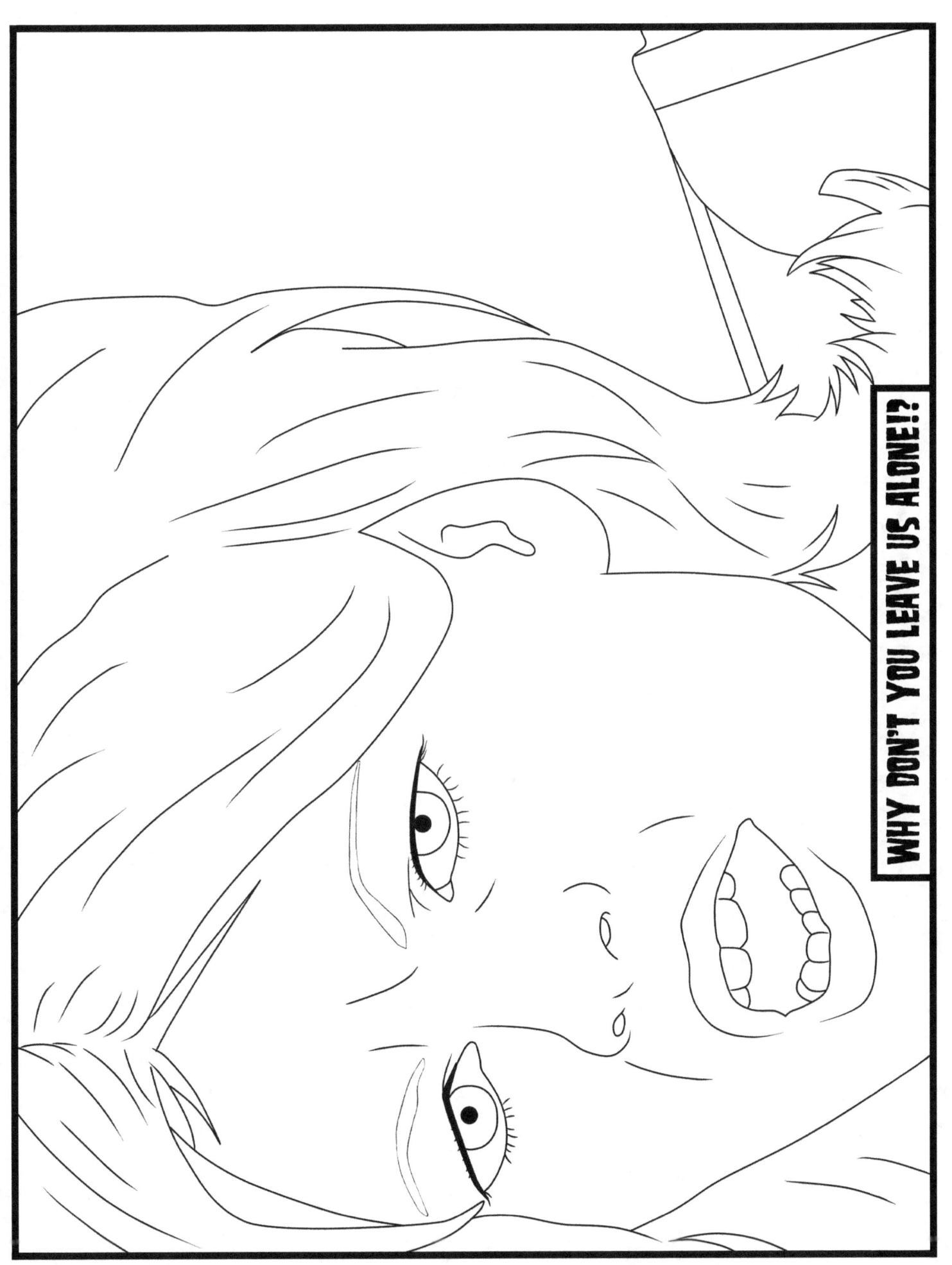

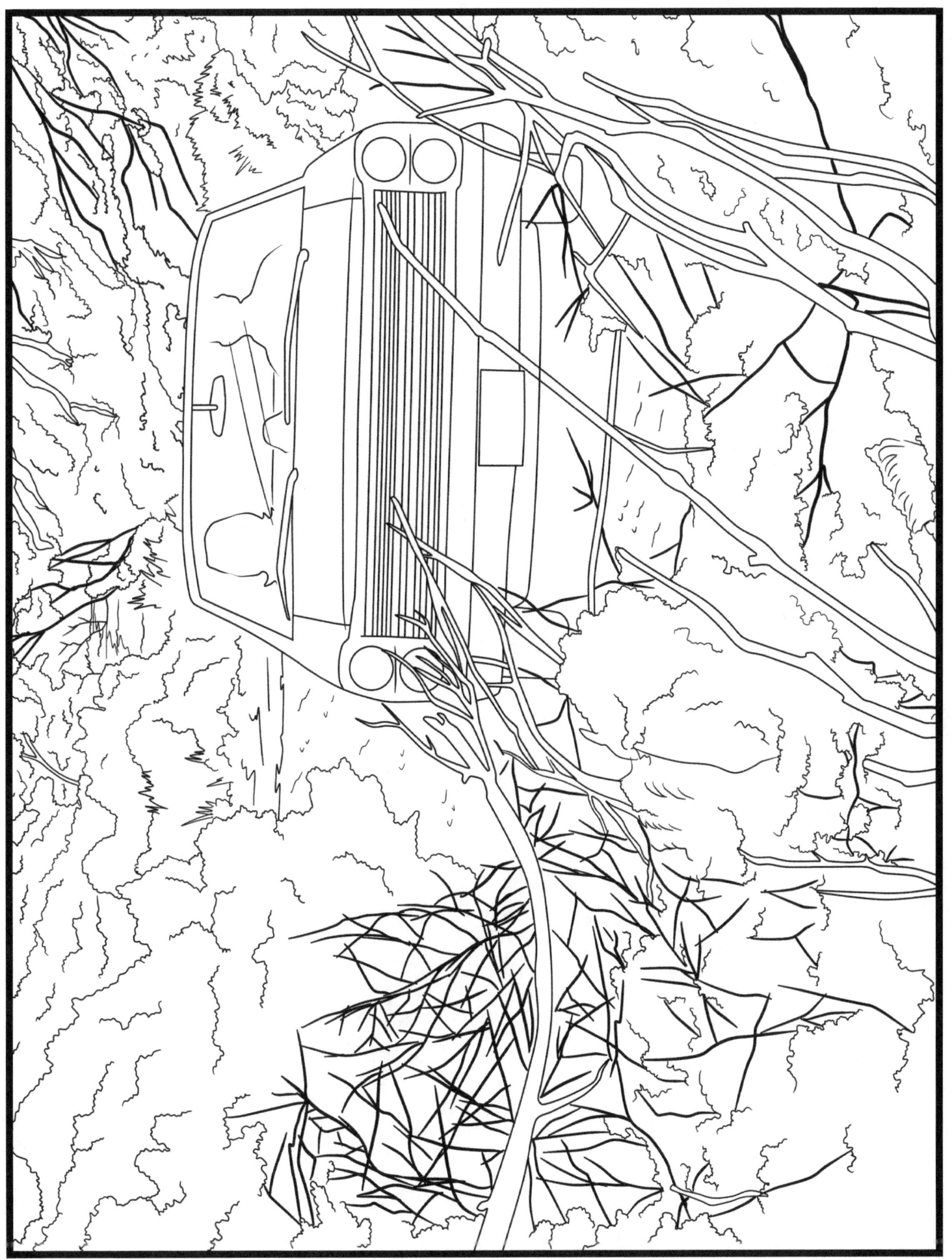

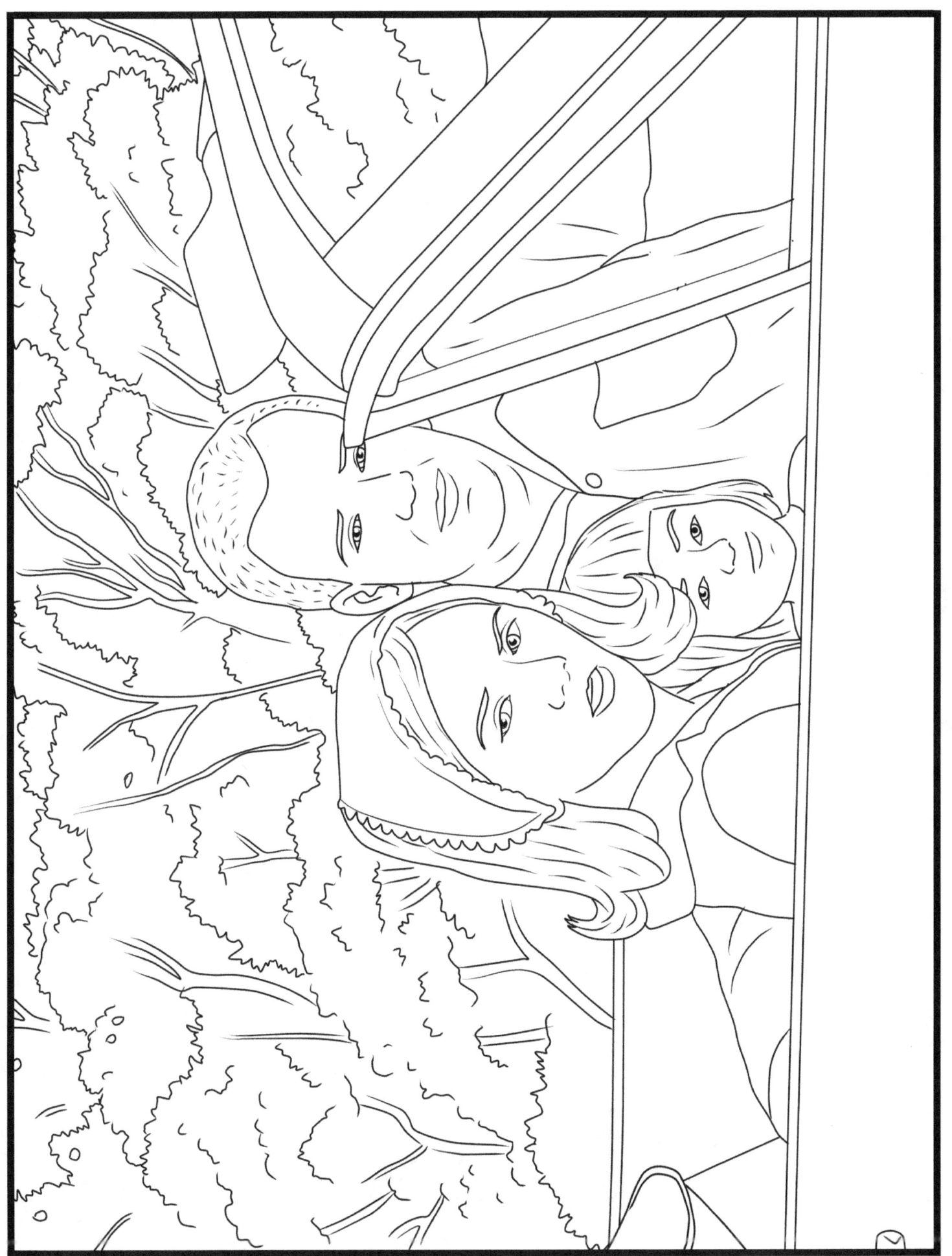

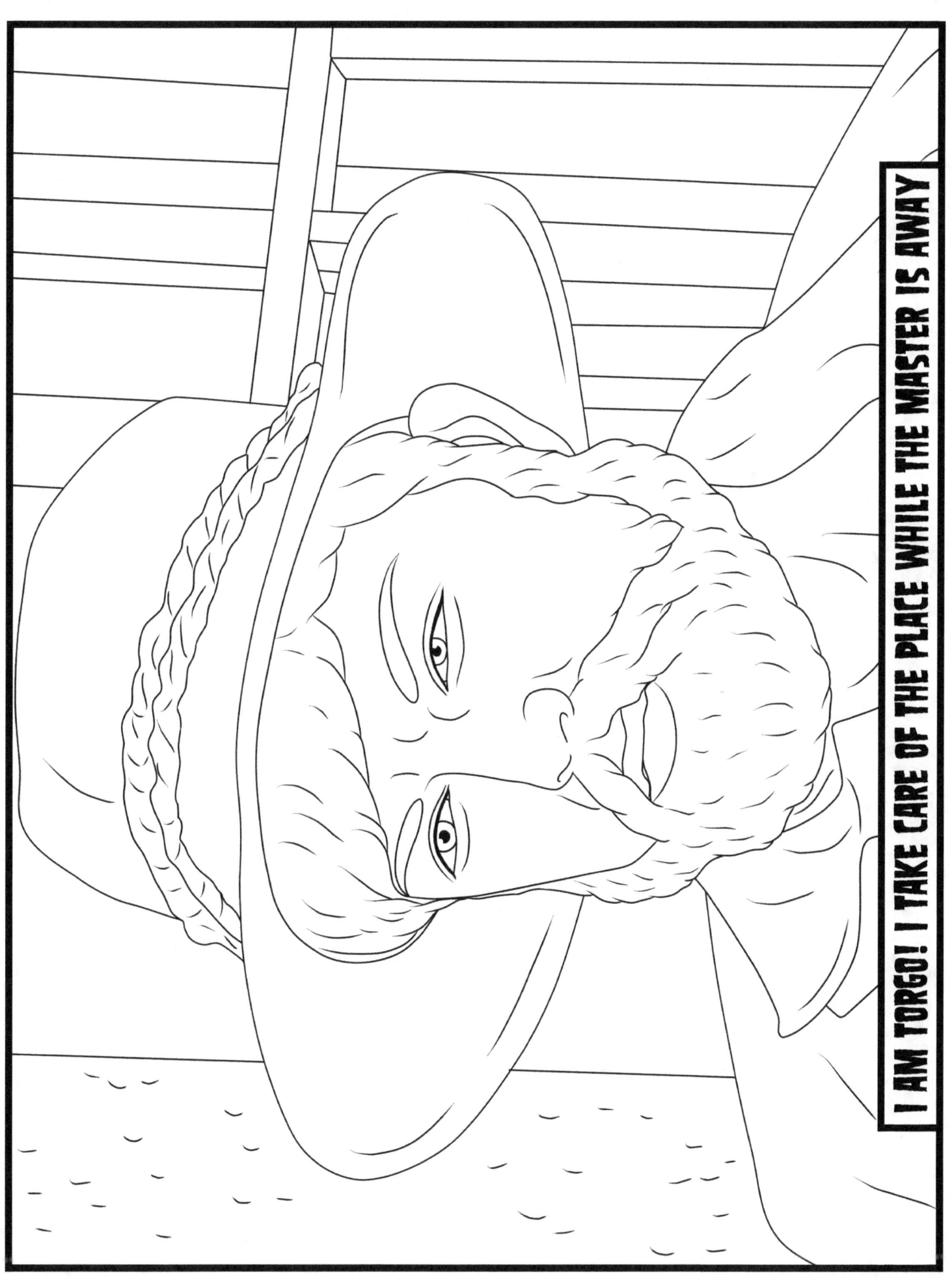

I AM TORGO! I TAKE CARE OF THE PLACE WHILE THE MASTER IS AWAY

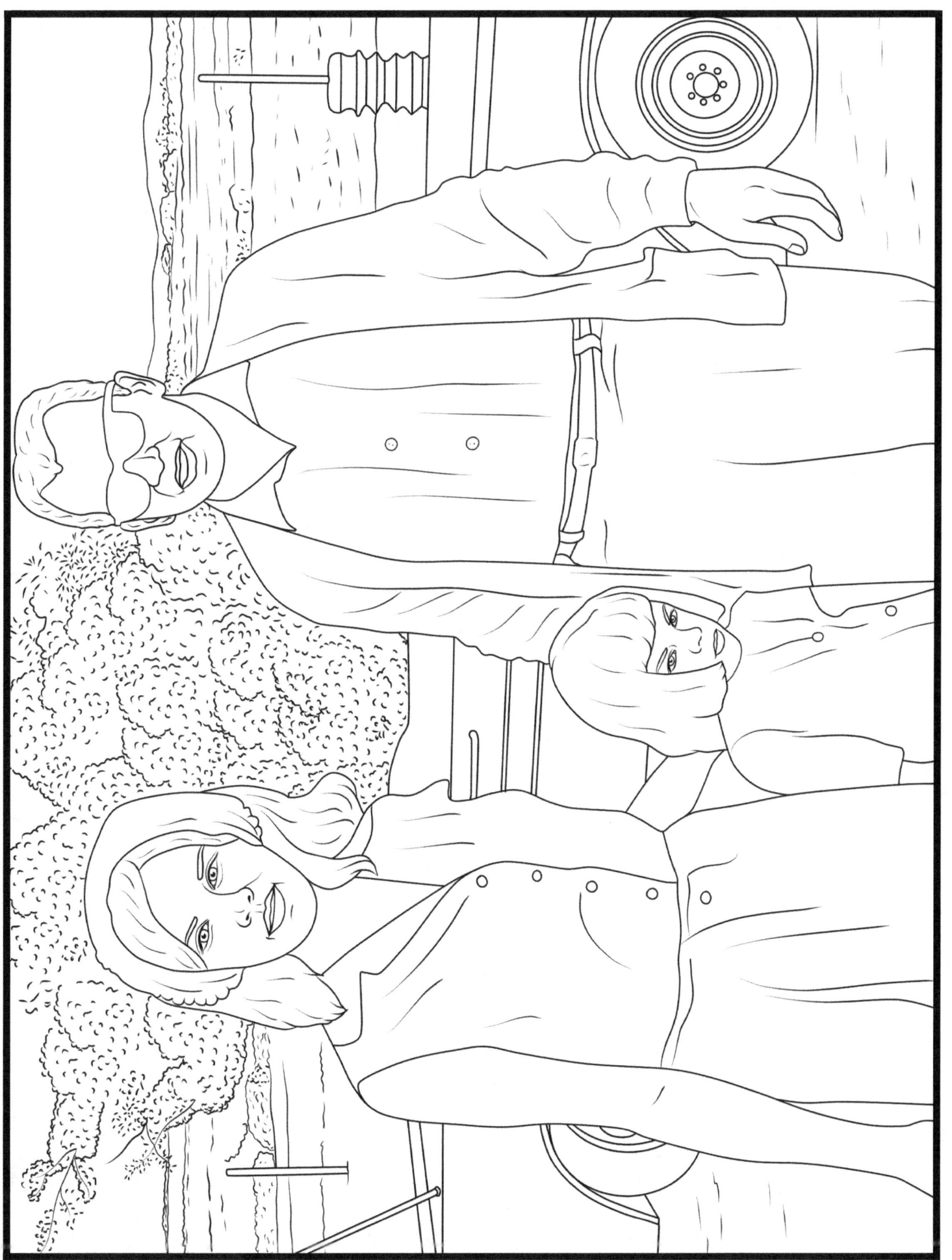

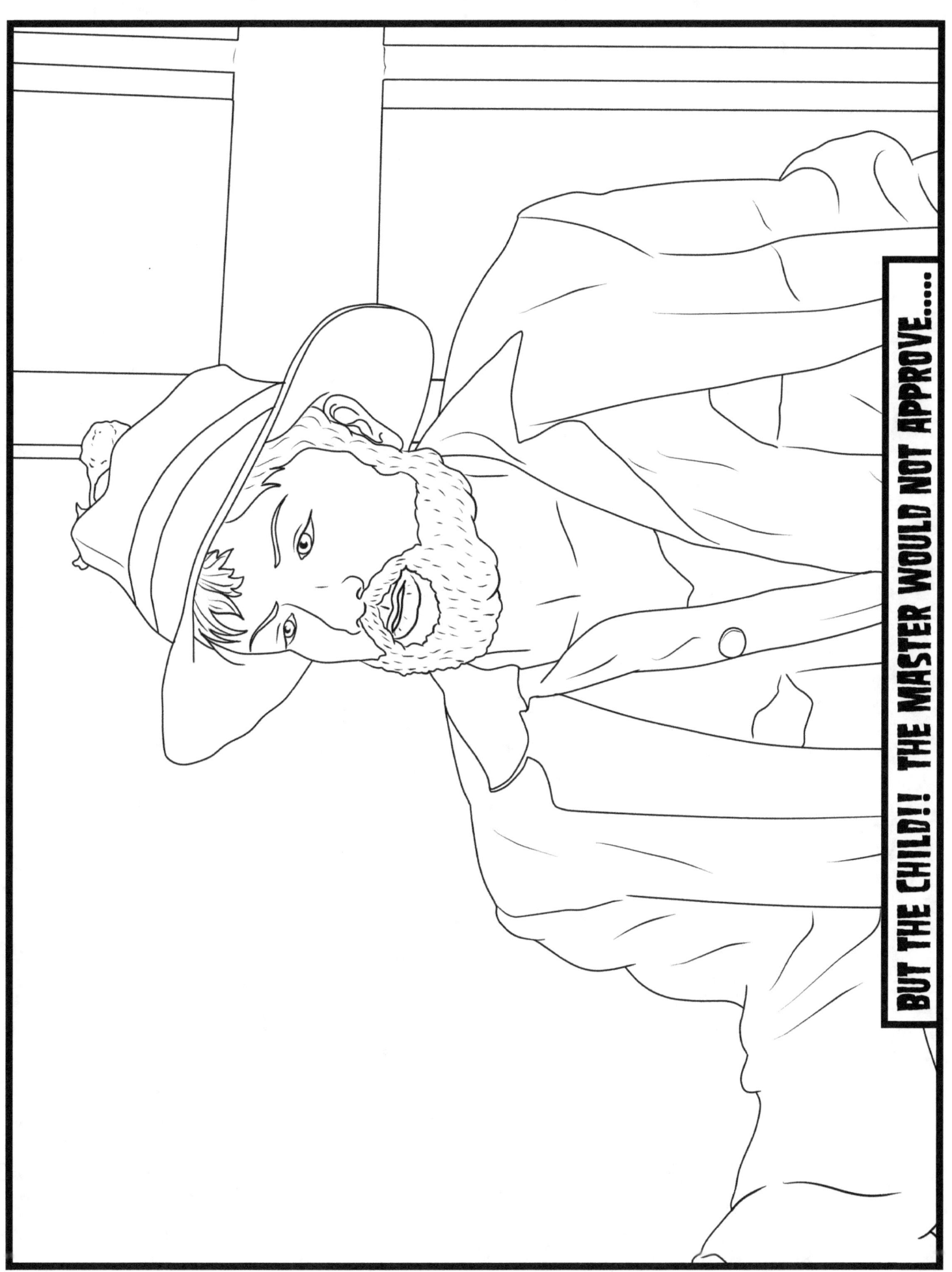

BUT THE CHILD!! THE MASTER WOULD NOT APPROVE.....

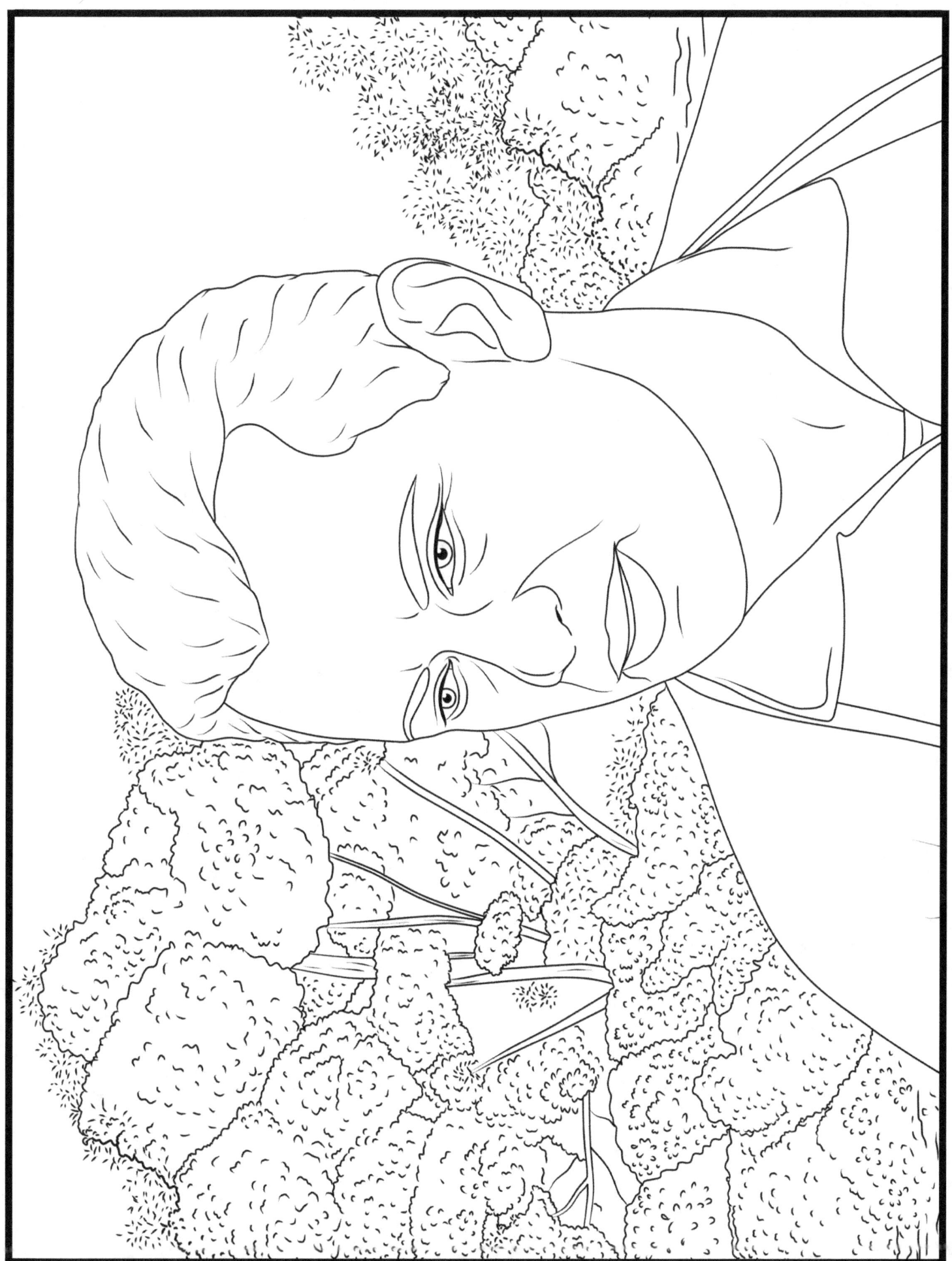

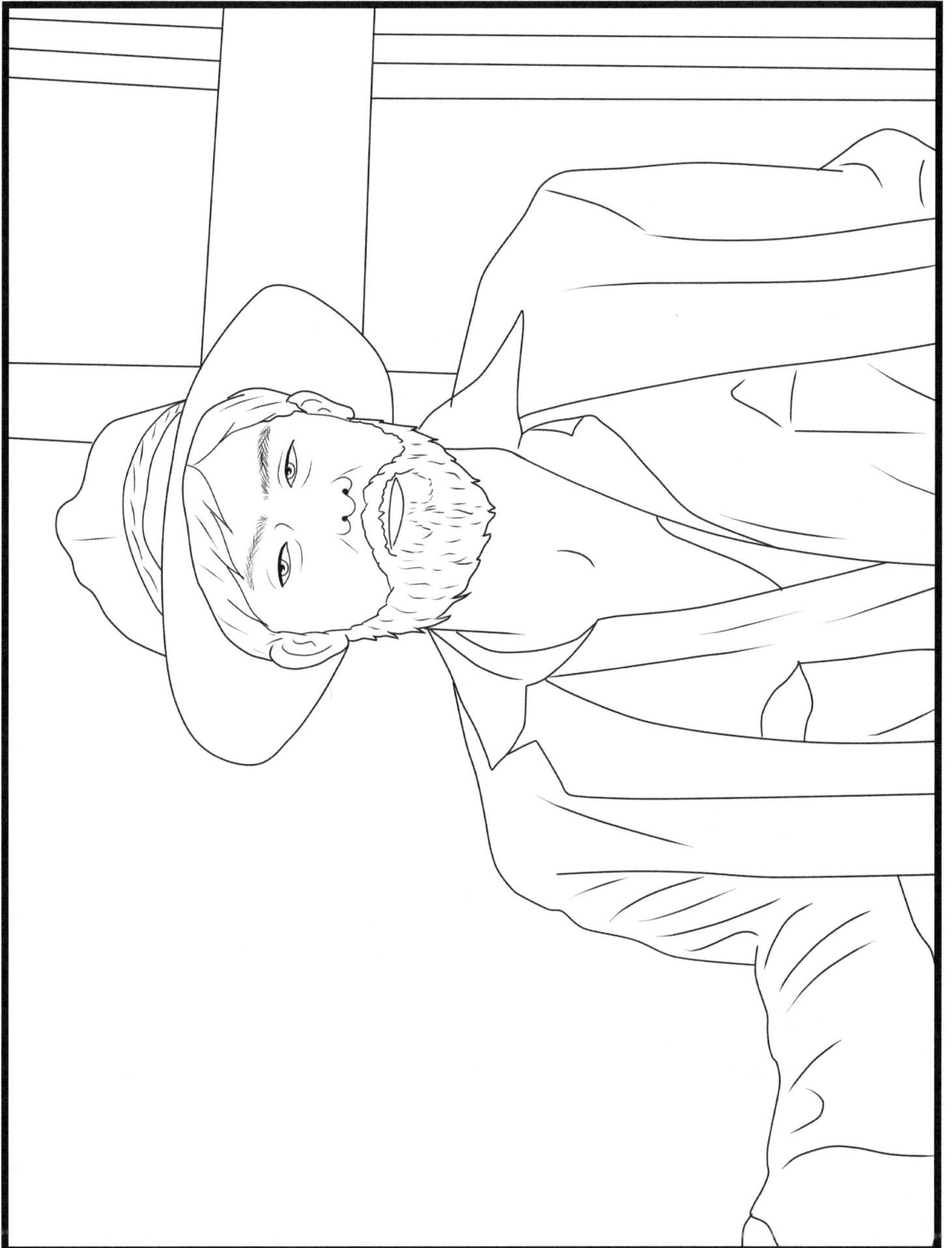

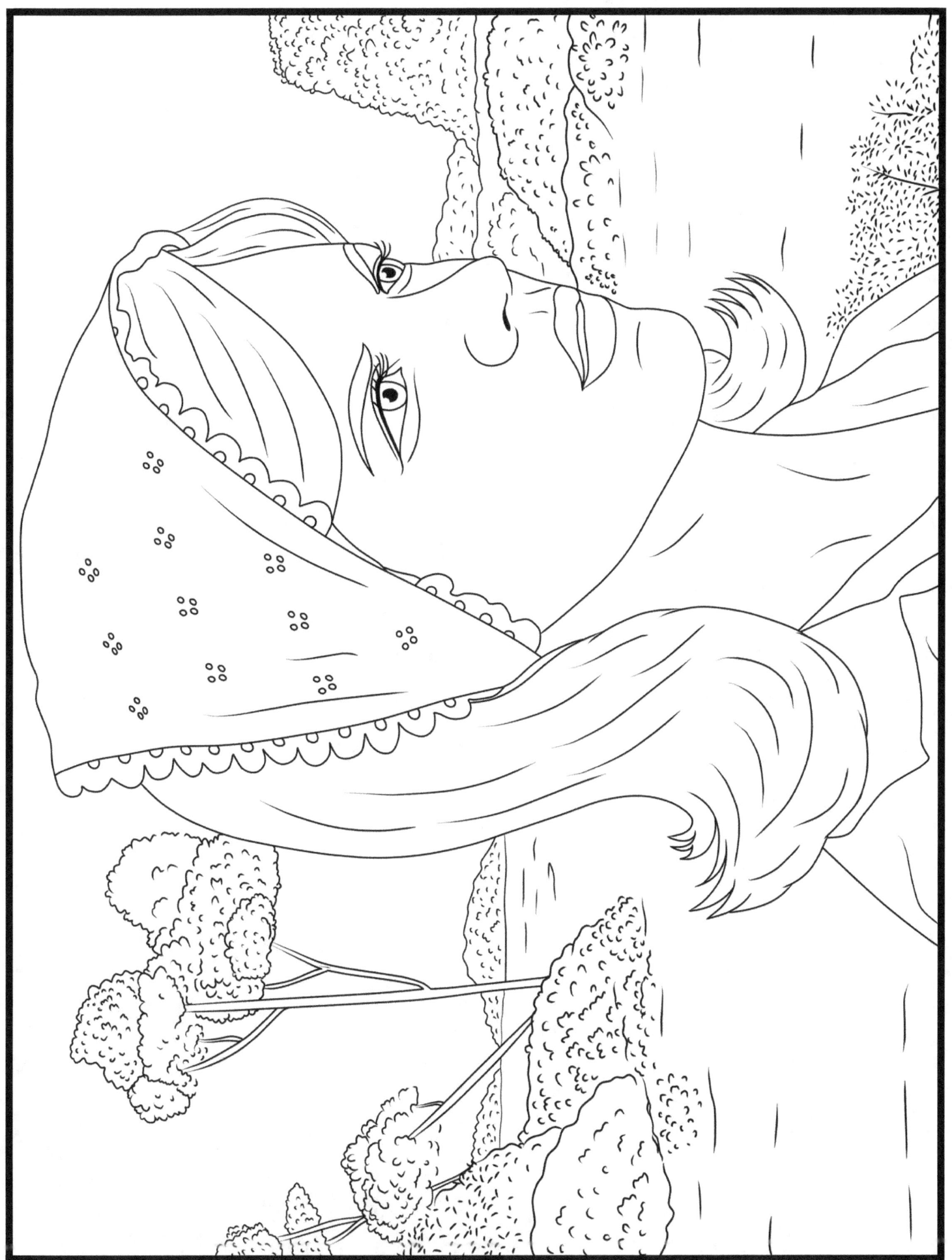

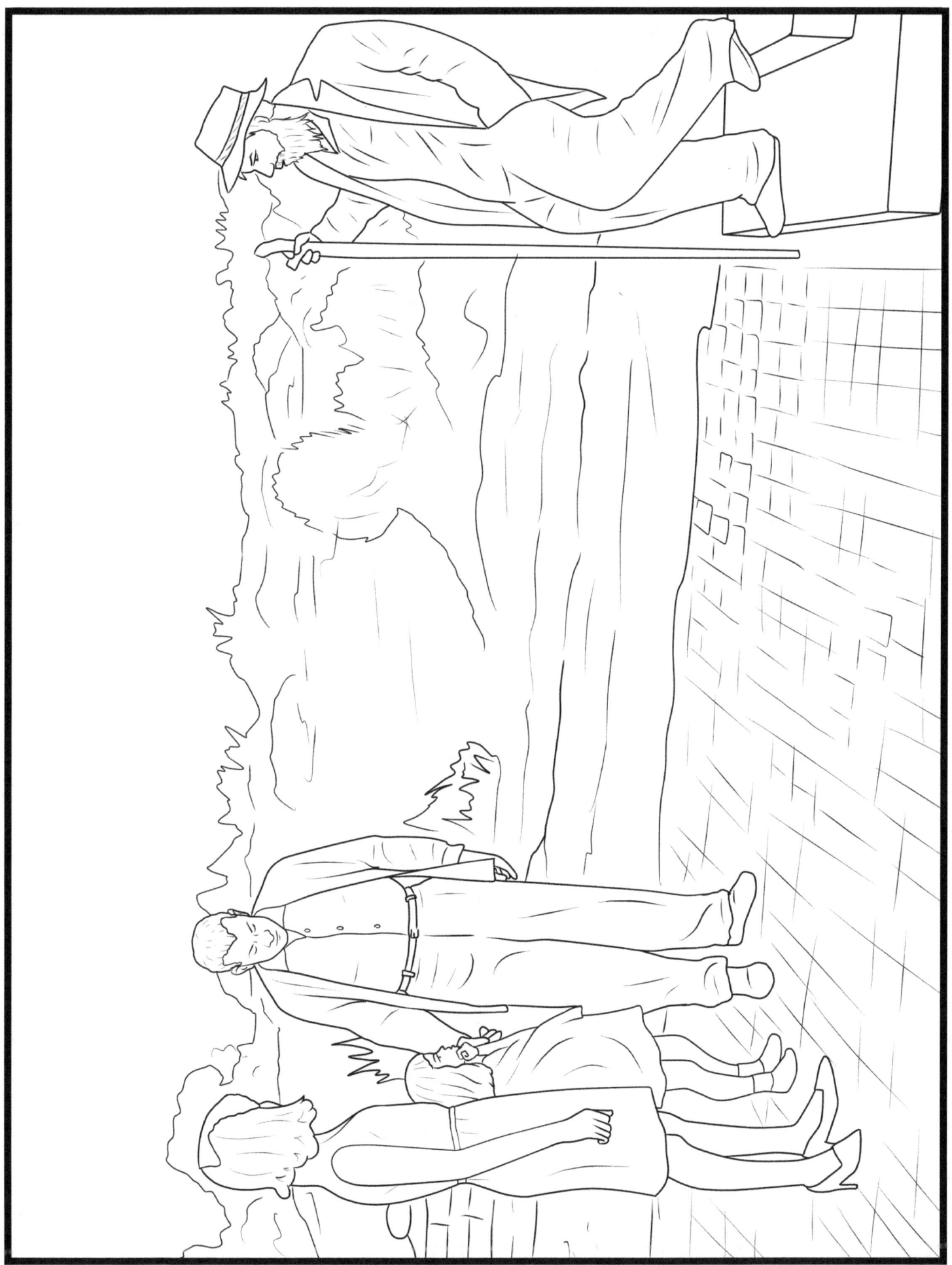

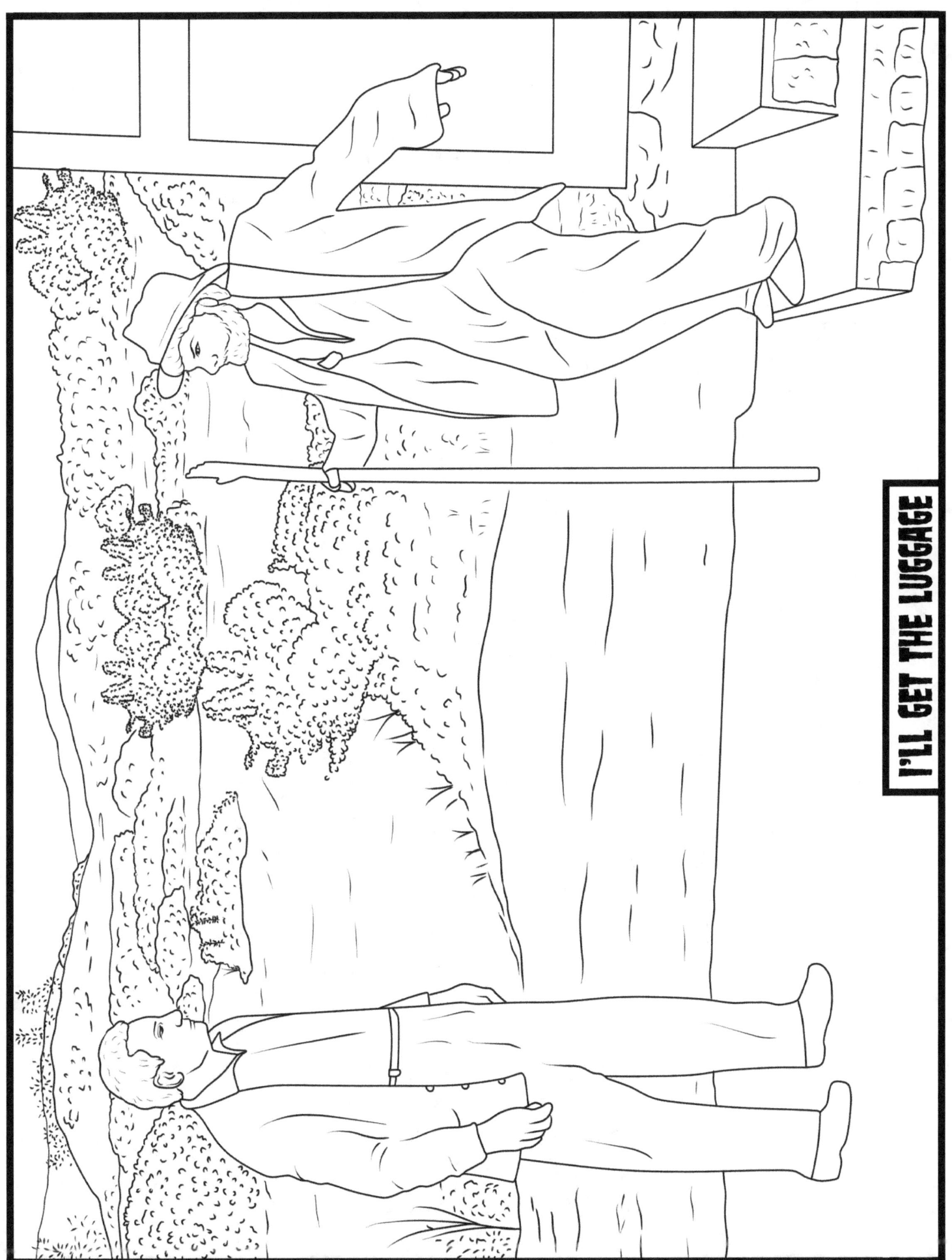

I'LL GET THE LUGGAGE

WHILE TORGO GETS THE LUGGAGE
(IT'LL TAKE AWHILE)
TRY AND FIND THE HIDDEN WORDS IN THIS WORD SEARCH!

```
W  E  W  P  B  W  W  G  O  U  P  C  O  V  O  E  C  N  Y  G
B  U  G  Y  T  P  P  L  X  G  E  A  B  J  D  I  V  D  Y  W
C  A  J  R  C  H  T  W  R  F  Z  N  C  M  O  B  C  H  G  M
T  V  S  R  N  N  I  A  W  T  B  U  I  S  Y  B  L  N  K  C
V  V  U  B  O  V  A  L  L  S  Z  S  O  T  V  E  N  C  V  N
U  W  L  X  E  H  W  O  M  V  Z  O  V  R  L  D  E  C  W  Q
P  V  V  S  A  H  I  T  X  H  E  N  N  Q  N  S  M  J  M  S
P  V  L  N  G  D  F  X  G  F  H  A  B  X  U  J  Y  D  V  F
S  O  D  E  J  K  E  O  T  P  E  M  O  L  Z  O  S  N  A  F
W  S  E  I  A  L  Z  A  S  I  B  K  Q  D  N  U  U  O  Y  Q
A  R  E  K  M  H  J  N  V  L  W  P  U  P  P  Y  N  R  V  Z
G  K  C  N  K  I  C  T  P  B  A  B  C  R  V  W  X  D  L  M
M  C  L  P  K  D  E  I  E  D  T  I  Y  U  L  O  A  A  V  U
V  R  L  J  P  R  L  D  M  N  D  T  I  L  C  M  X  A  E  Y
K  E  P  X  A  T  A  N  W  H  S  U  L  C  G  Z  S  F  V  W
Y  T  A  G  V  S  J  D  T  G  J  I  F  I  S  S  M  E  L  J
S  S  R  M  A  S  H  W  D  O  K  I  T  Z  E  Z  J  P  P  H
F  A  B  V  M  Q  L  E  L  C  R  D  H  I  N  P  K  X  H  Z
M  M  B  R  Q  Y  A  C  K  O  F  G  Z  H  U  I  R  V  X  Y
Q  W  D  L  T  P  Z  M  R  D  J  E  O  Y  M  A  S  J  G  L
```

TORGO	WIFE
MASTER	DARKNESS
MICHAEL	KILL
DEBBIE	PUPPY
MARGARET	WIVES
MANOS	HANDS

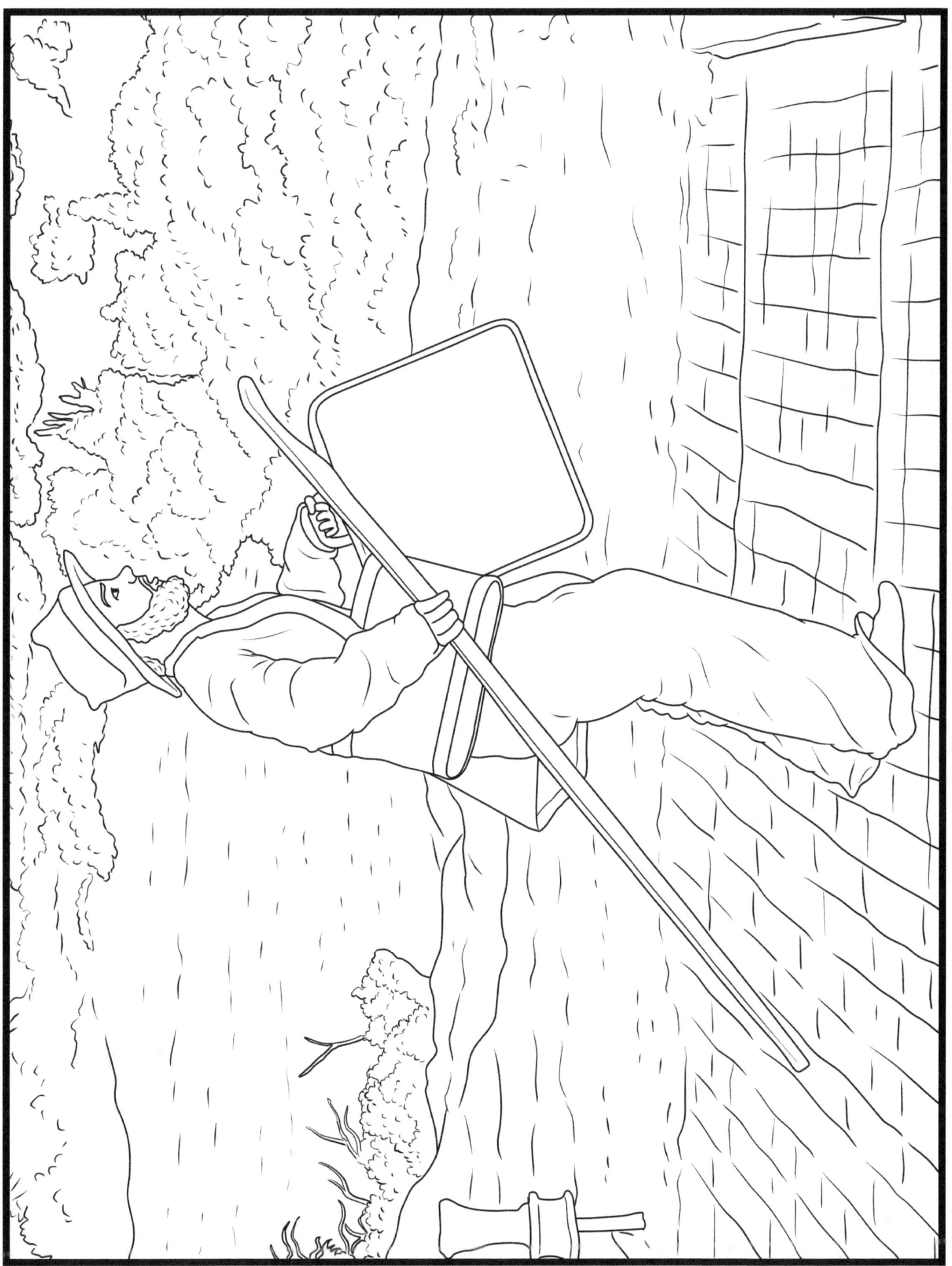

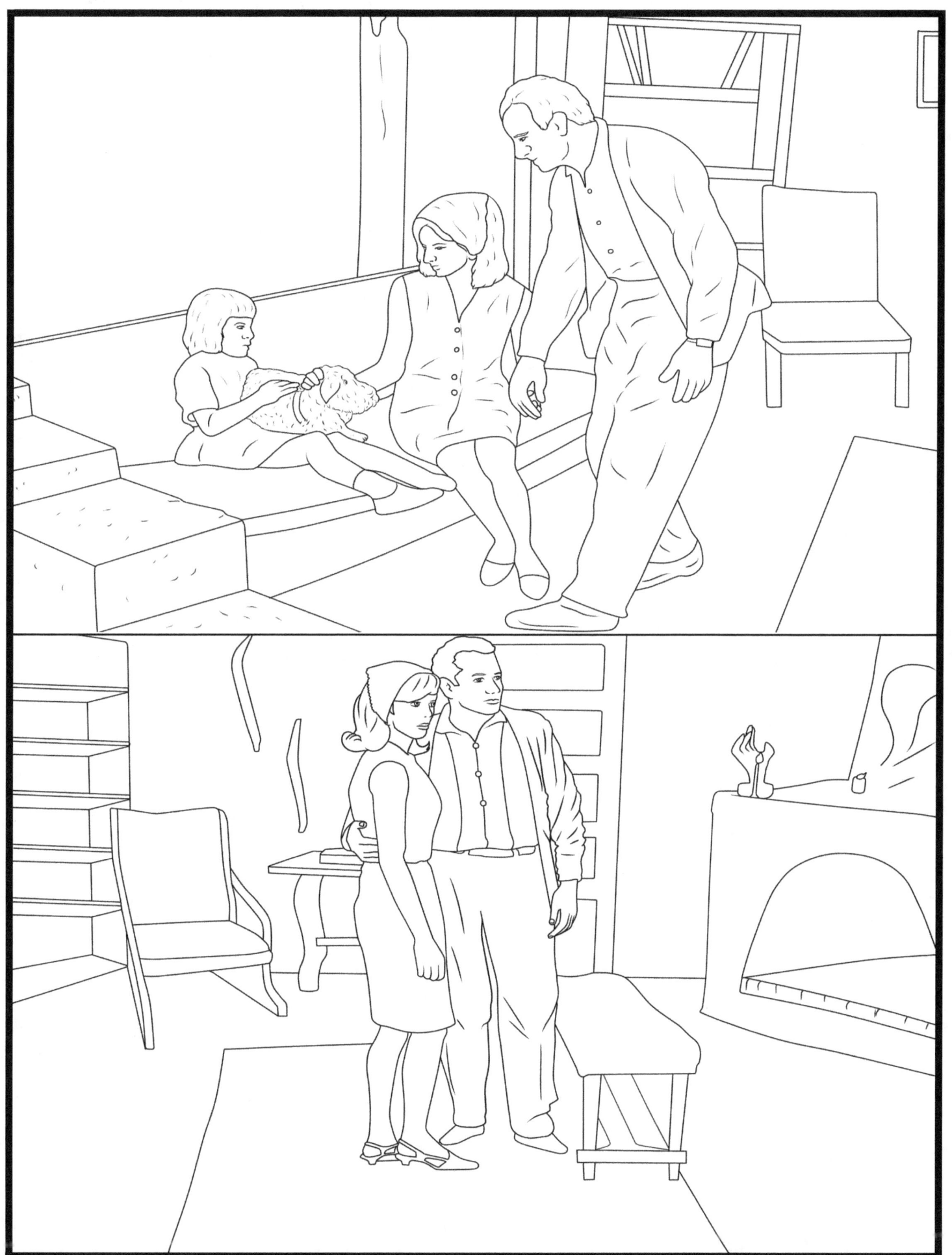

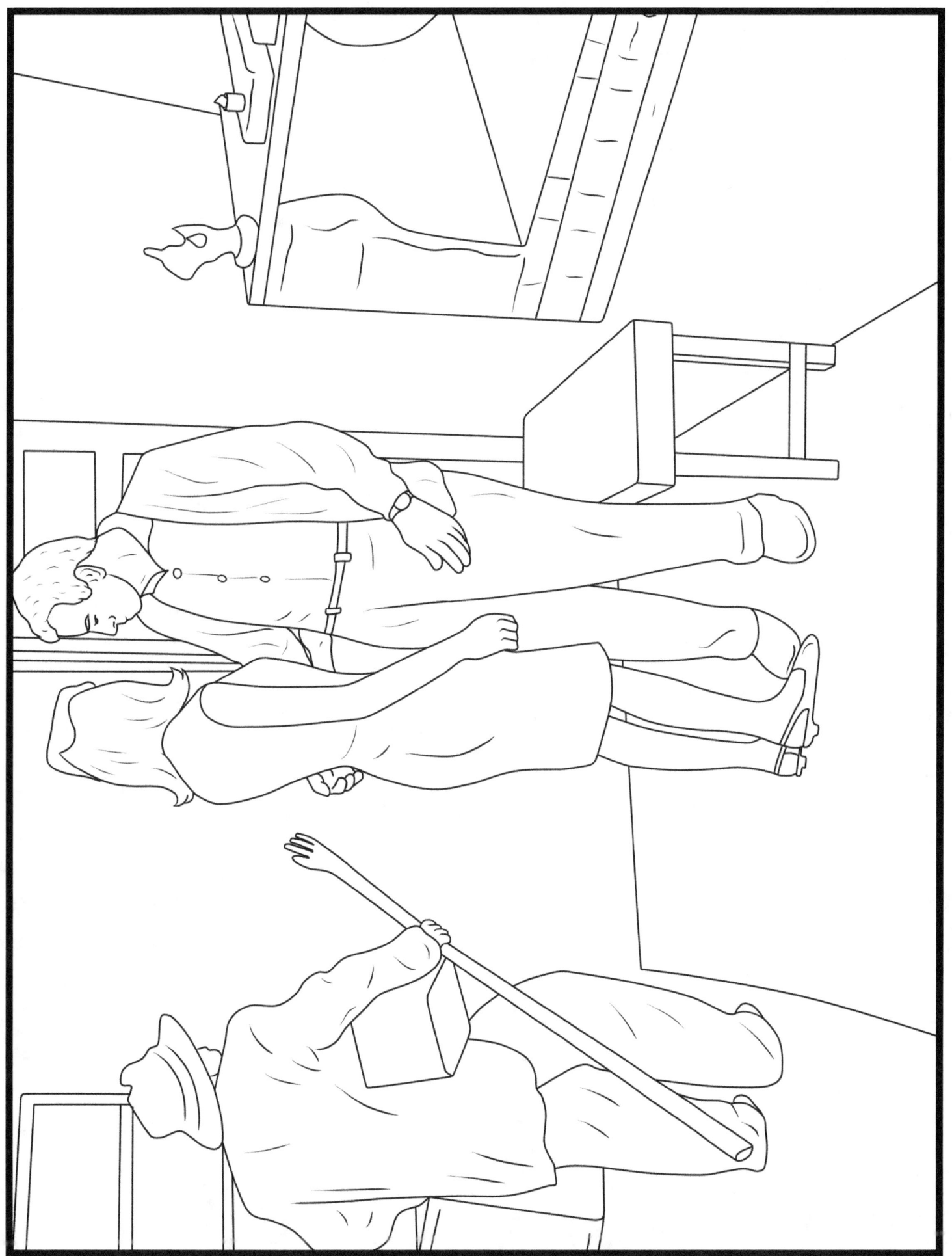

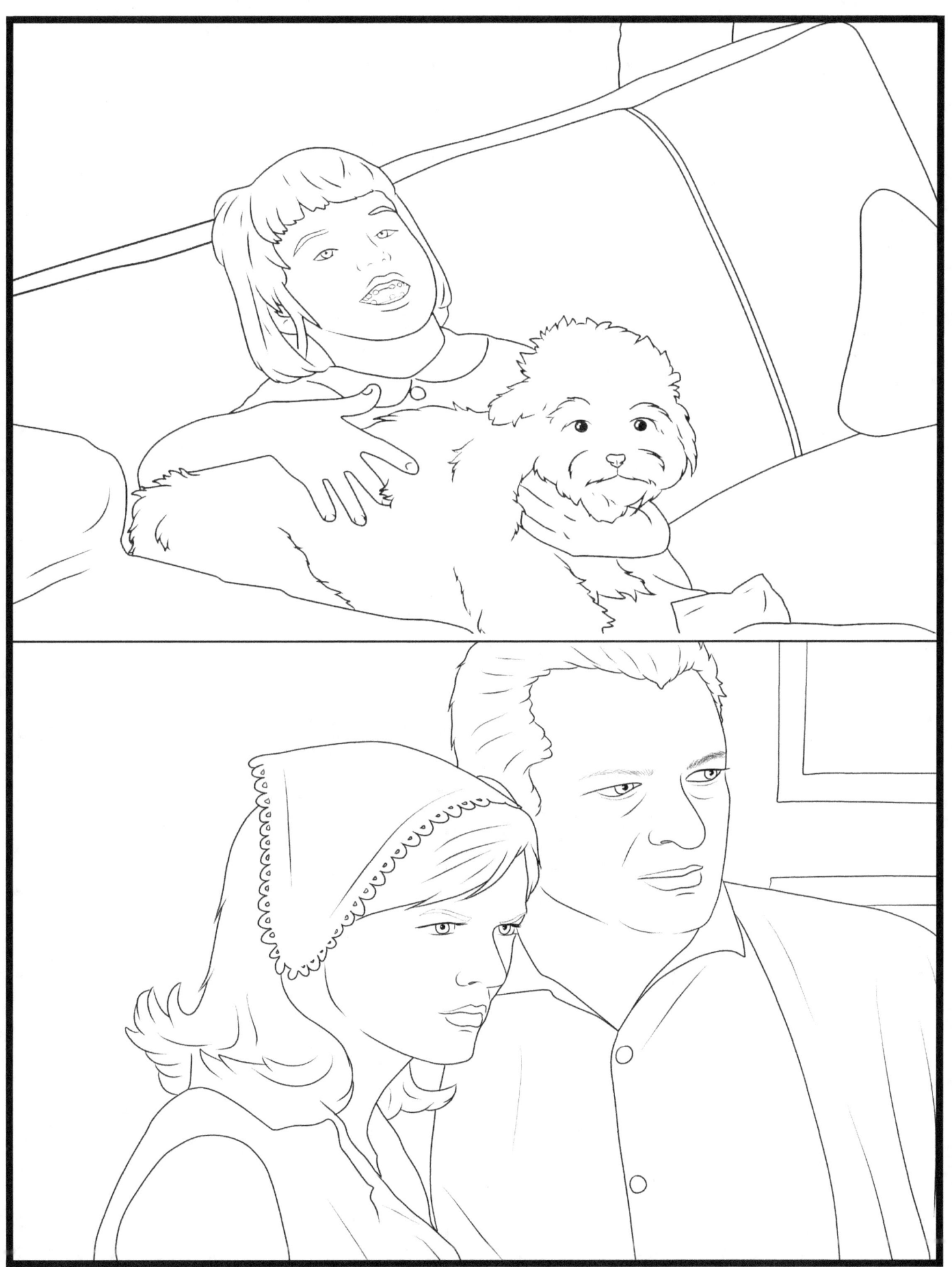

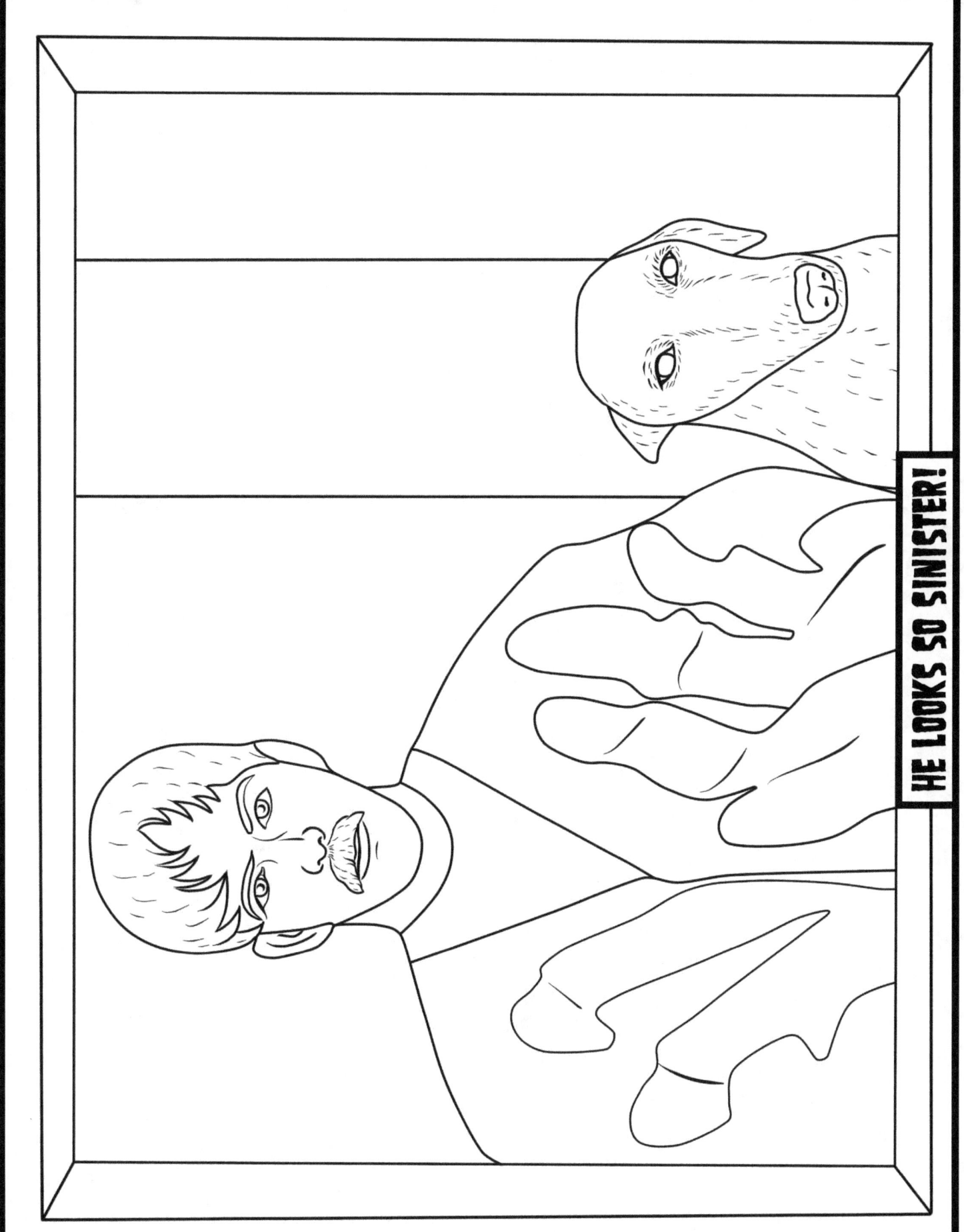

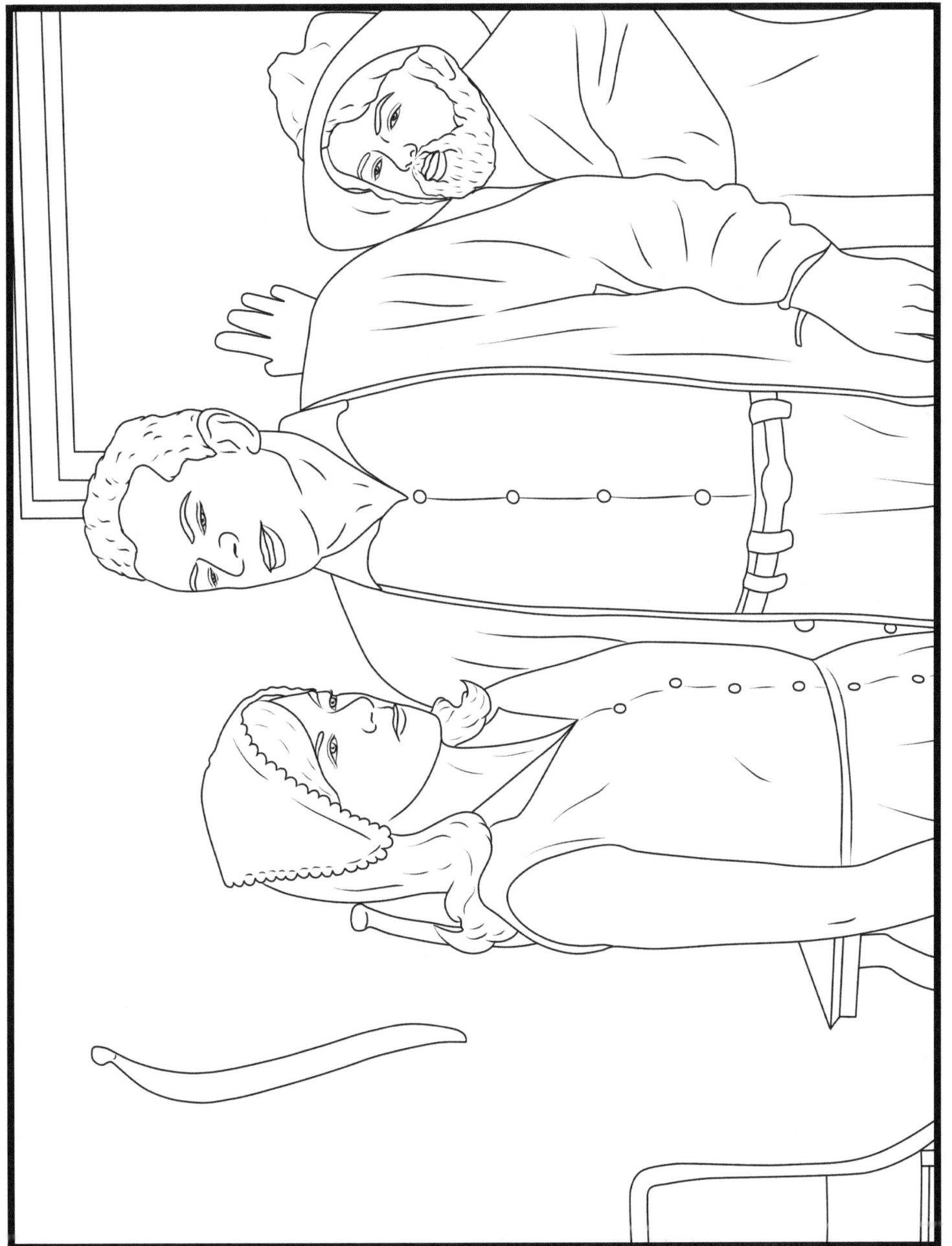

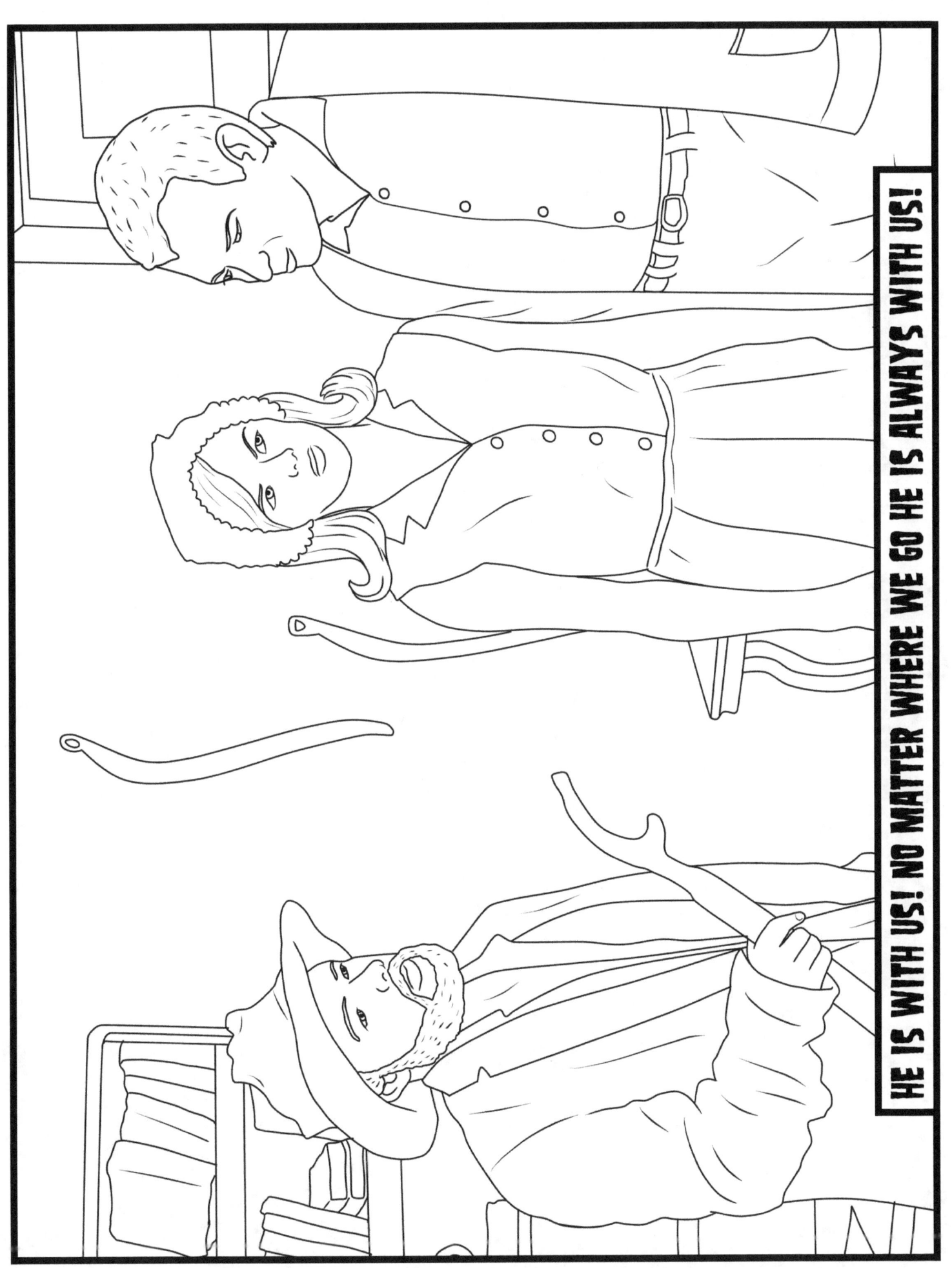

HE IS WITH US! NO MATTER WHERE WE GO HE IS ALWAYS WITH US!

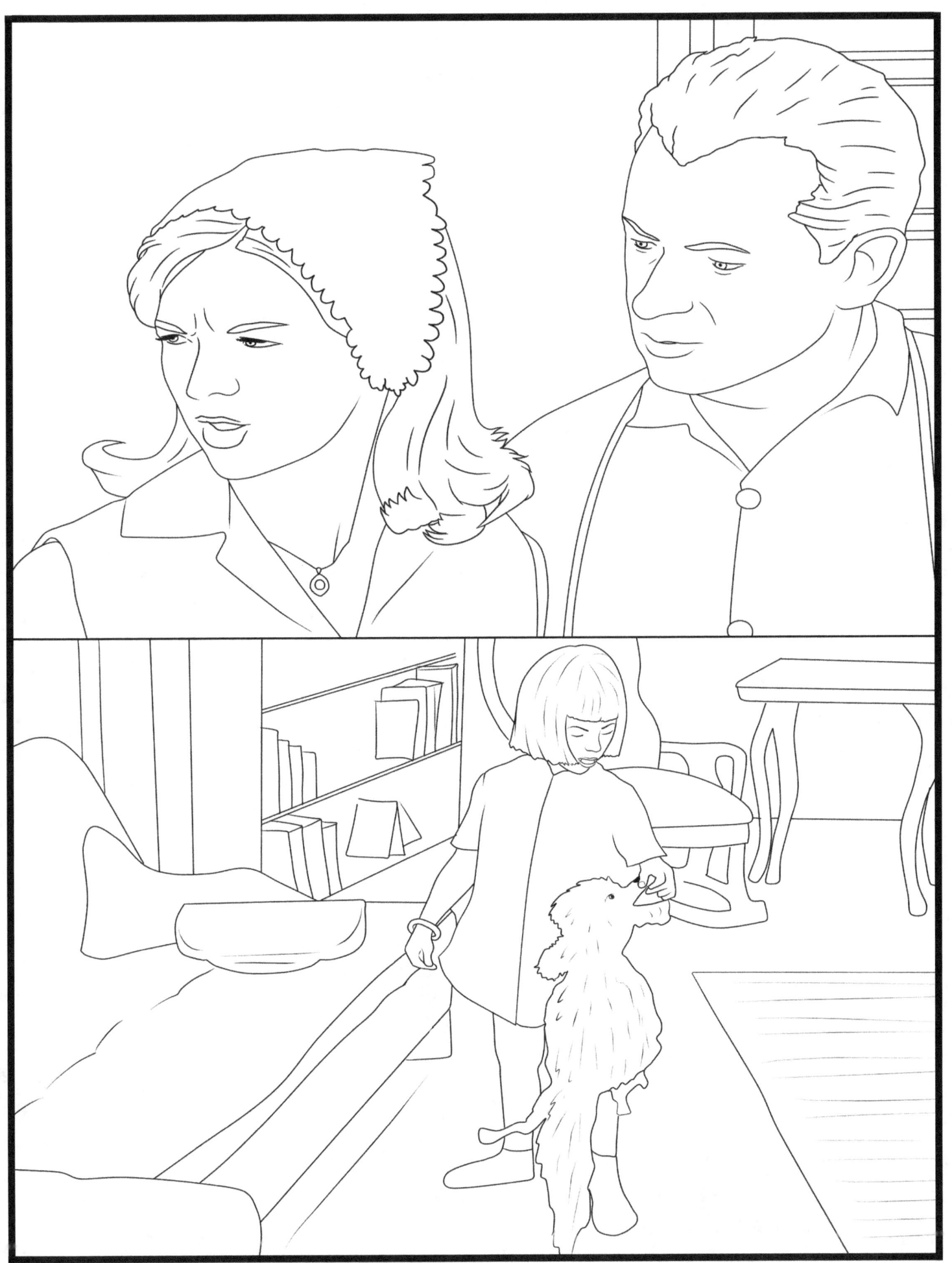

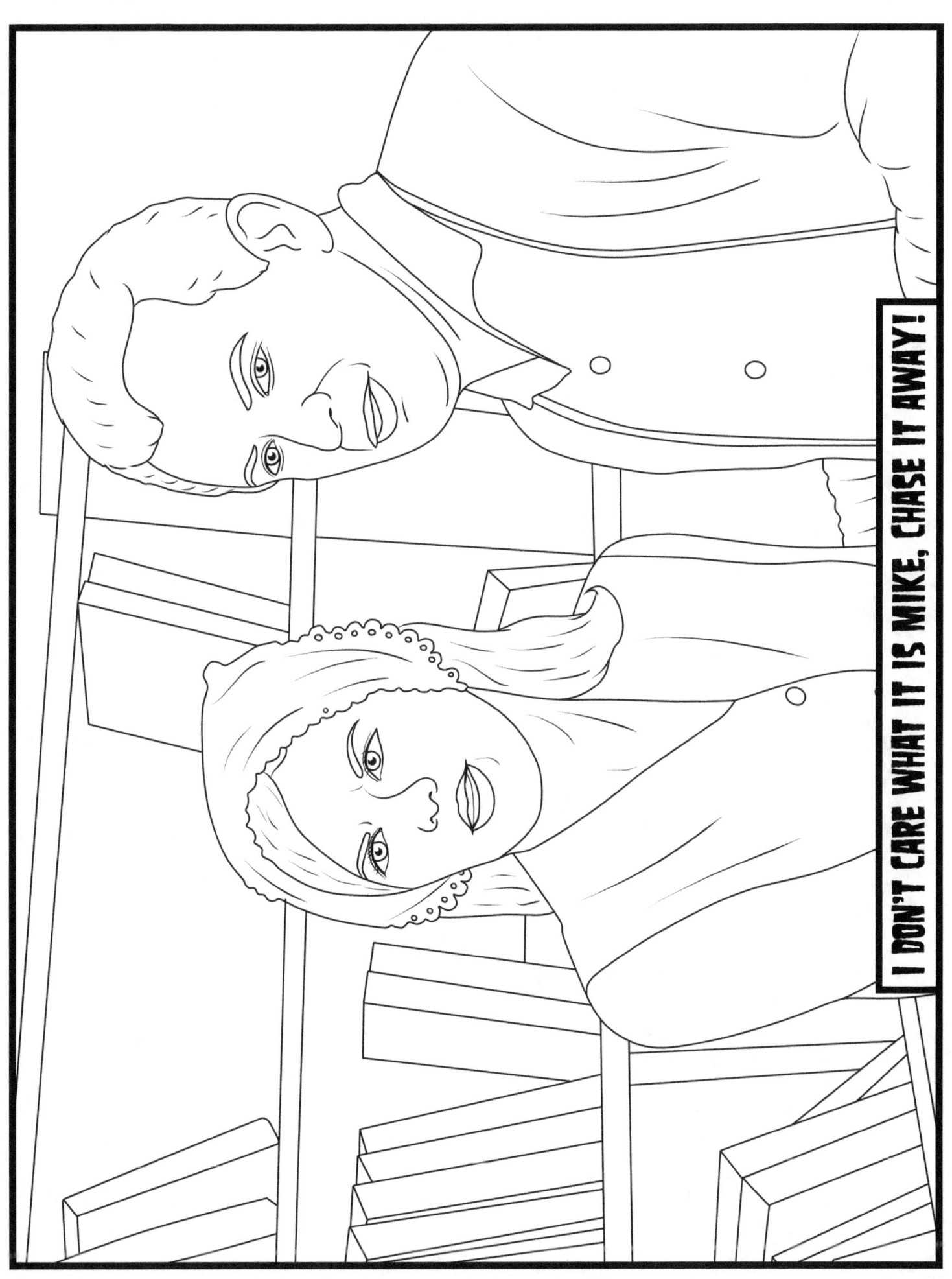

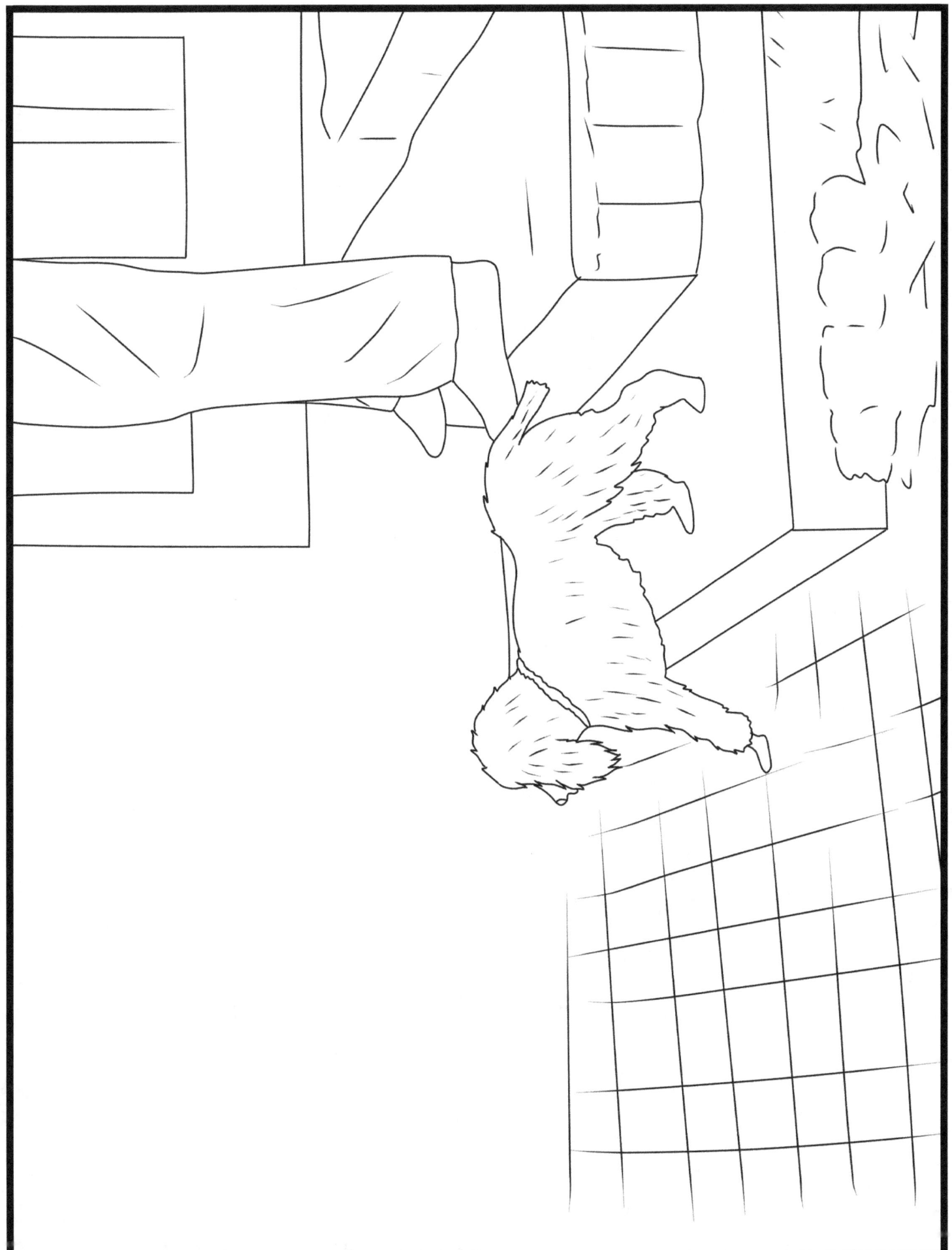

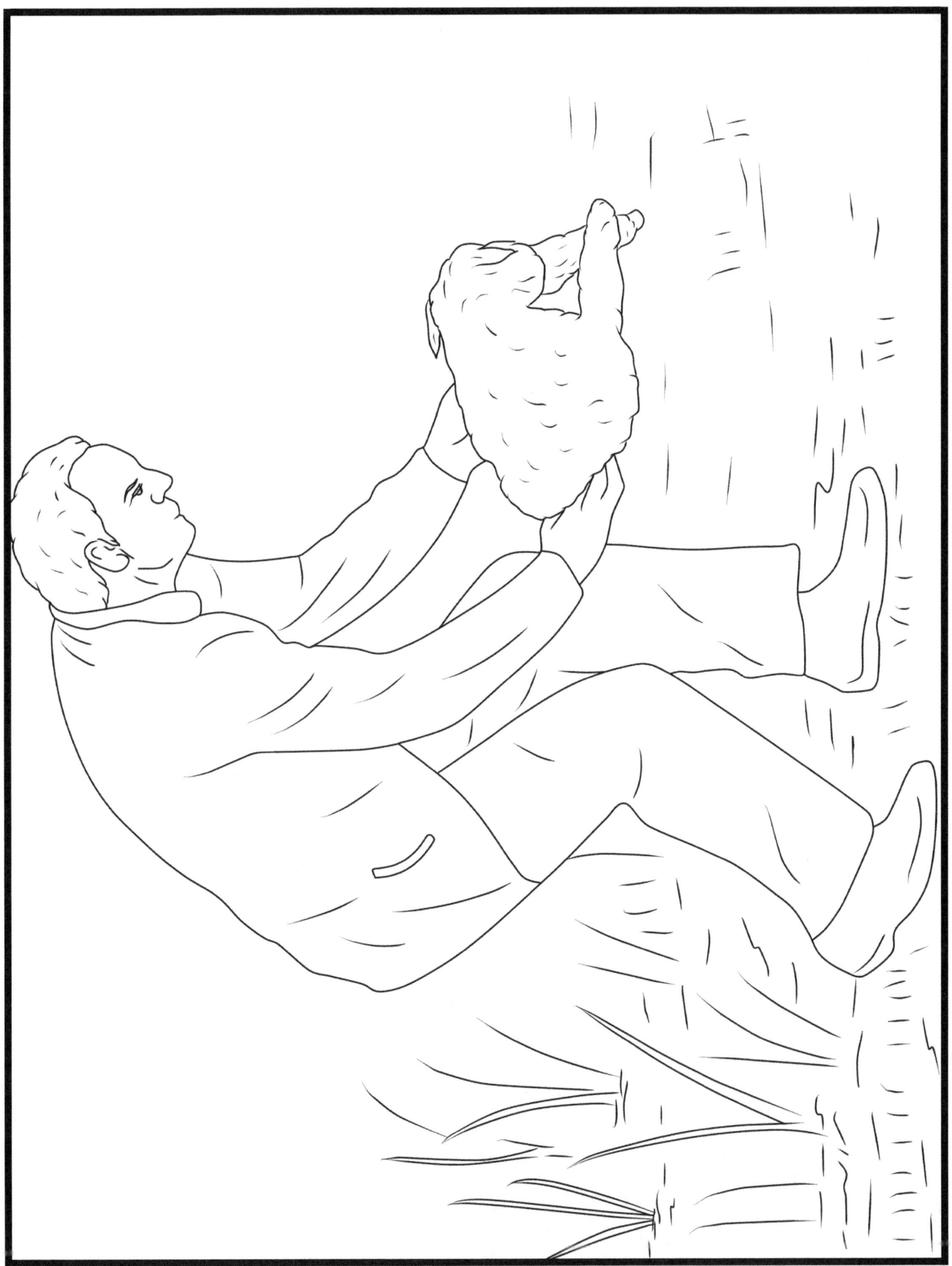

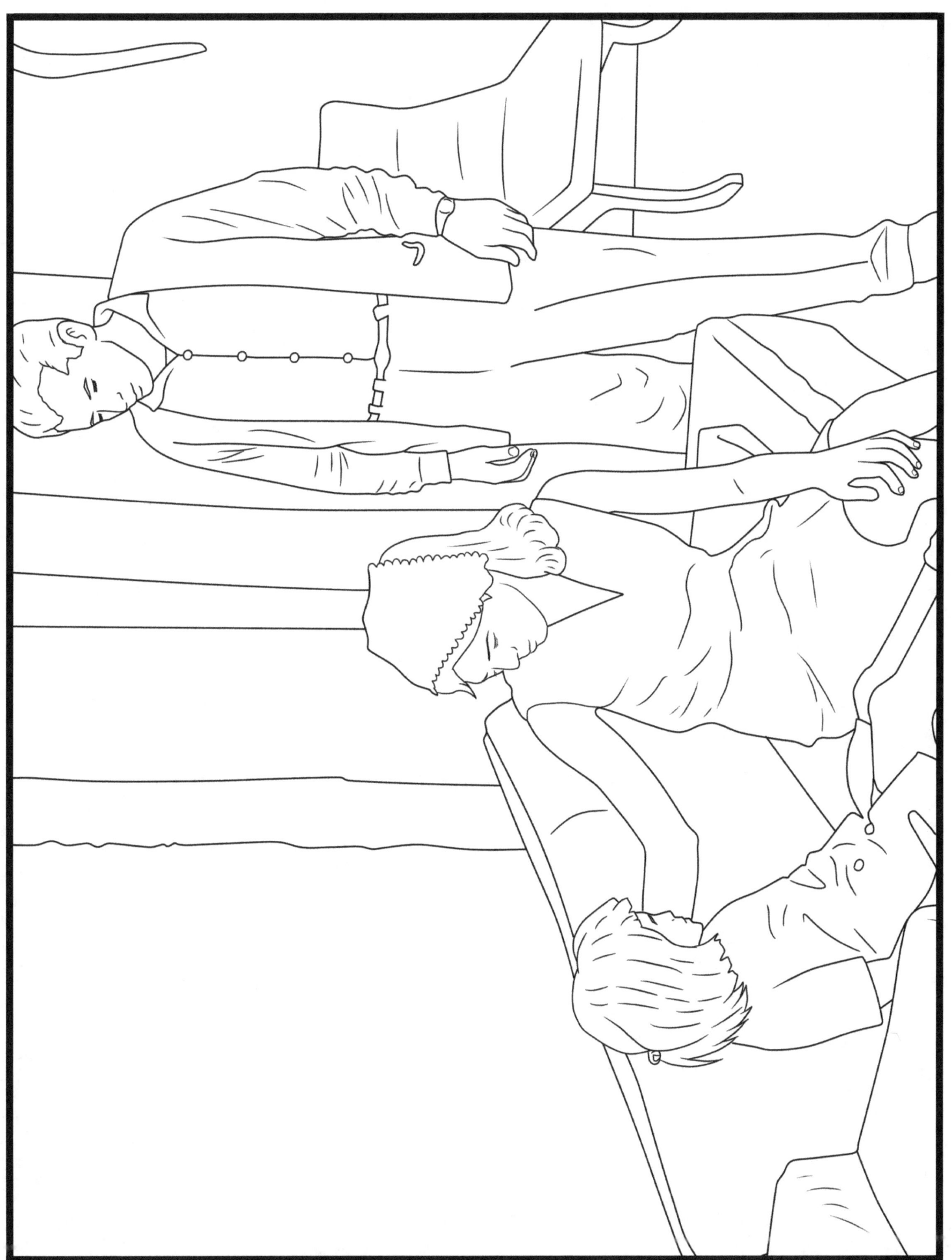

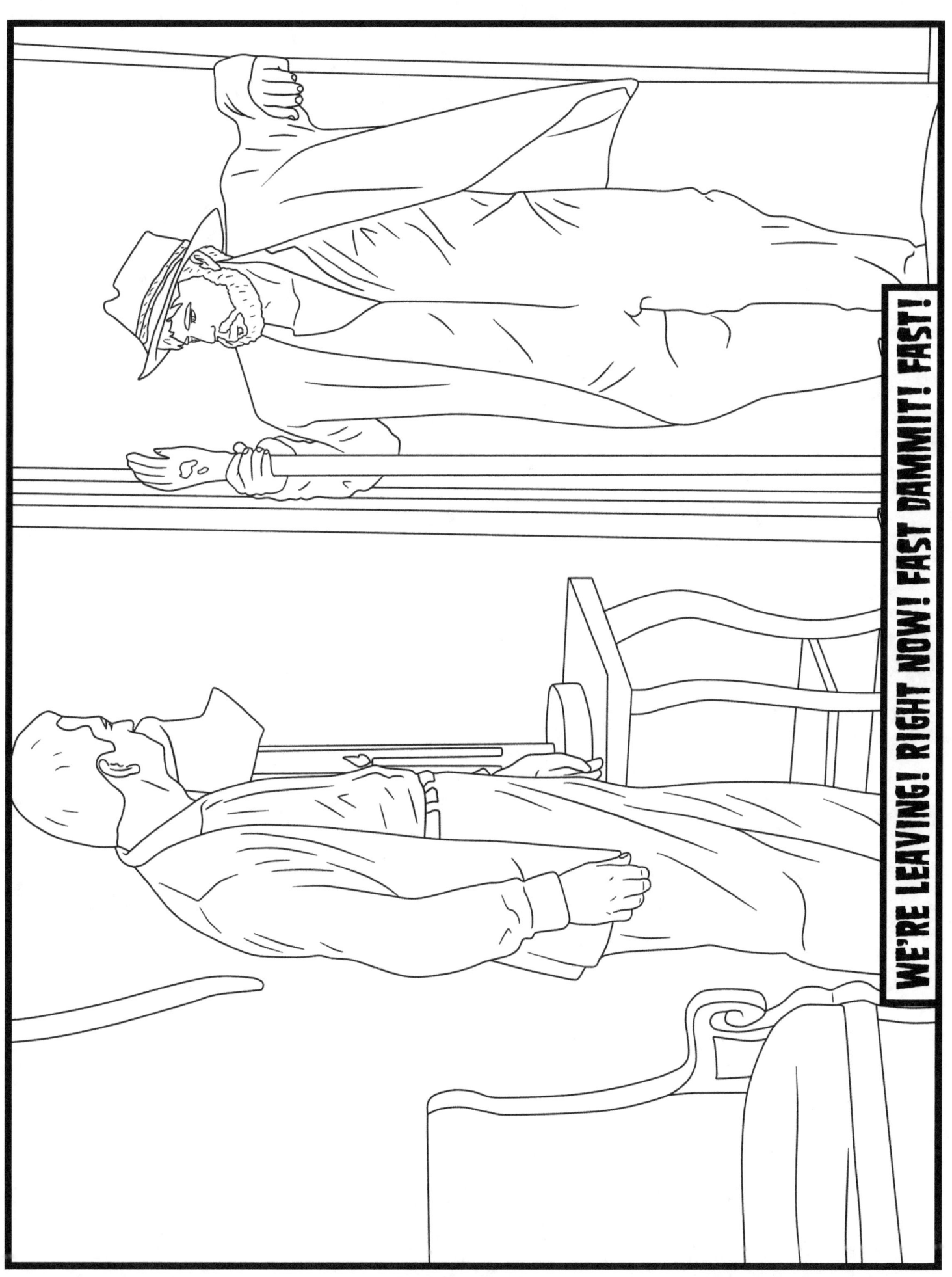

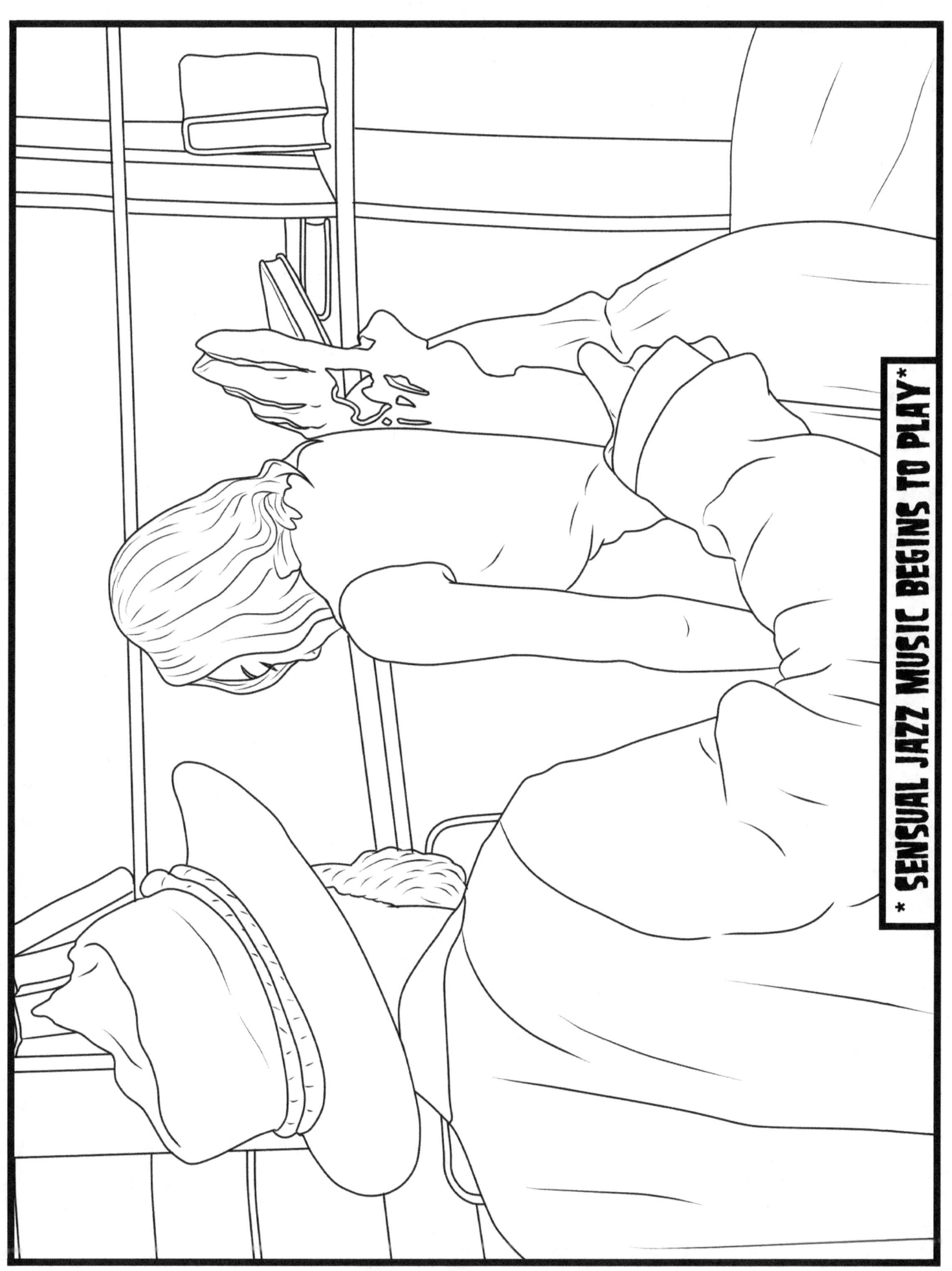

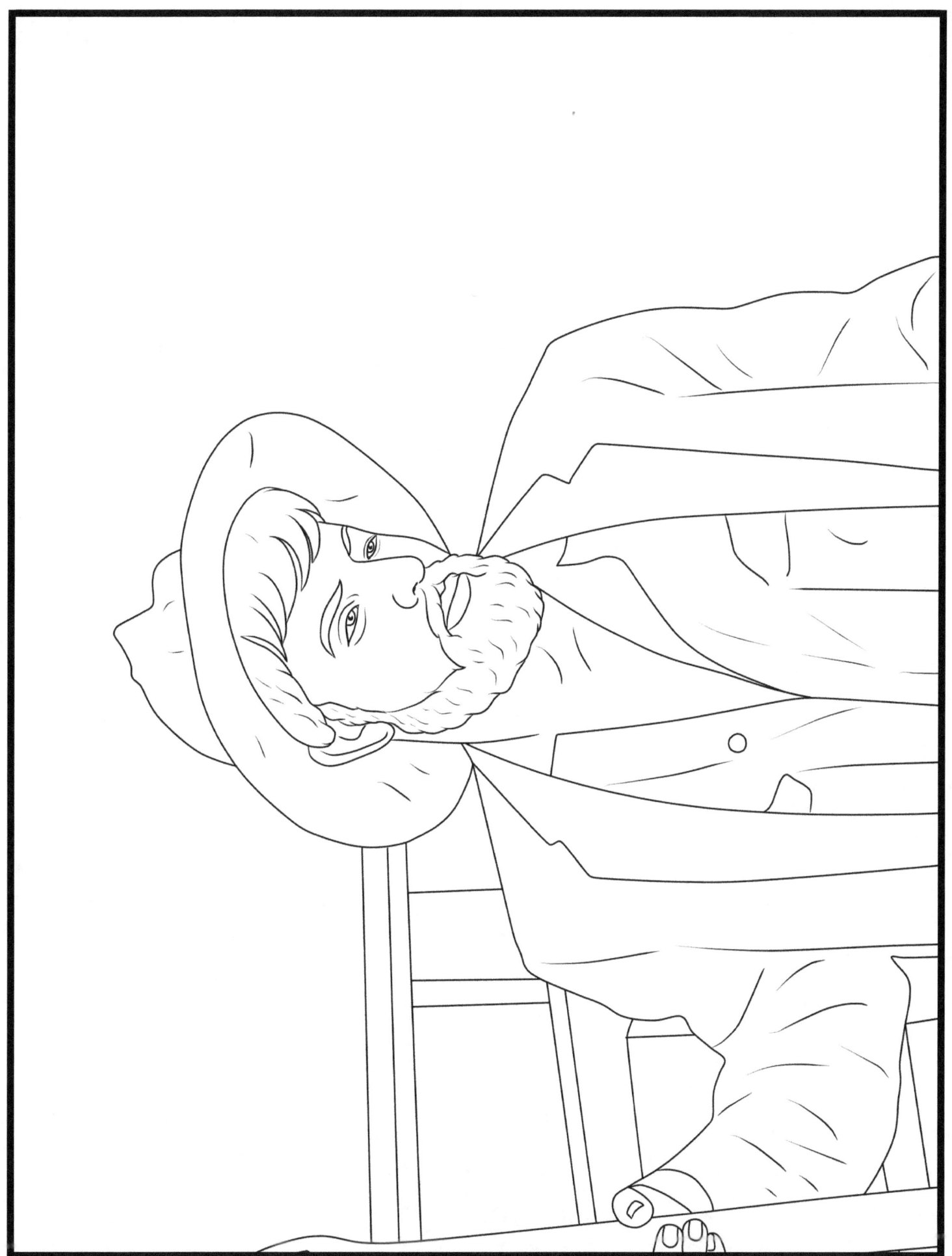

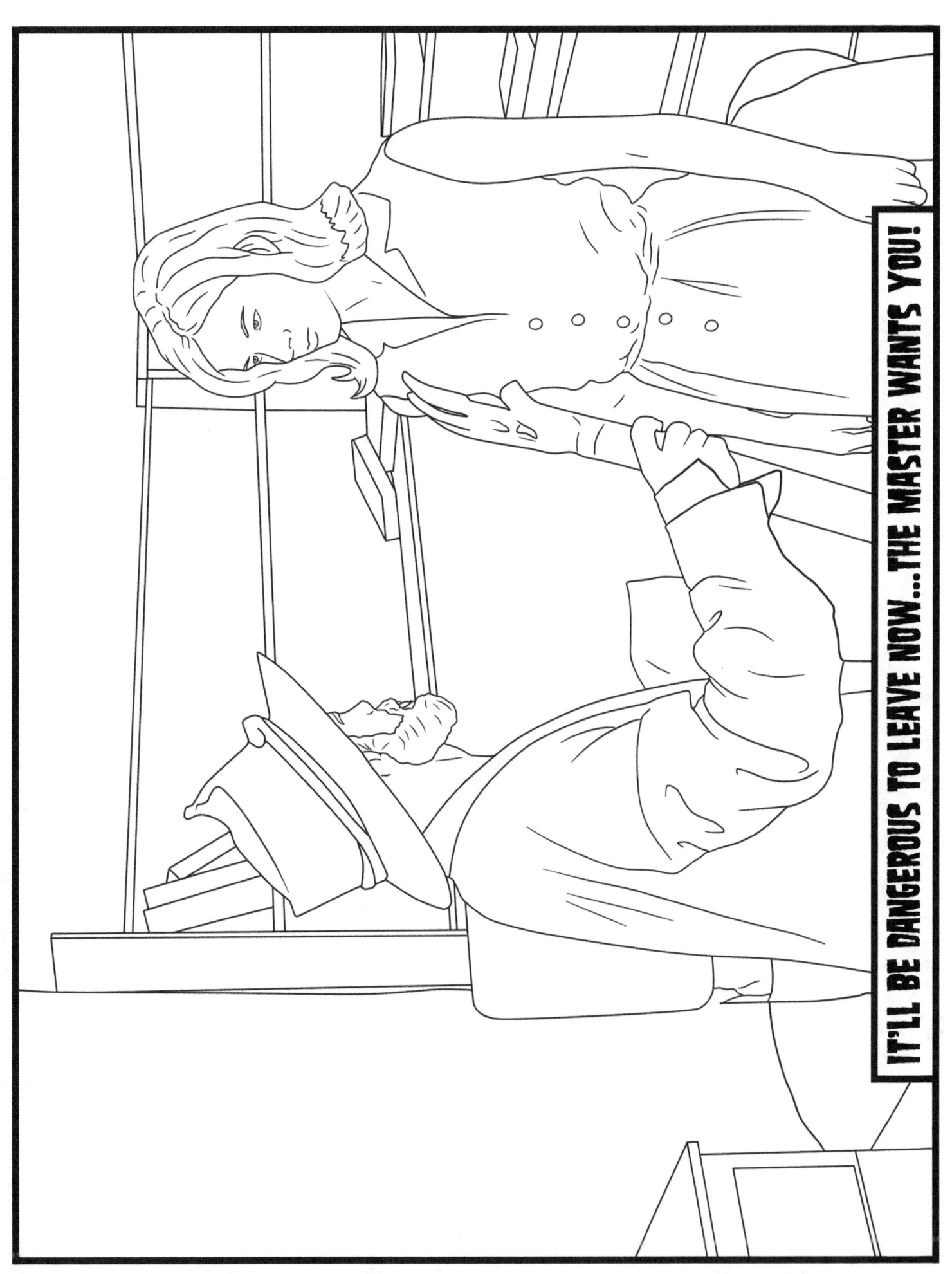

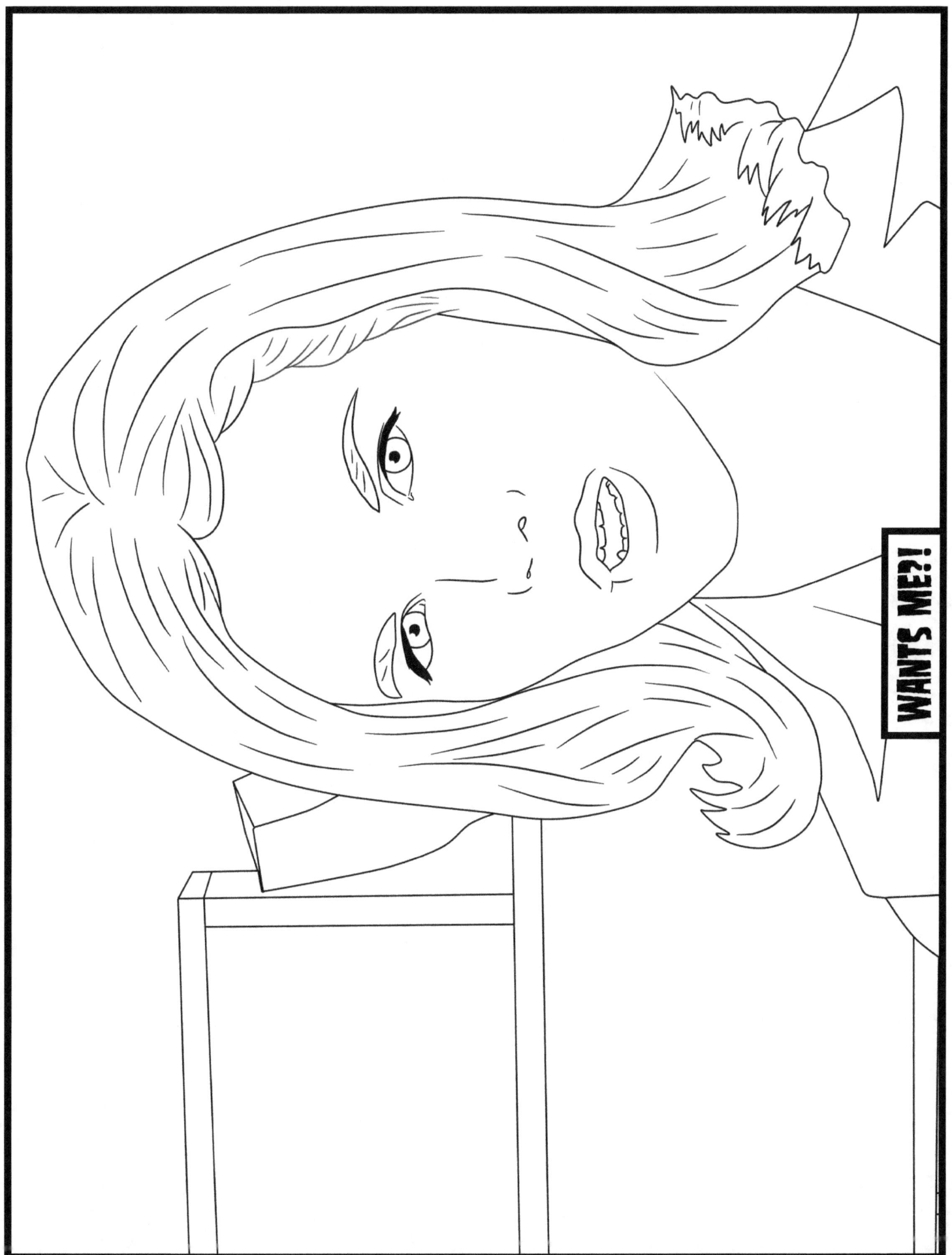

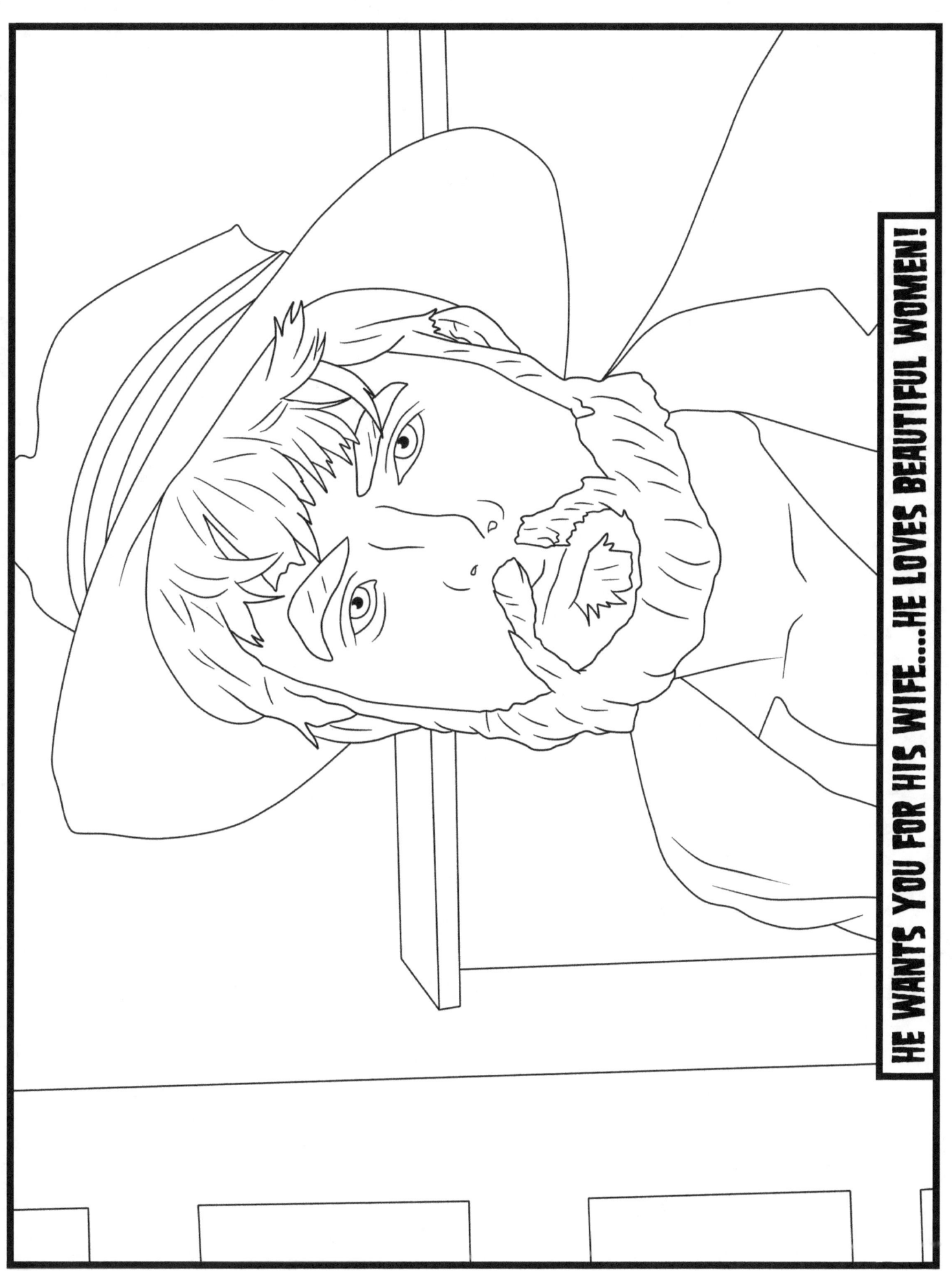

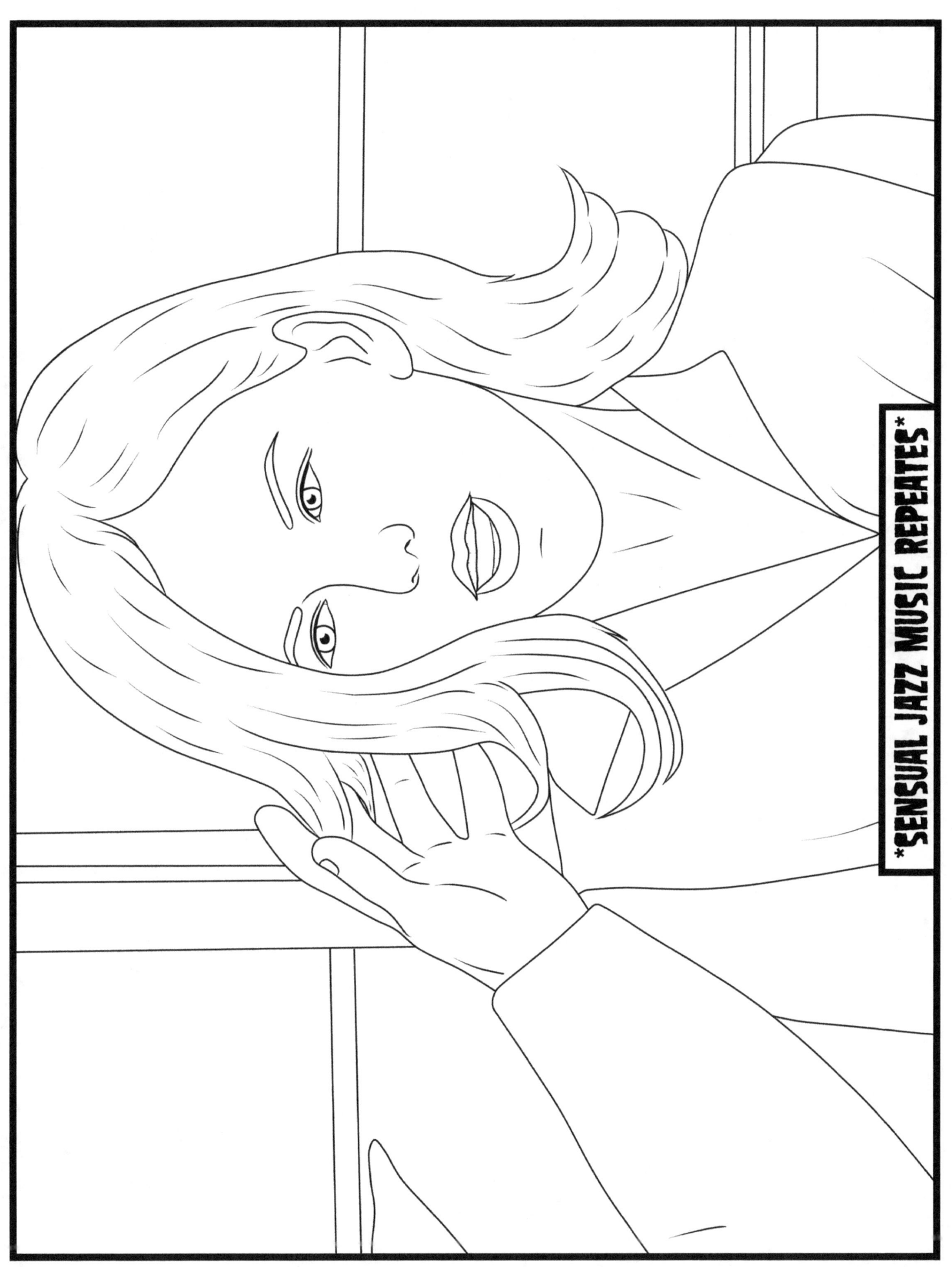

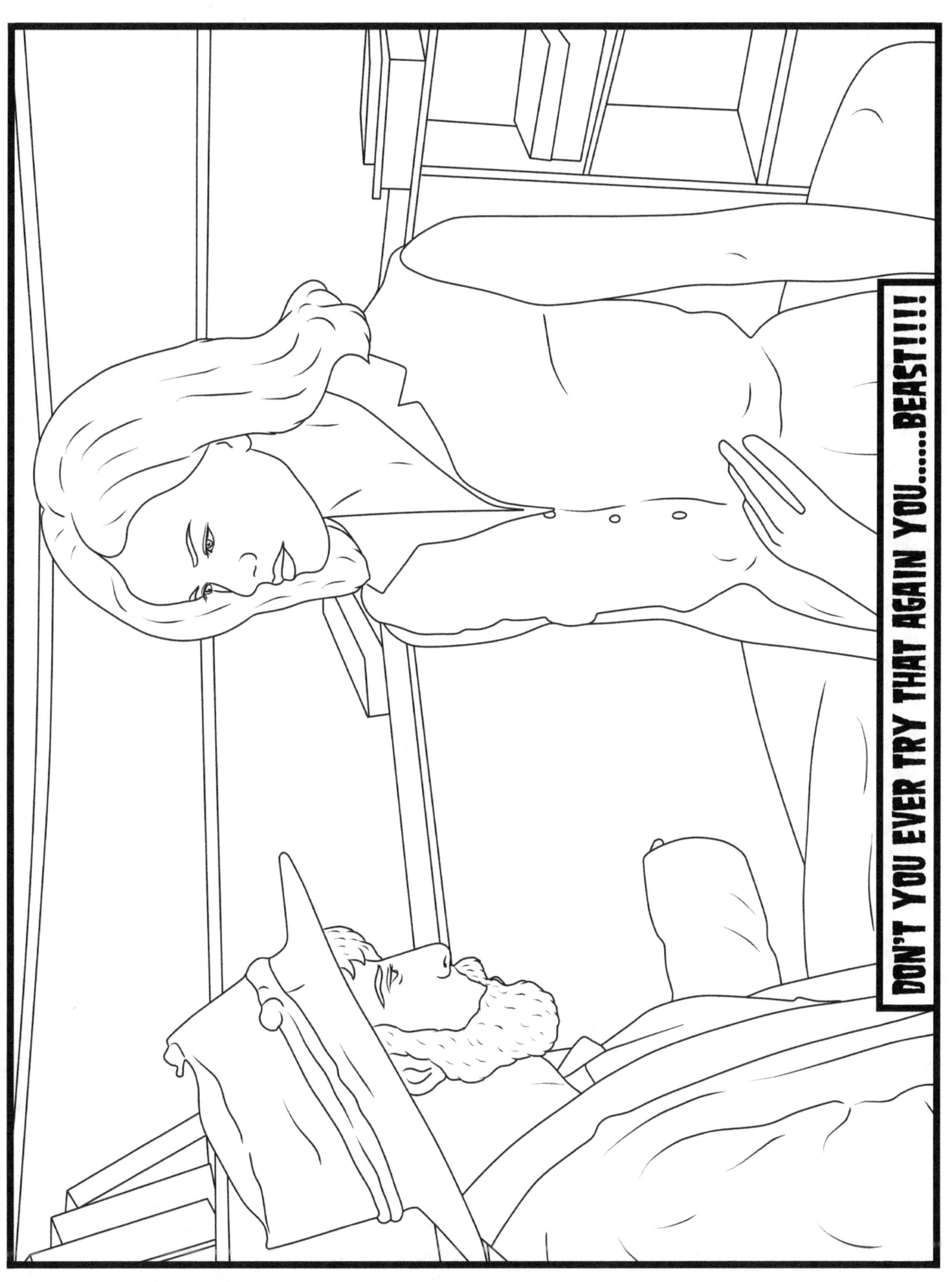

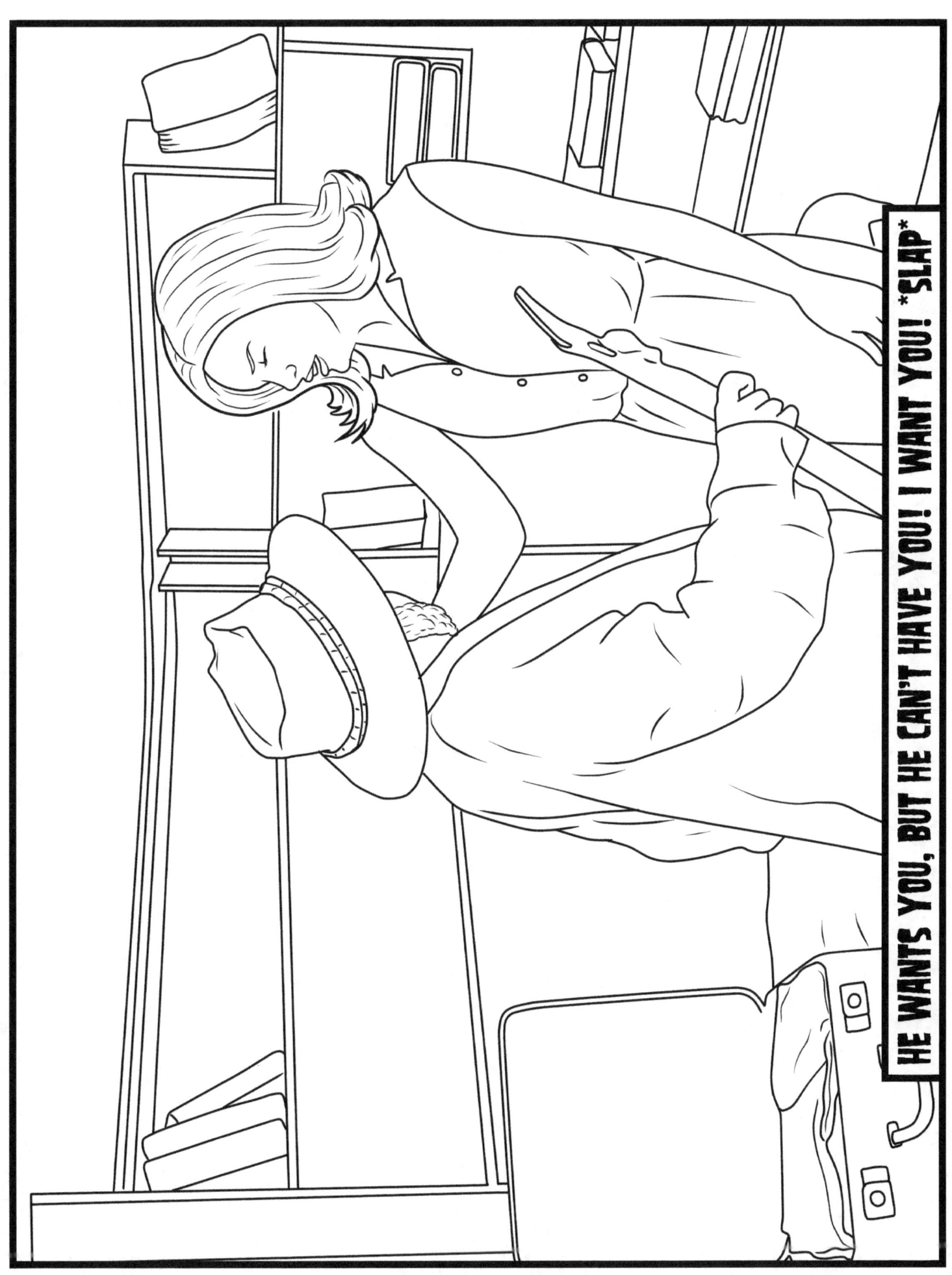

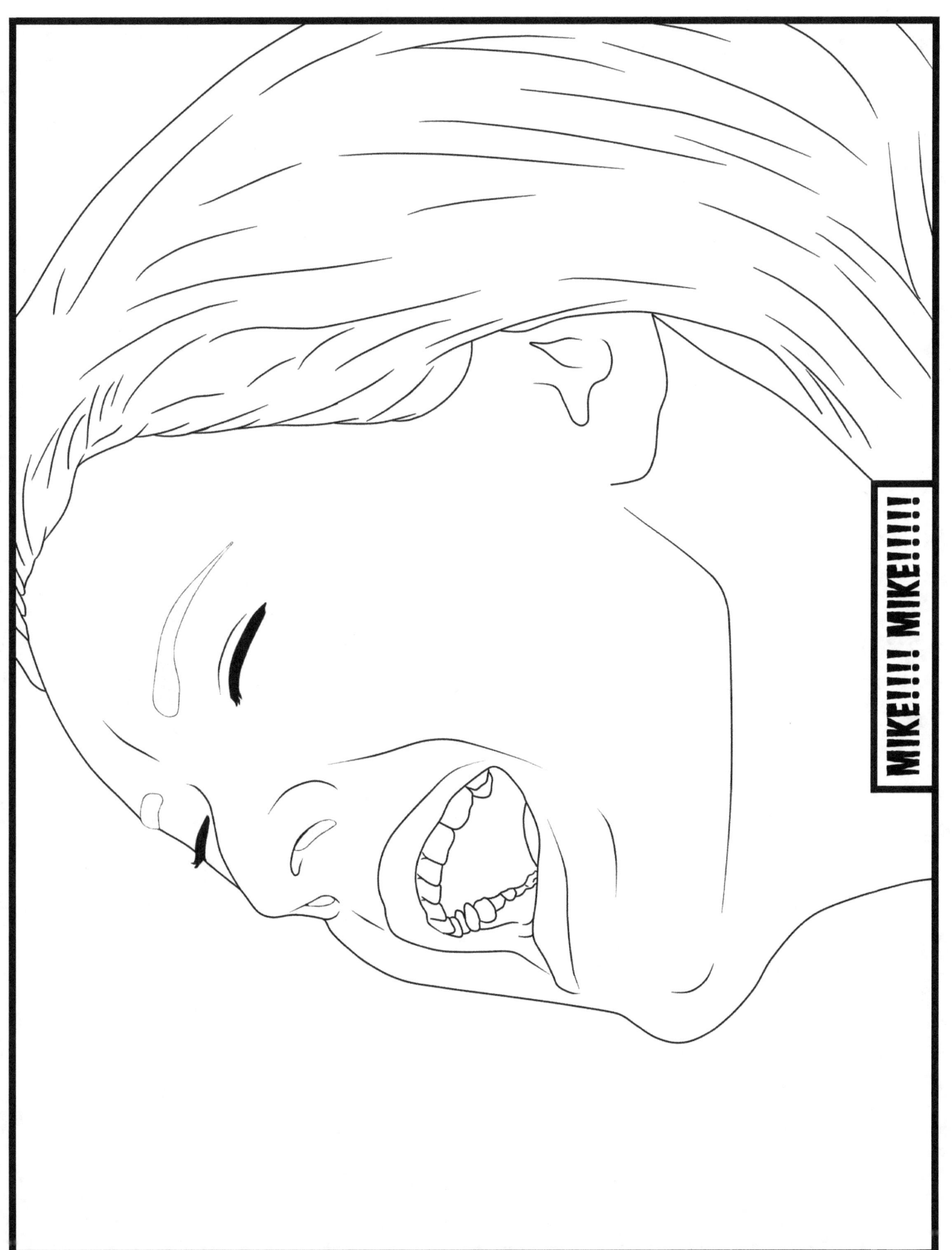

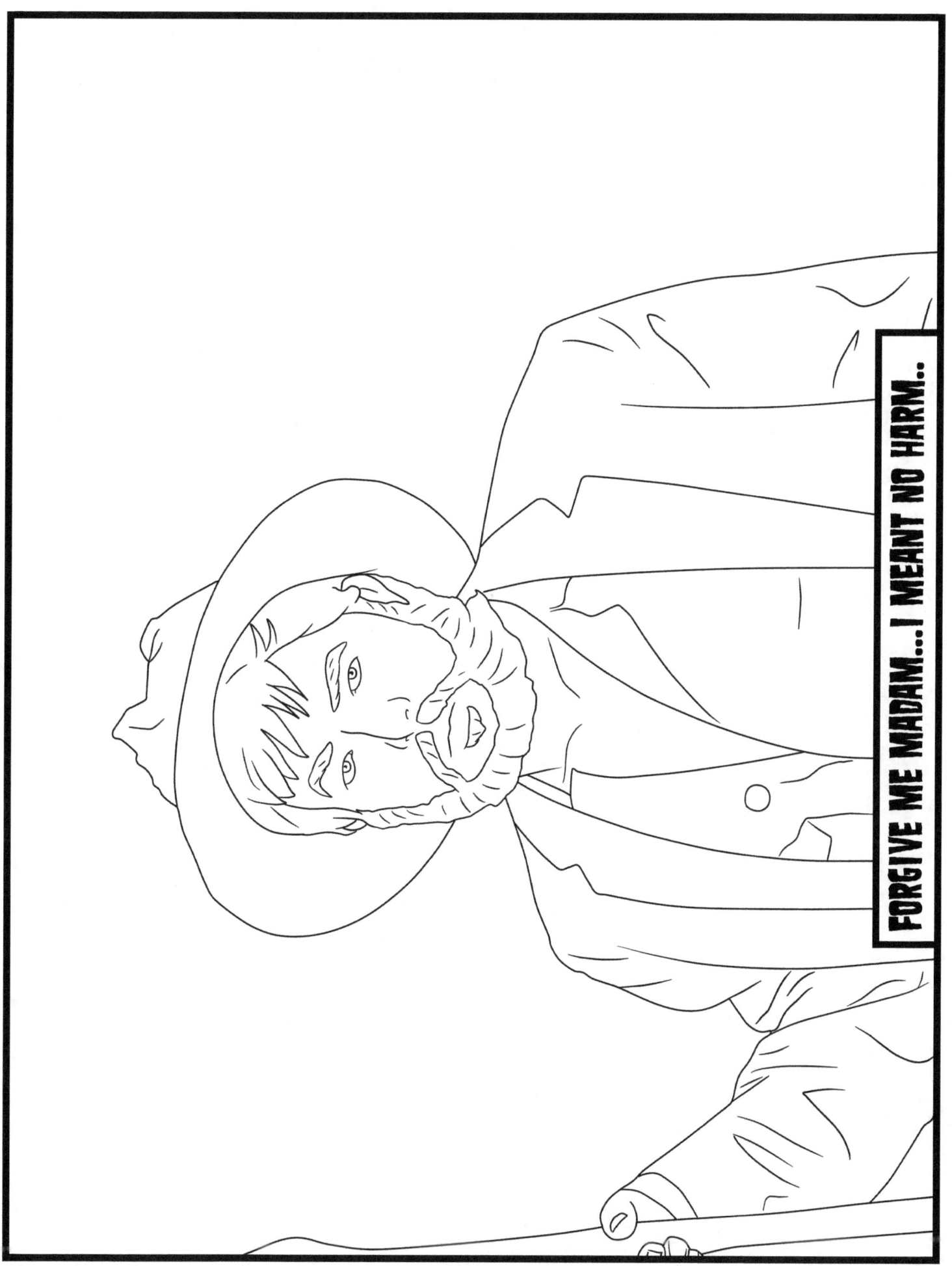

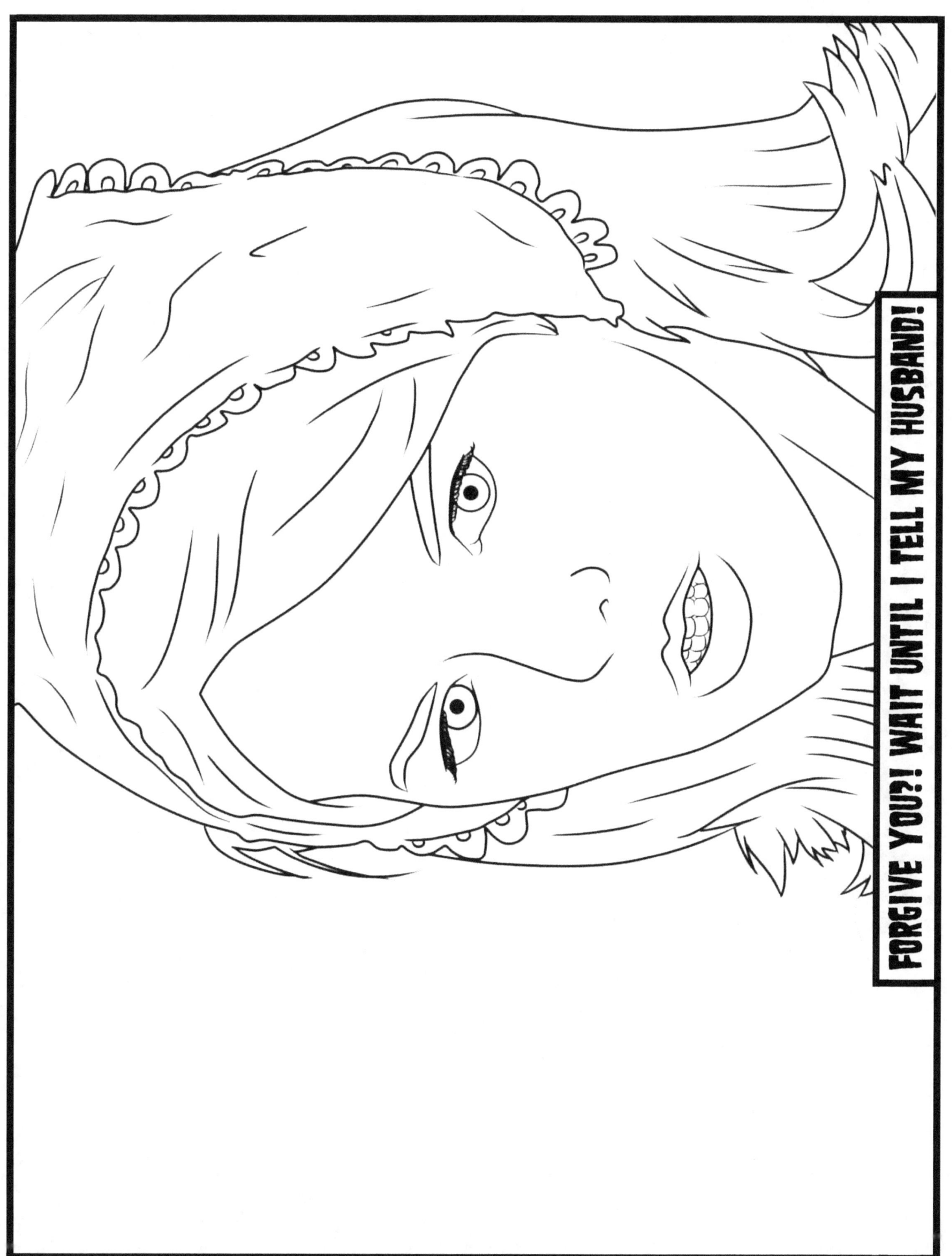

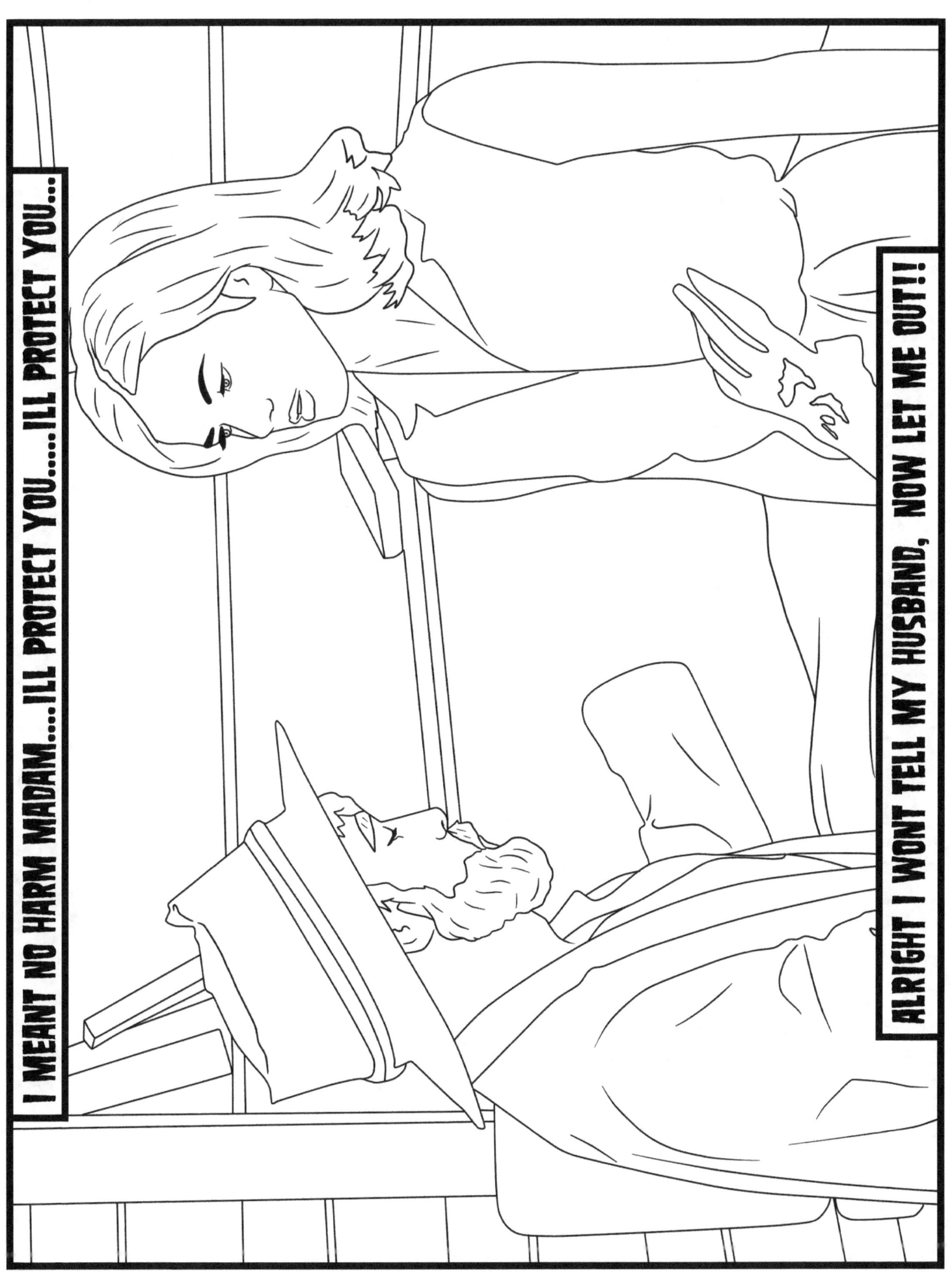

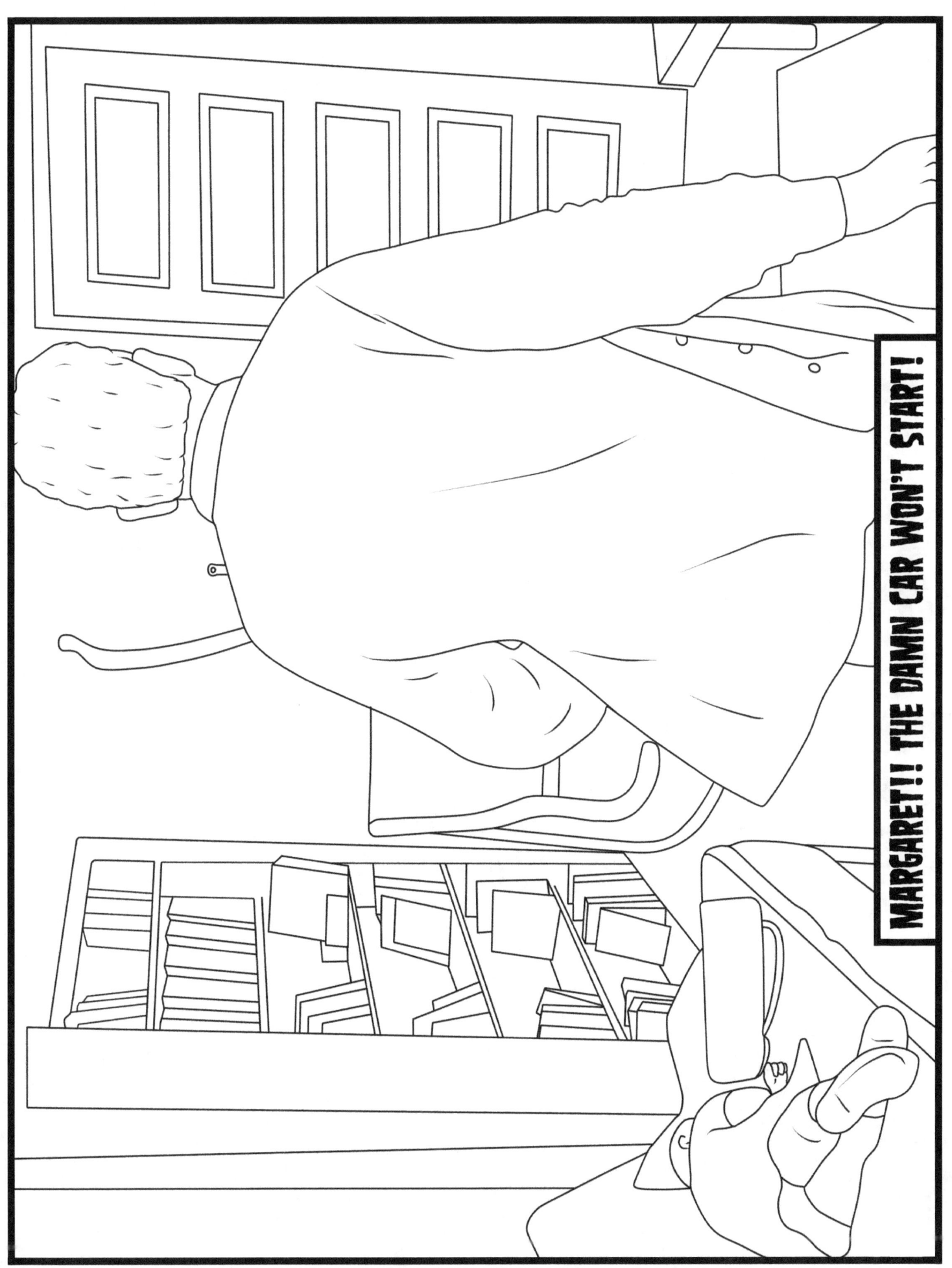

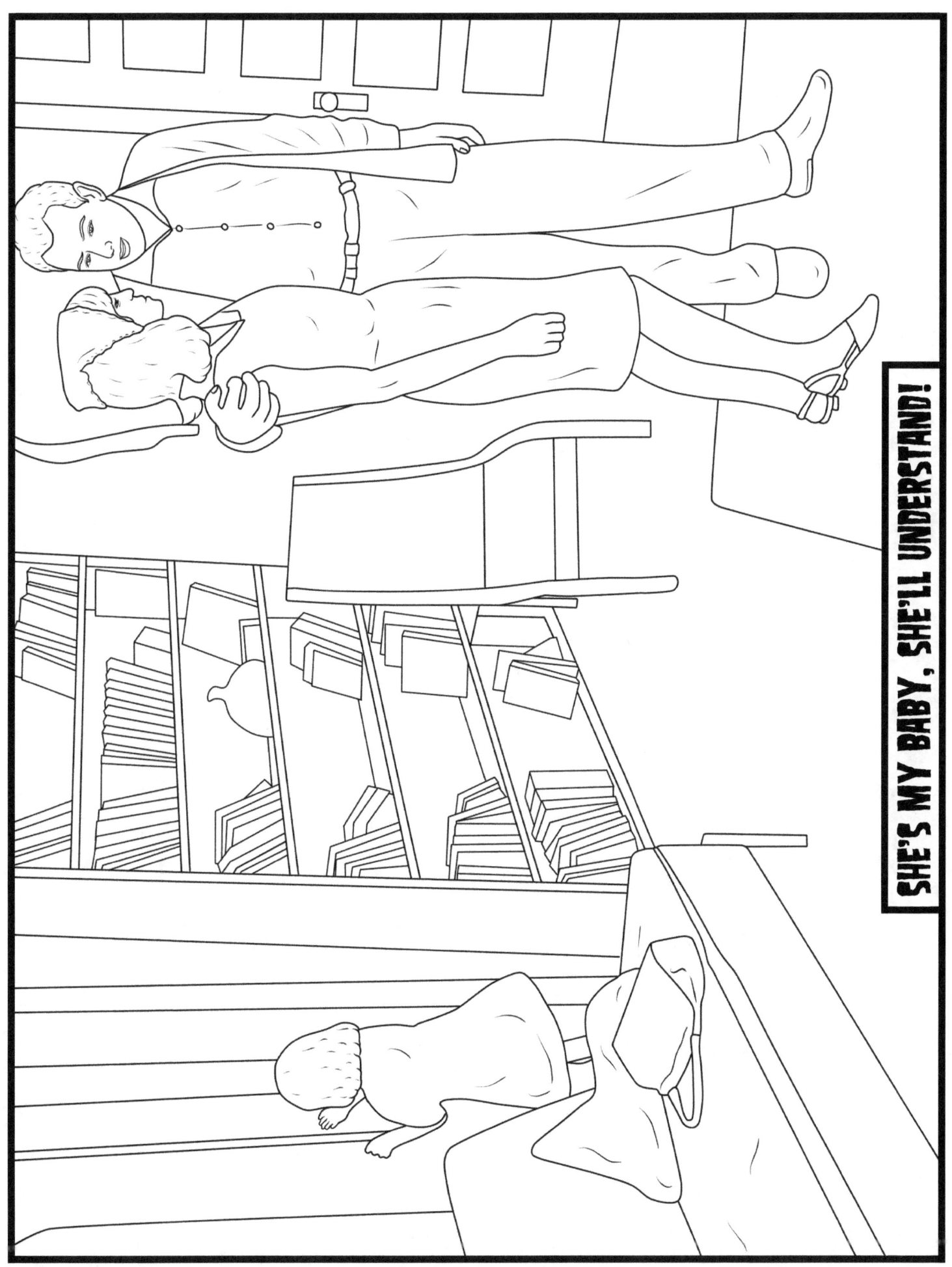

SHE'S MY BABY, SHE'LL UNDERSTAND!

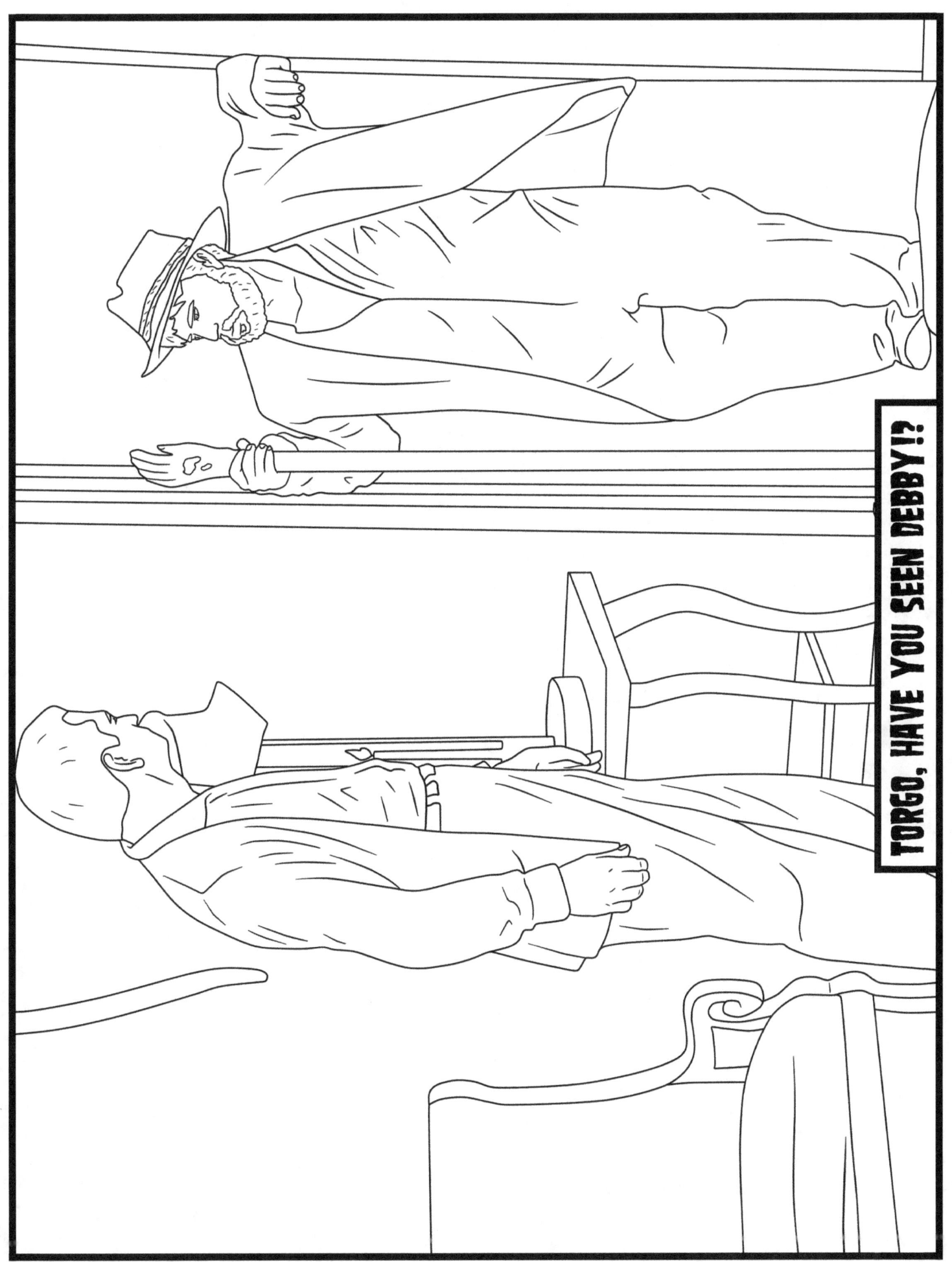

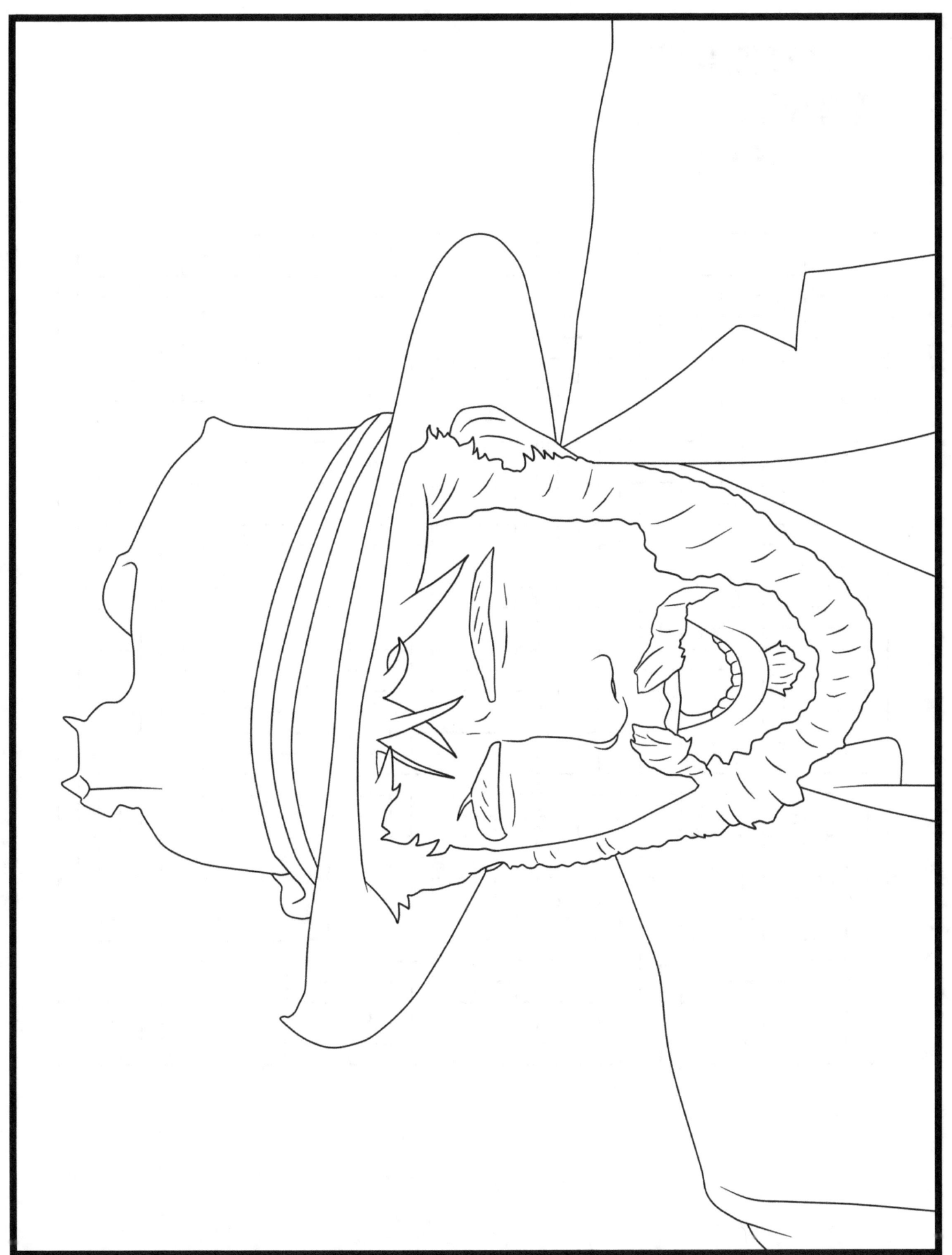

HELP MARGARET AND MICHAEL FIND DEBBY!

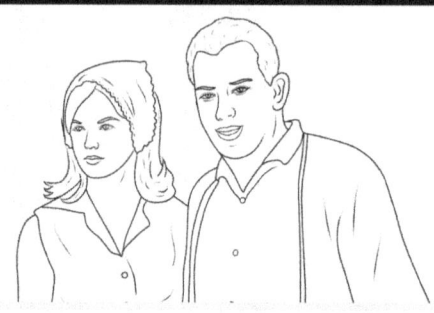

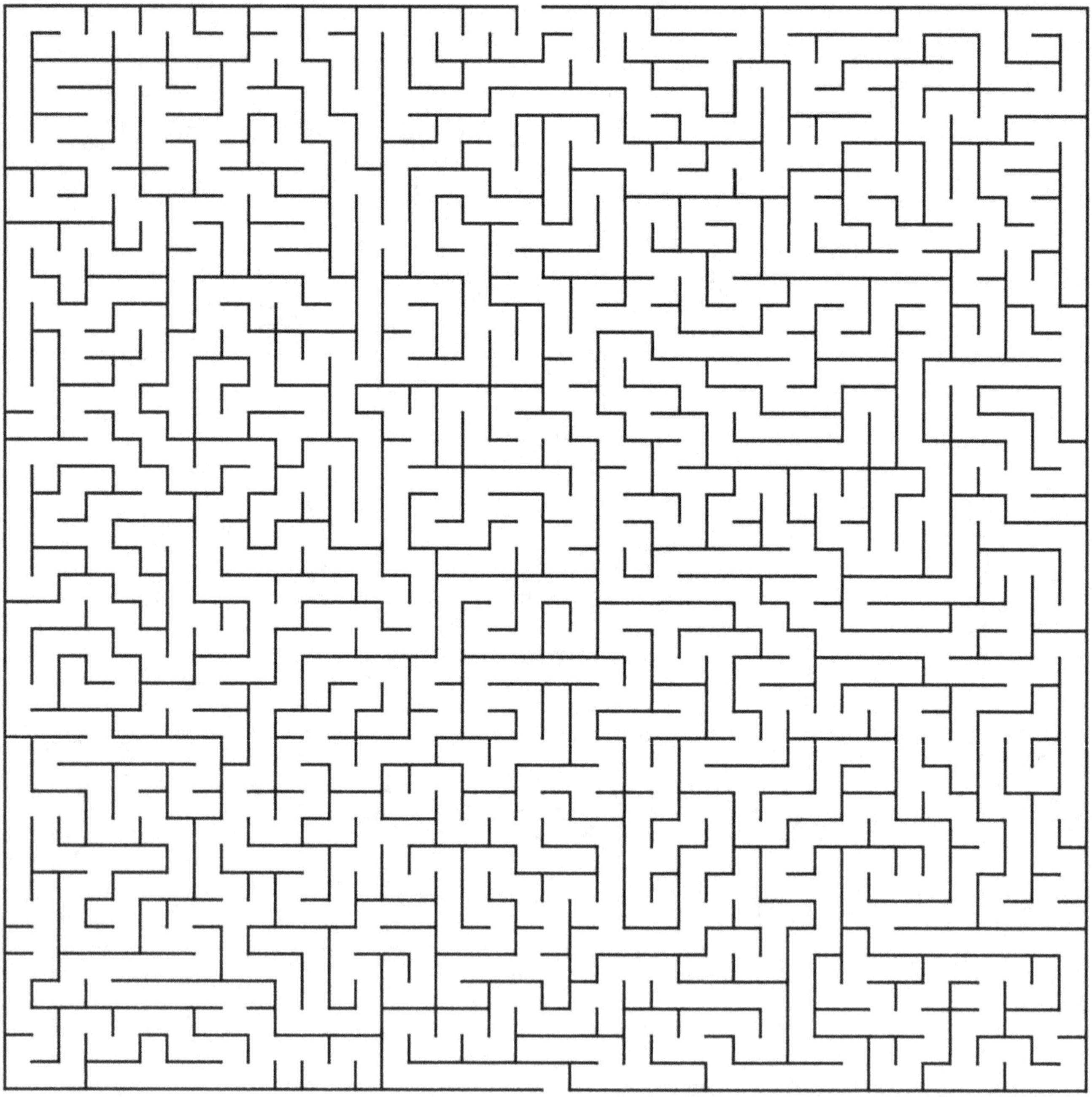

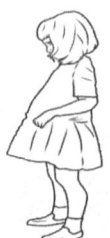

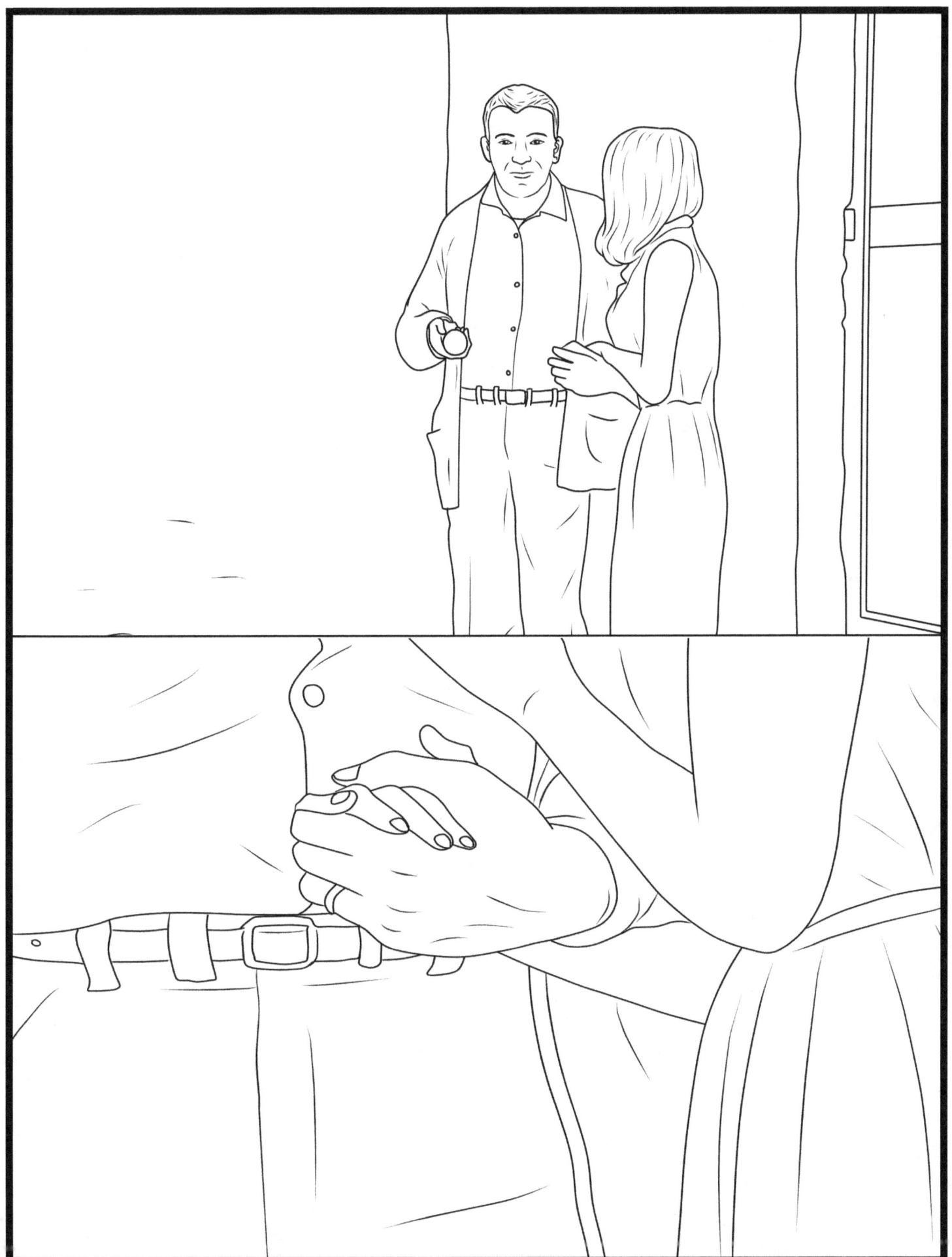

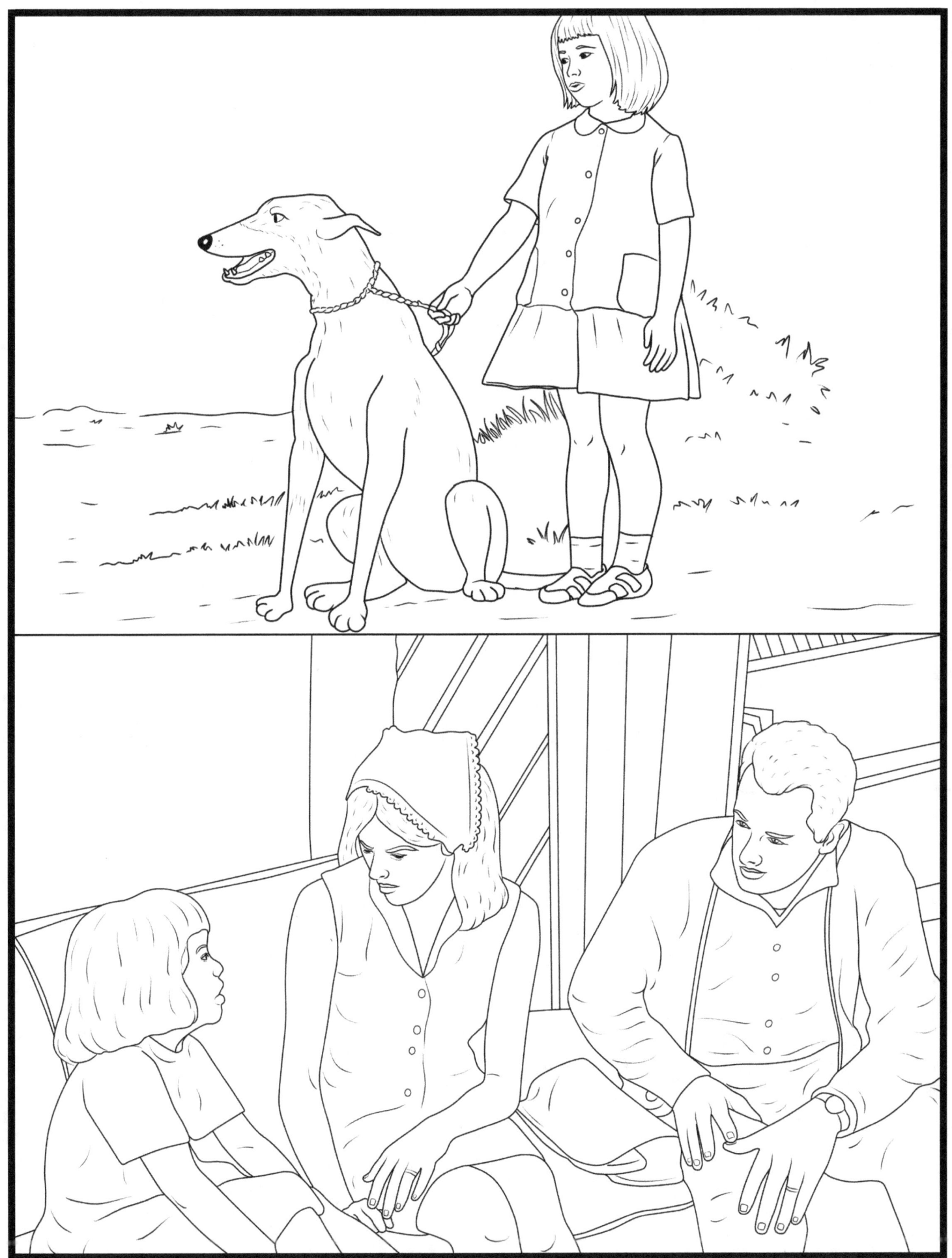

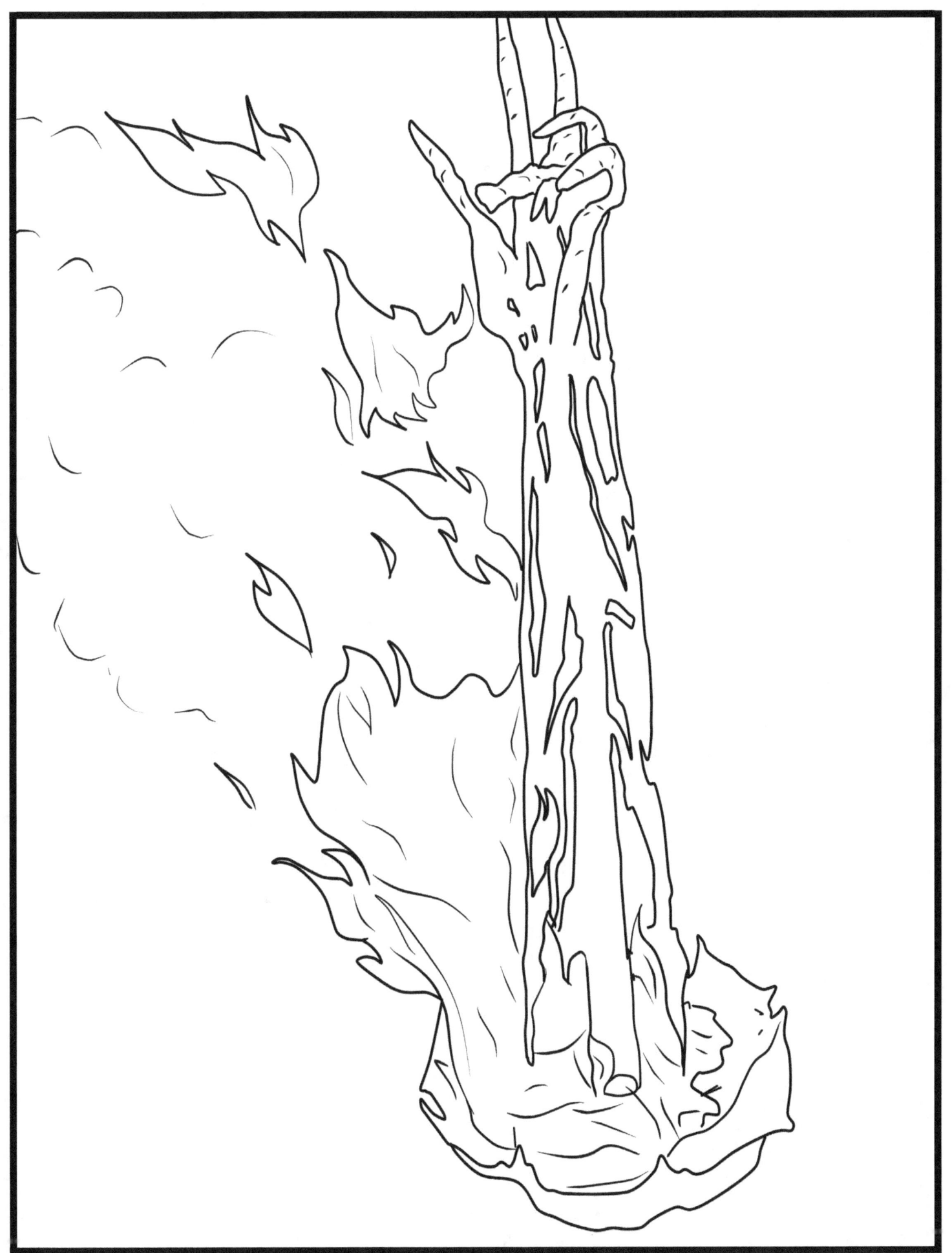

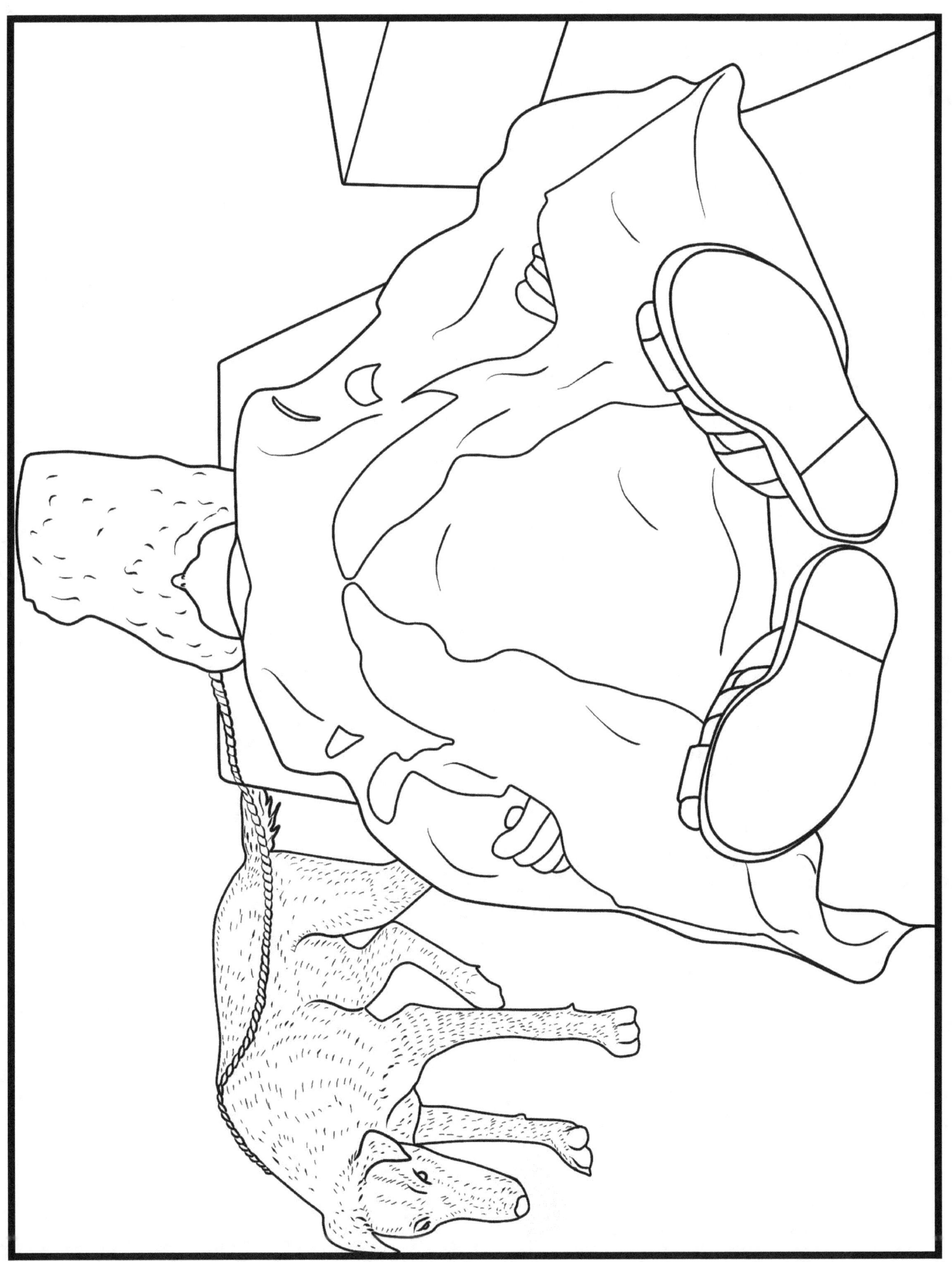

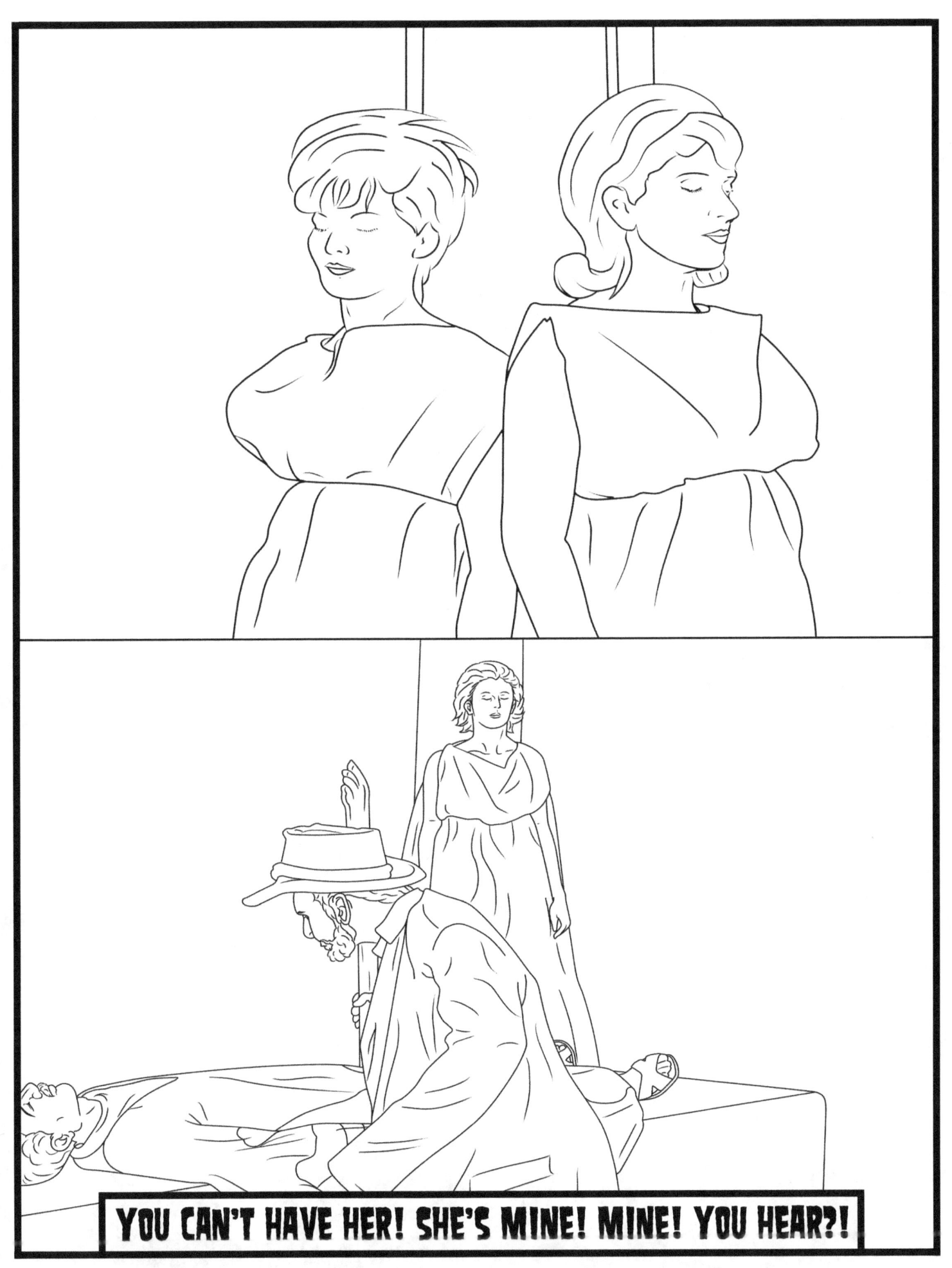

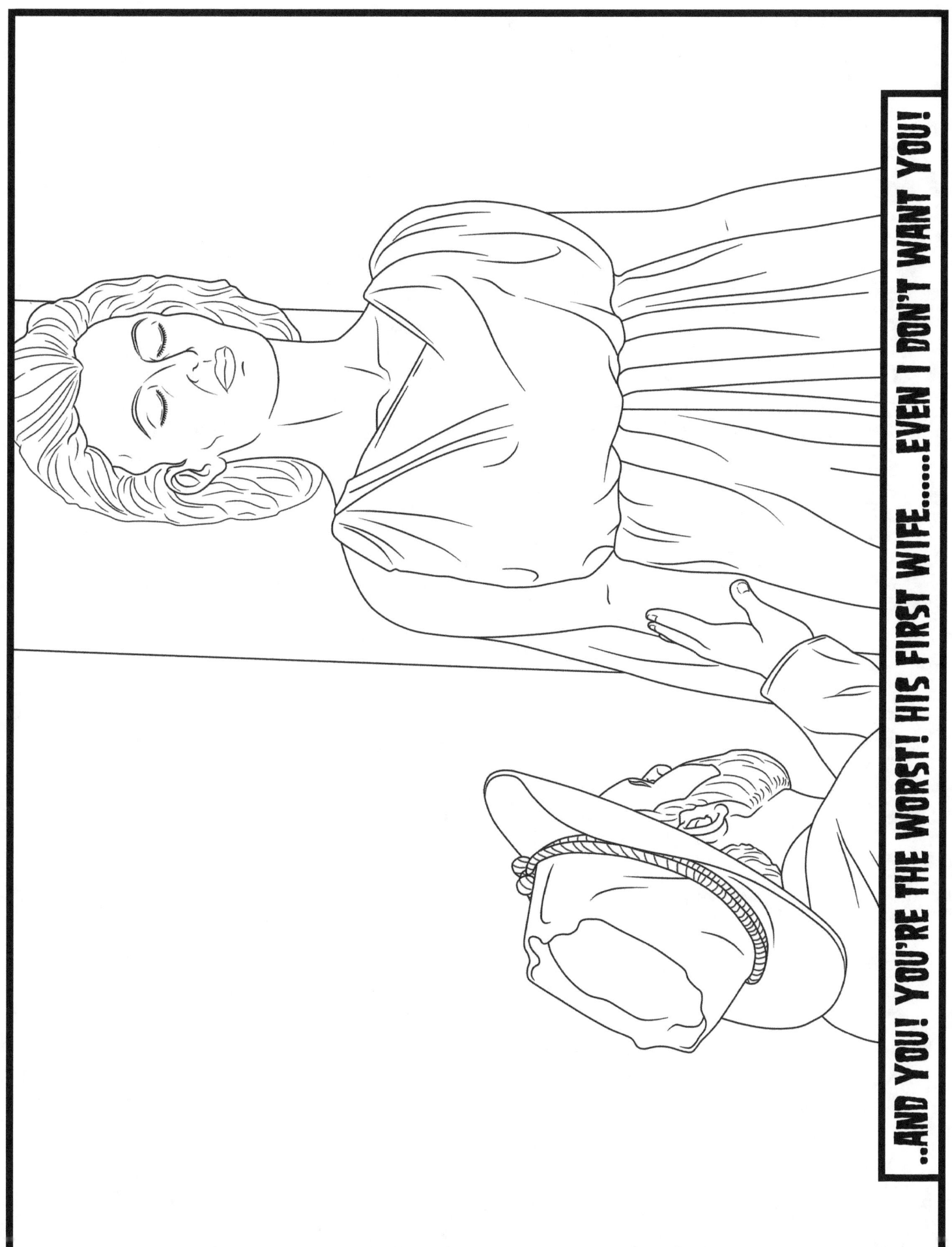

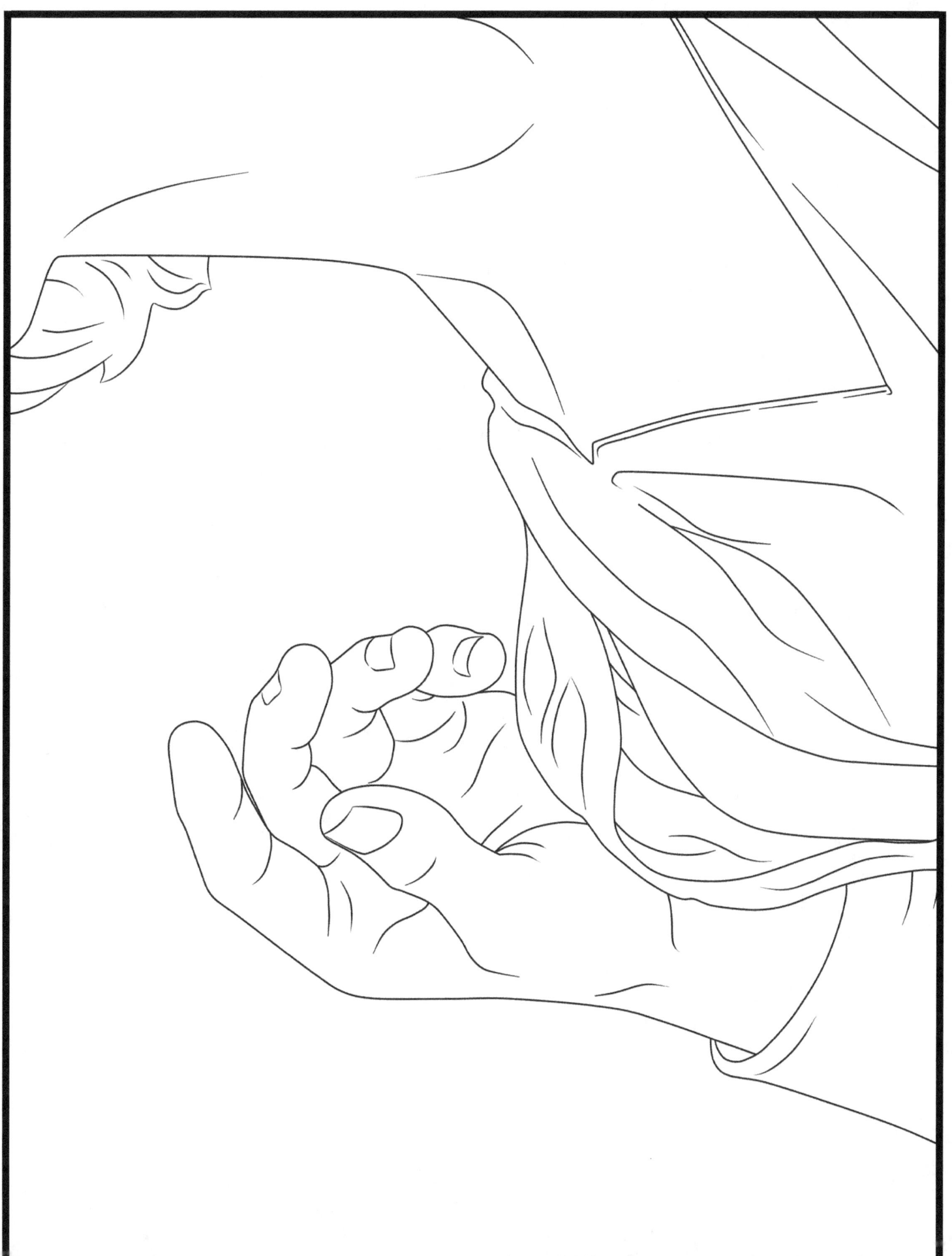

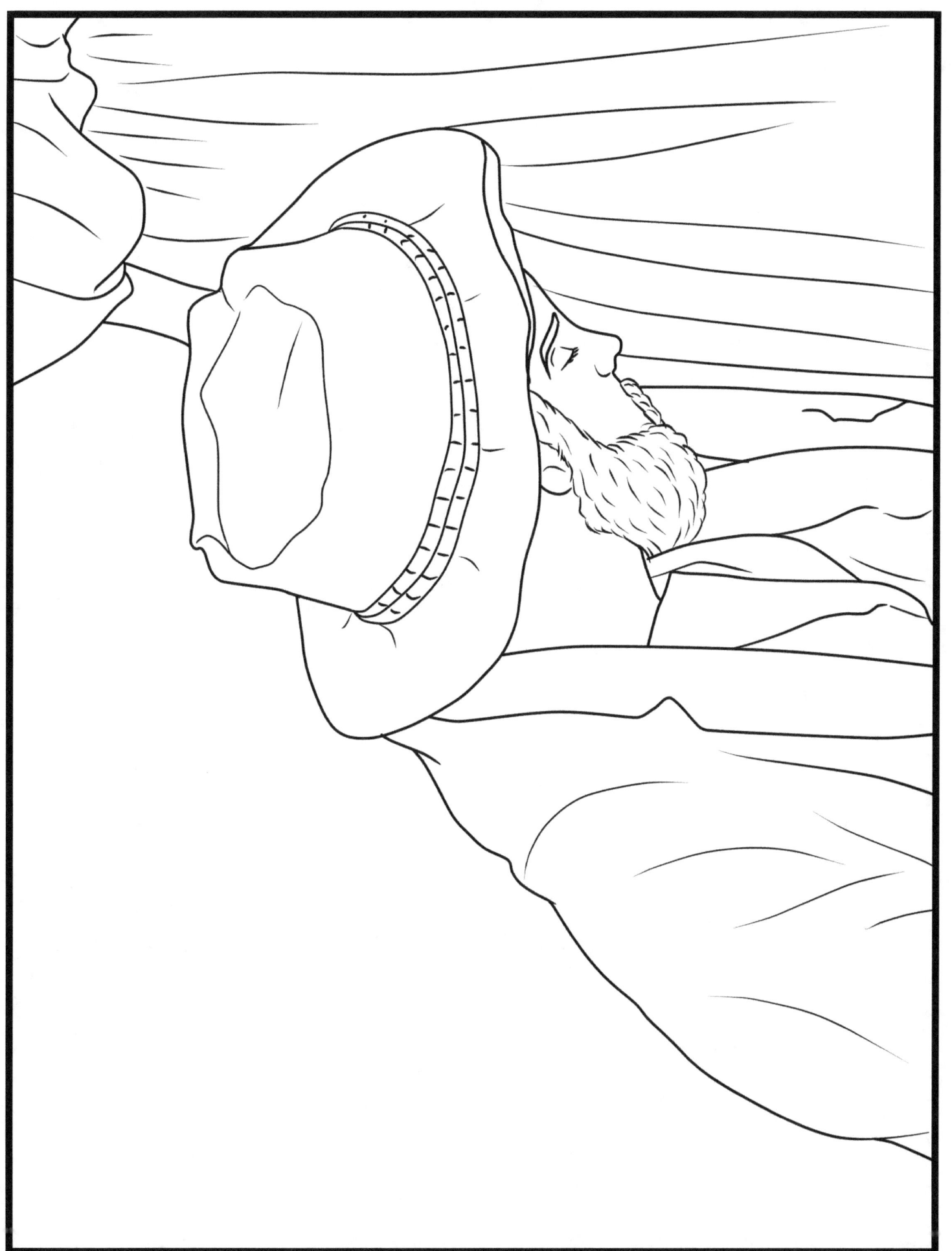

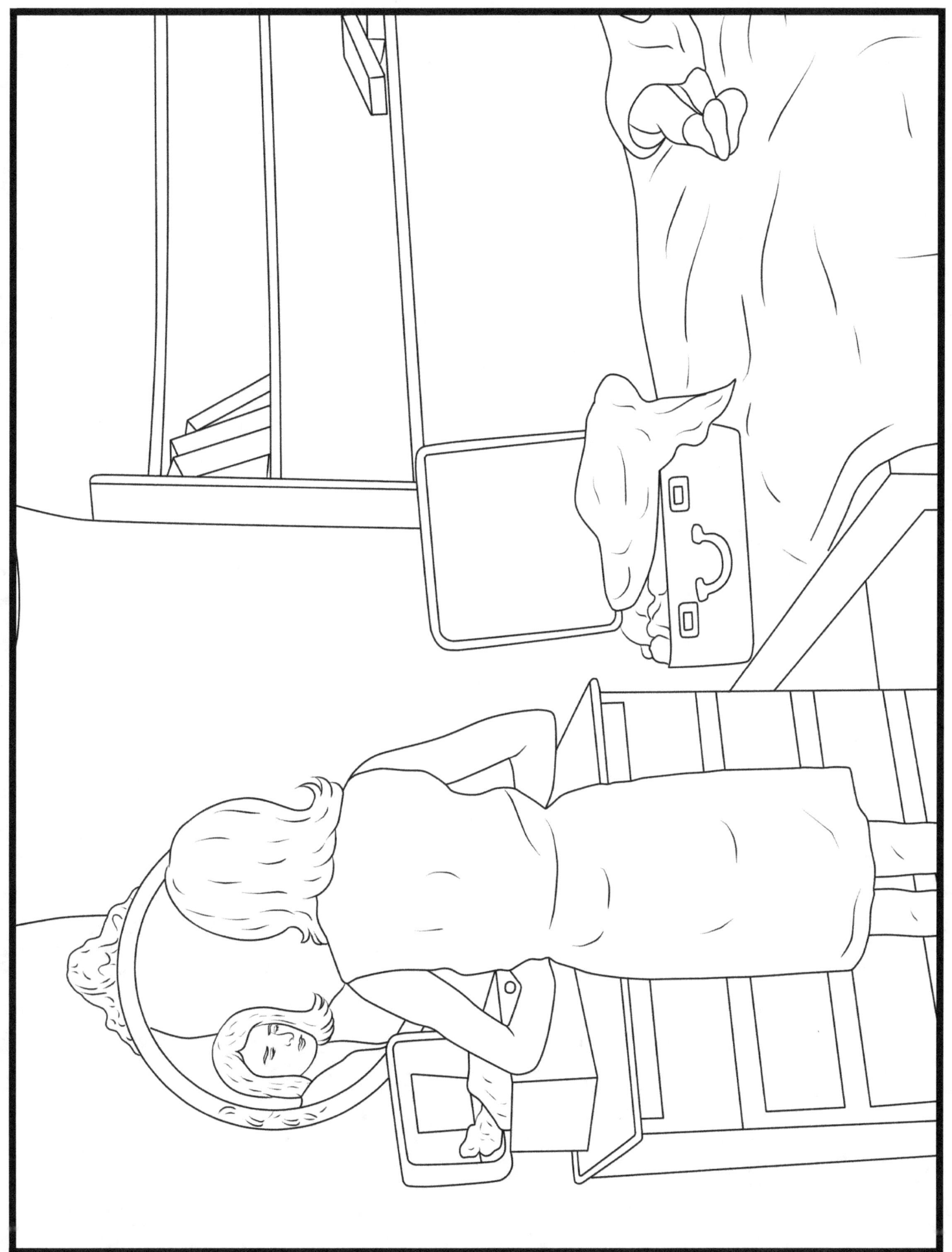

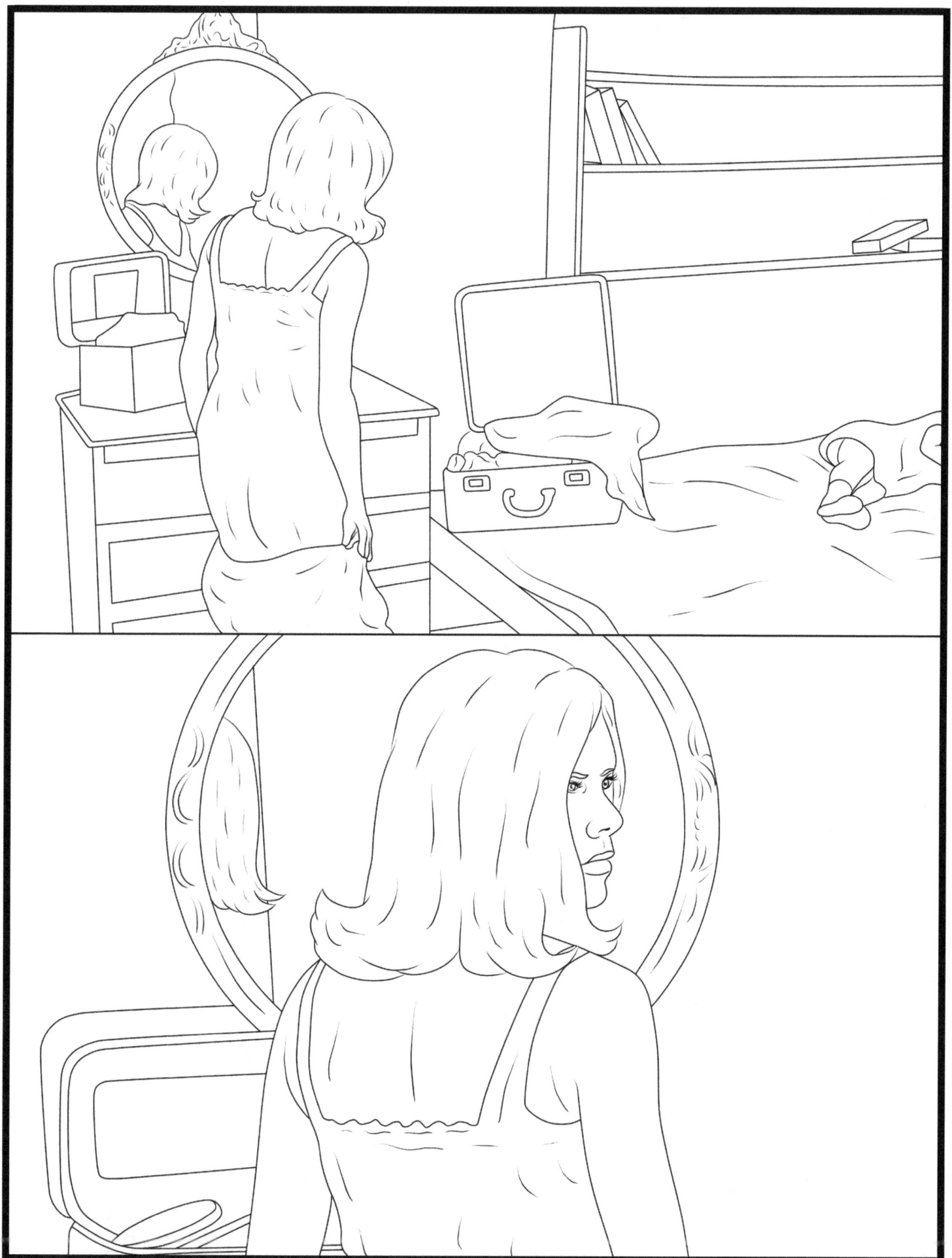

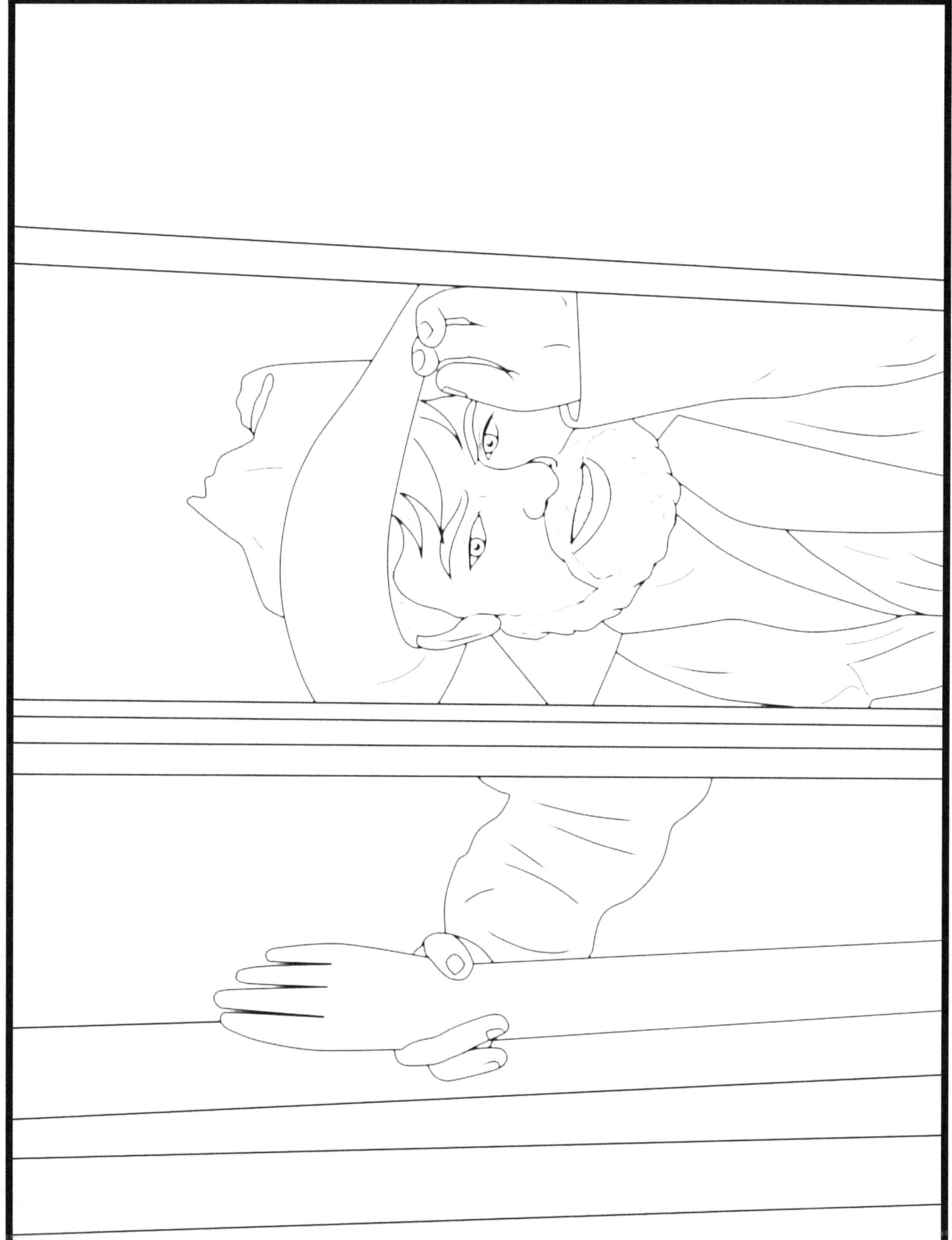

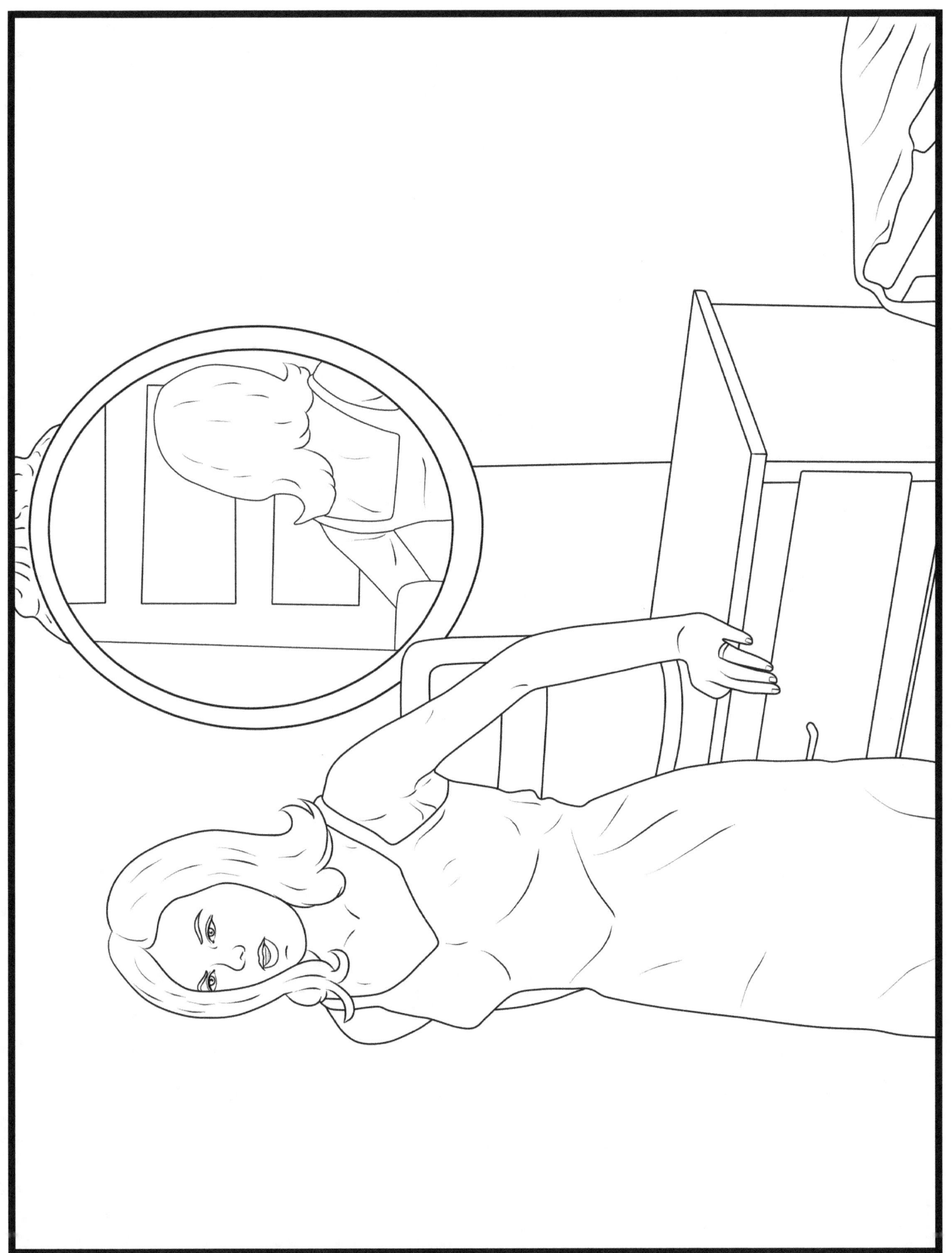

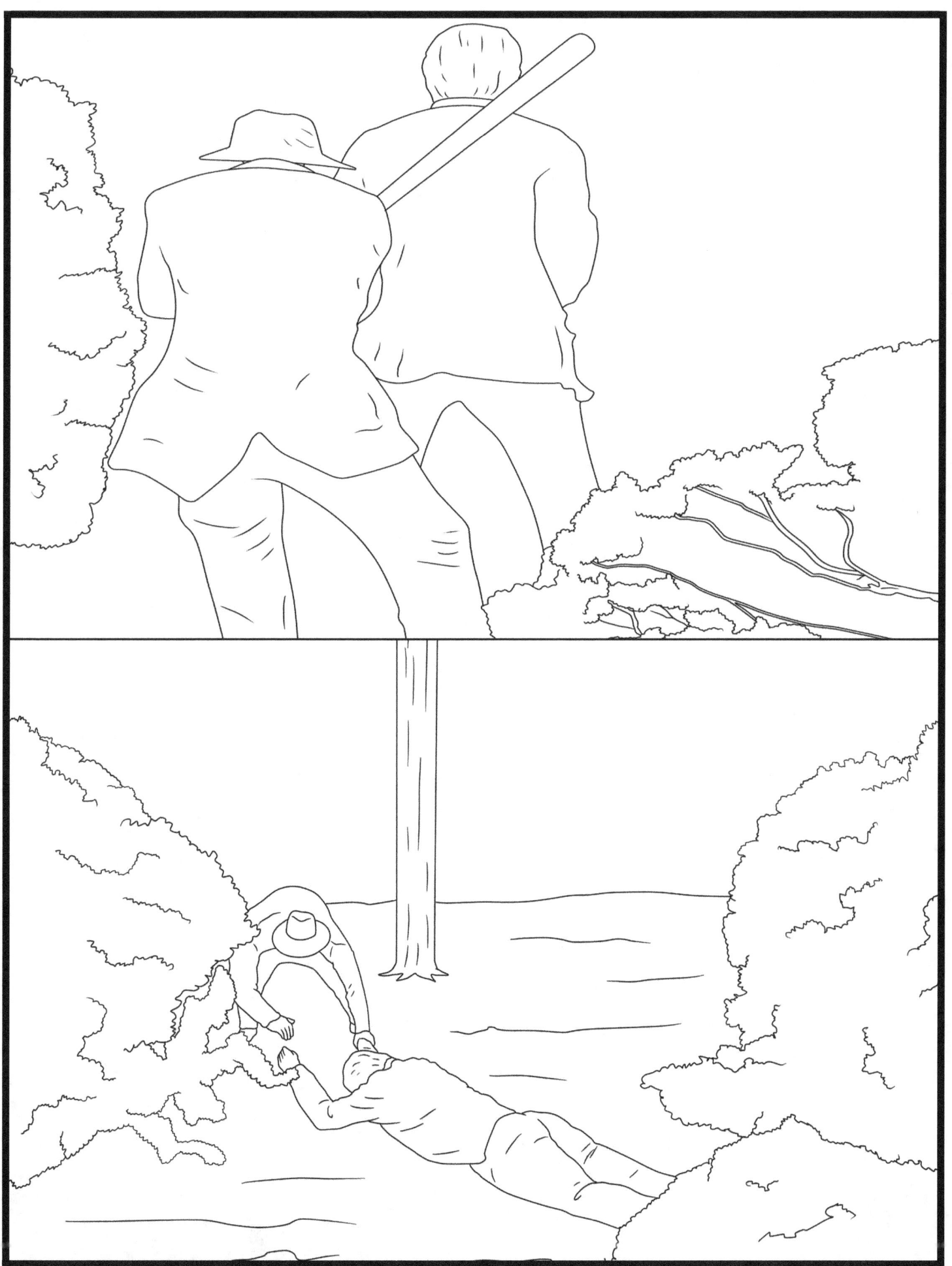

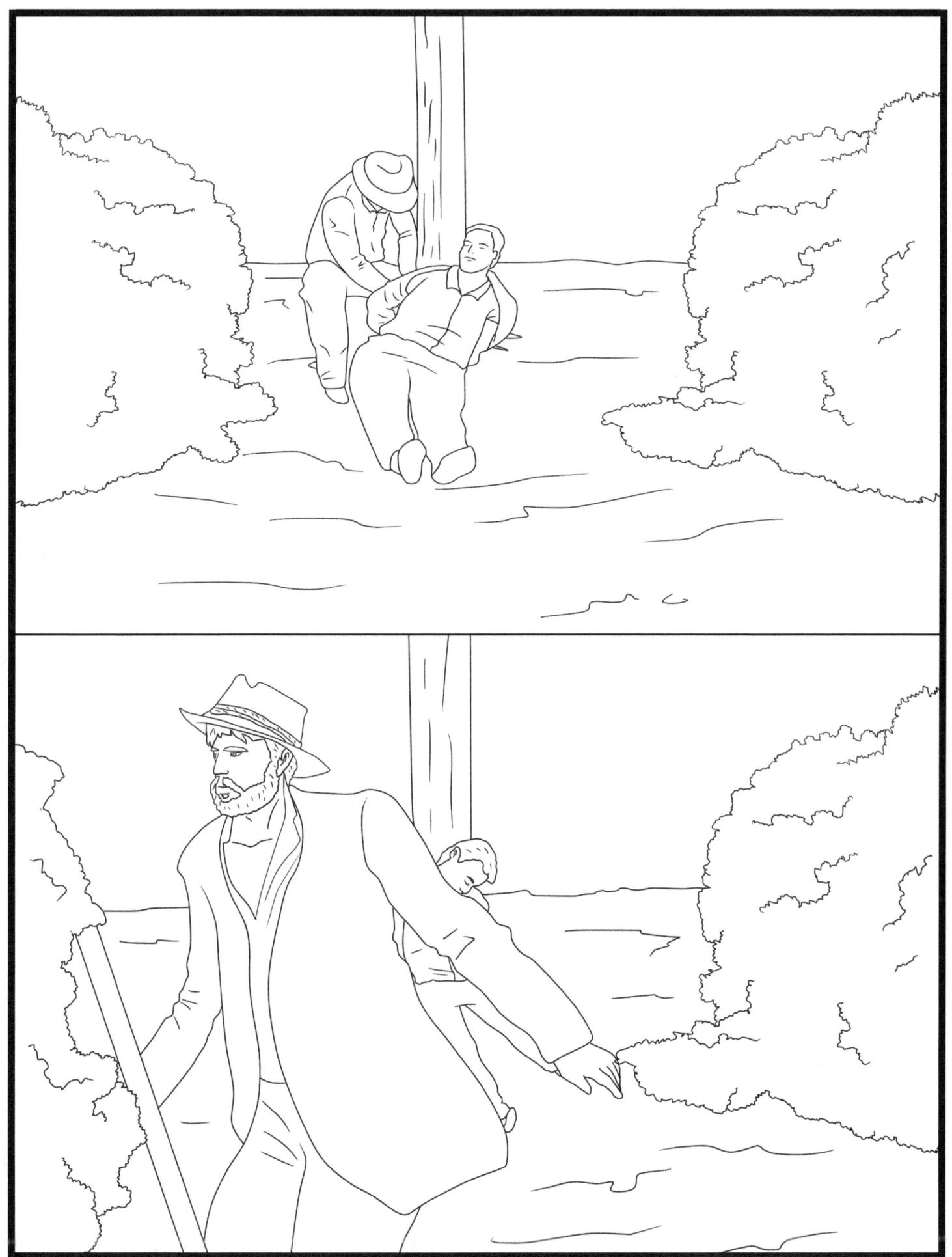

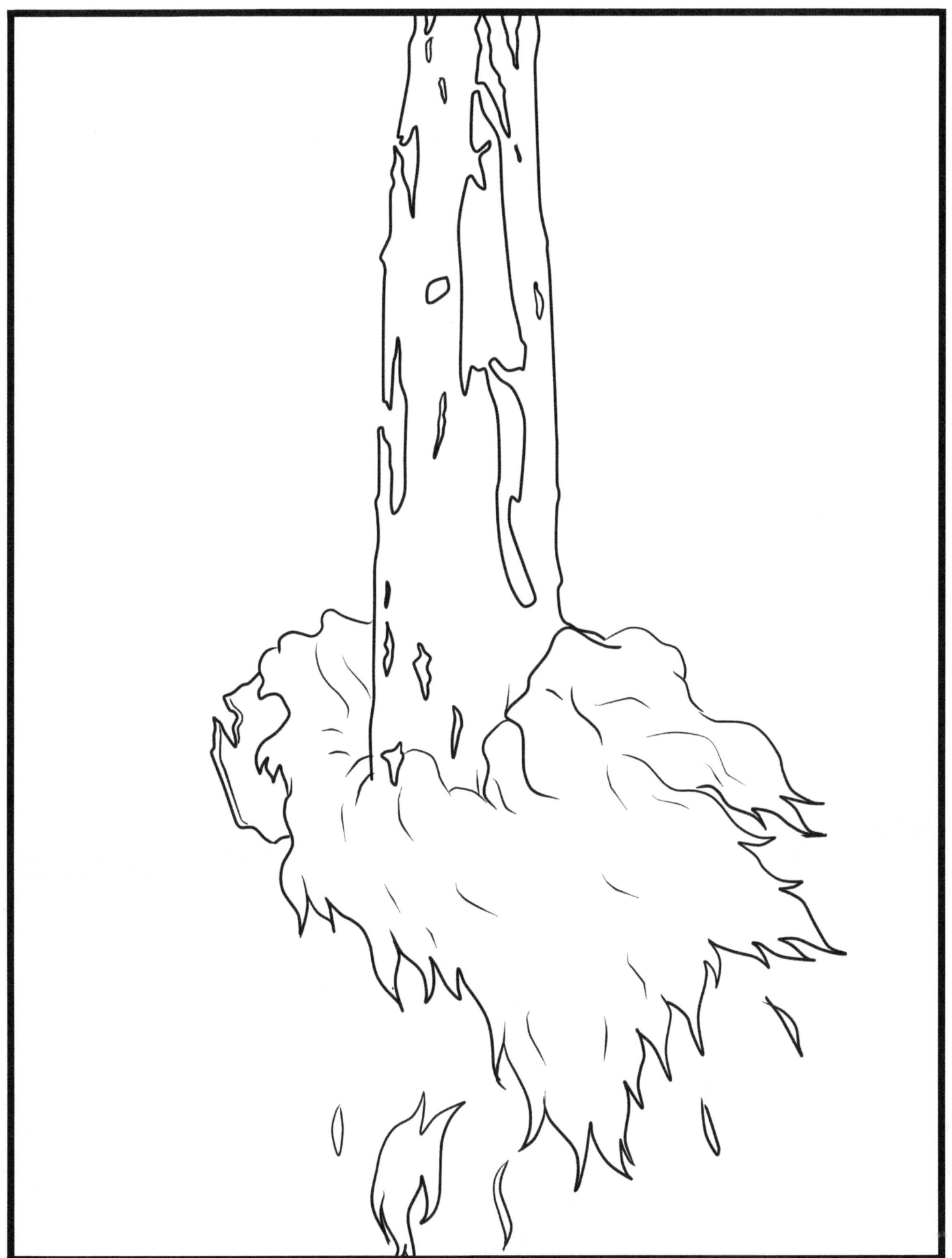

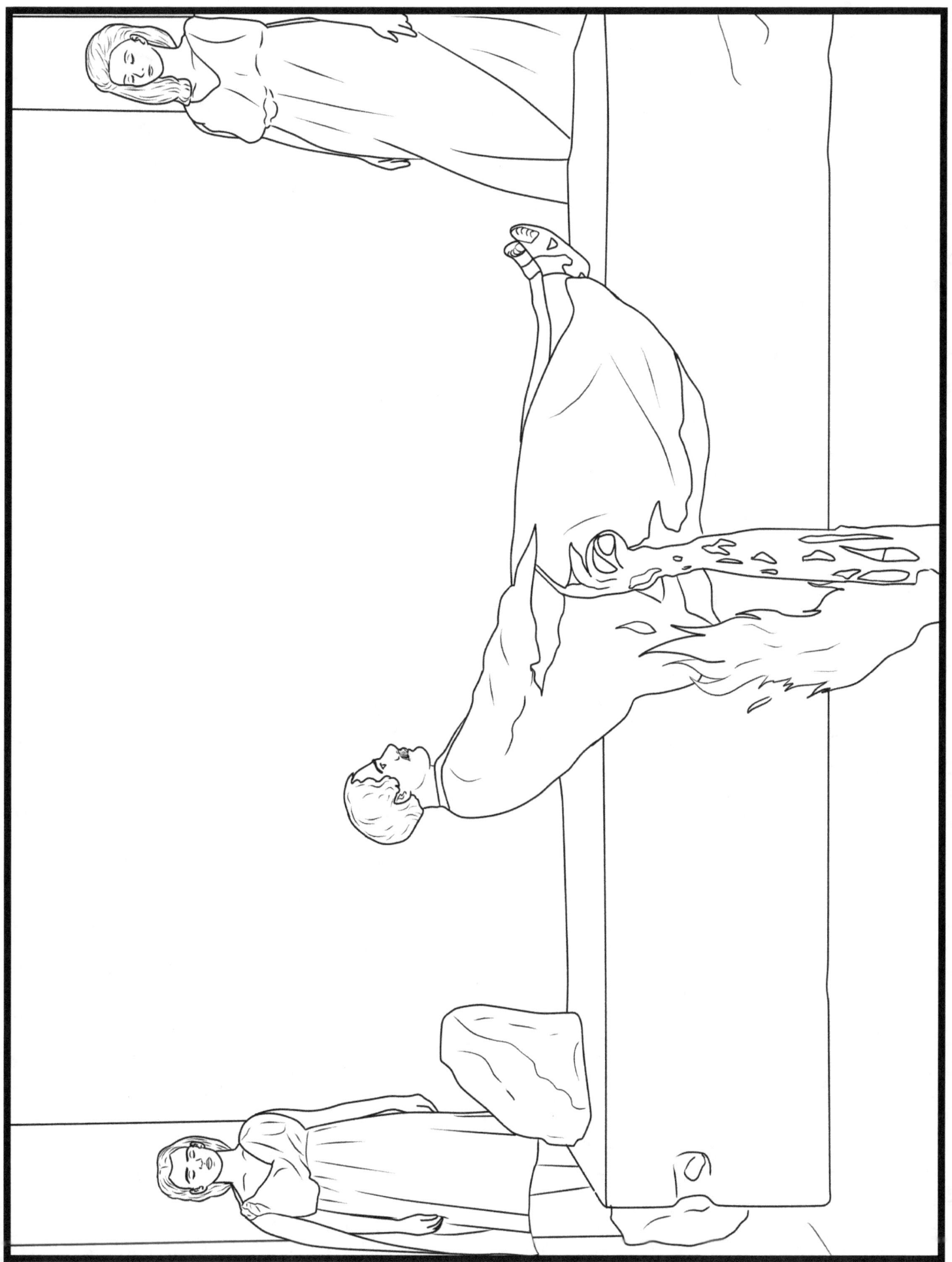

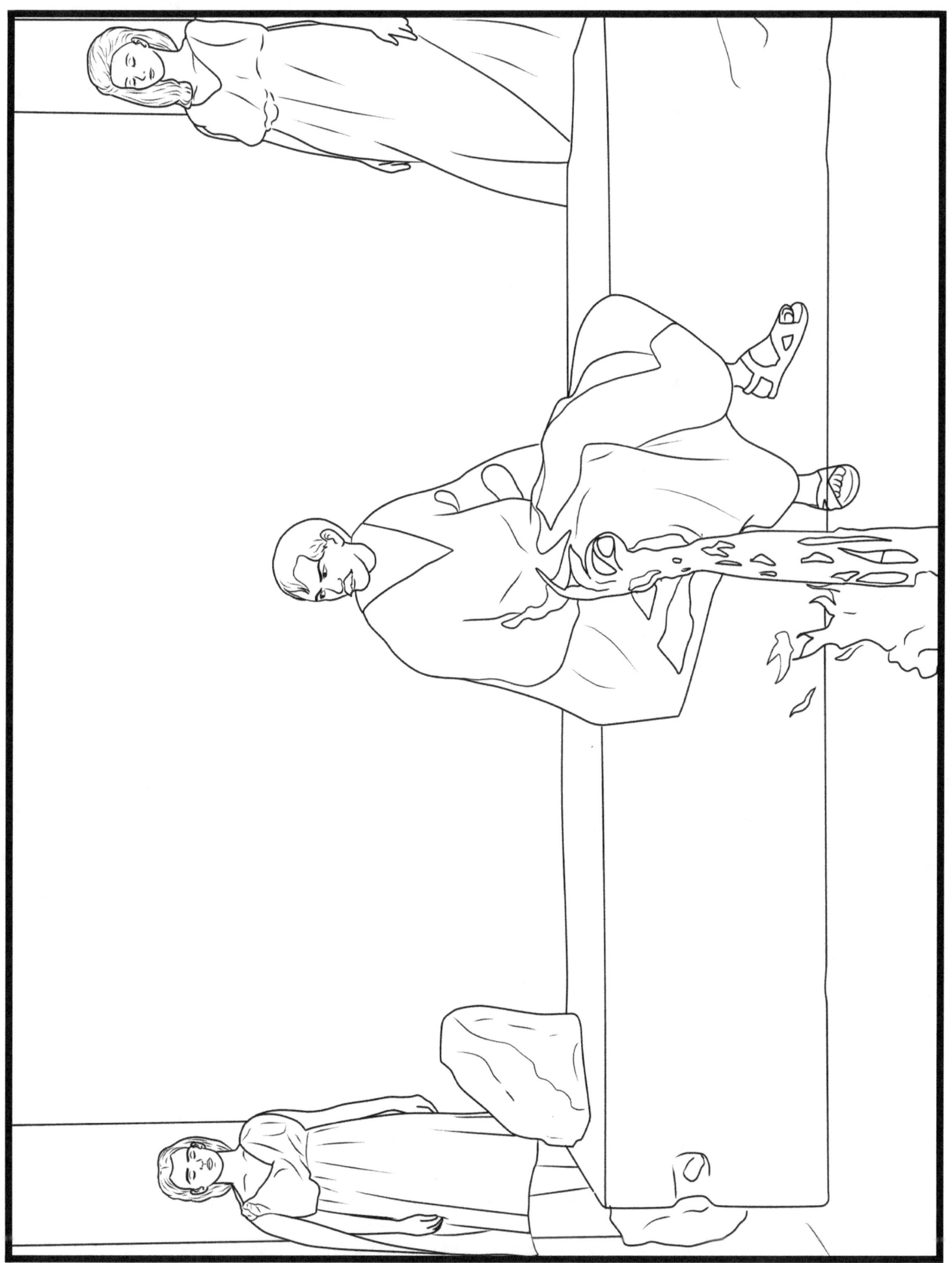

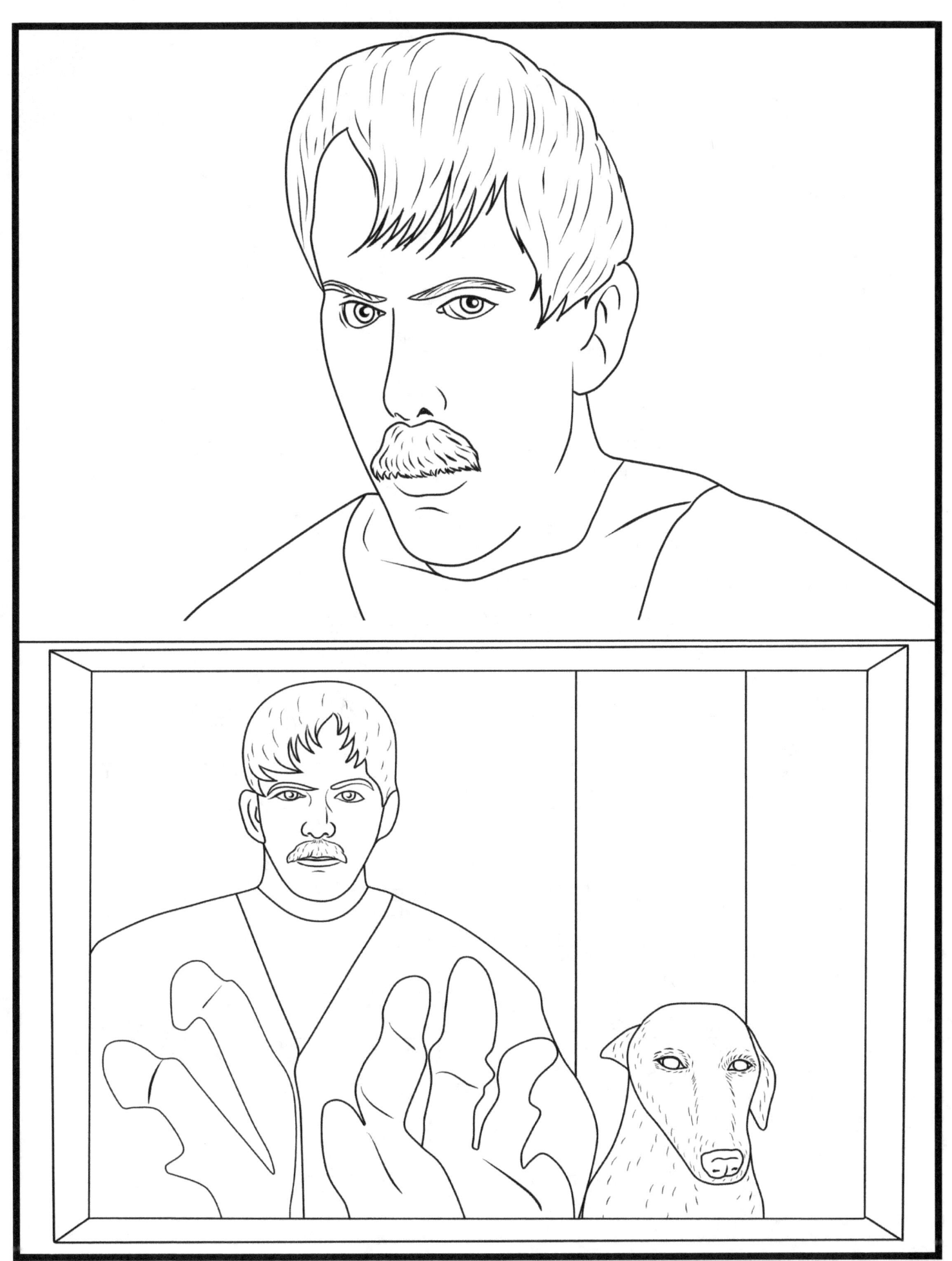

A	B	C	D	E	F	G	H	I	J	K	L	M	N	O	P	Q	R	S	T	U	V	W	X	Y	Z
12												3	7	24					1						

O__ M A N O S . . . ___ O _____ O _____ M A ___ A __ N
24 3 12 7 24 1   19 10 24 23   24 17   5 25 18 3 12 8   13 12 25 9 7 15

S S ! ___ O _____ O _____ N
1 1   19 10 24 23   22 10 24   13 22 15 8 8 15 19 10   18 7   19 10 15

_____ O _____ N _____ S ___ N
13 15 5 19 10   24 17   19 10 15   23 7 18 20 15 25 1 15   18 7   19 10 15

A _____ A S M S O ___ N _____ ! ___ O
4 8 12 14 9   14 10 12 1 3 1   24 17   7 18 2 10 19   19 10 24 23

O _____ S O _____ M O _____ A __ N
22 10 24   4 15 1   19 24 22 15 19 10   19 10 15   3 24 19 10 15 25   13 12 25 9 7

S S ___ O N ___ A , ___ O
15 1 1   23 5 24 7   19 10 16   17 12 18 19 10 17 23 8   19 24

_____ N A _____ N _____ N .
8 18 20 15   15 19 15 25 7 12 8 8 16   18 7   10 15 25   9 15 15 5 18 7 2

O _____ O S ___ M A _____ M M O S _____ S S
19 10 24 23   13 24 1 19   3 12 9 15   10 18 3   3 24 1 19   4 8 15 1 1 15 13

O _____ ! A N _____ O _____ O _____ O S
17 24 25 15 20 15 25   12 7 13   19 10 24 23   22 10 24   13 24 1 19

S _____ N A _____ N N
14 23 25 1 15 13   22 18 19 10   15 19 15 25 7 12 8   4 23 25 7 18 7 2

O S _____ O M _____ A N S _____ S S
8 18 17 15   19 10 24 1 15   22 10 24 3   19 25 12 7 1 2 25 15 1 1

A __ A N S _____ ! O ___ A _____ O ,
12 2 12 18 7 1 19   19 10 15 15   10 24 8 16   12 25 19   19 10 24 23

O ___ A _____ O , O ___ A _____ O !
10 24 8 16   12 25 19   19 10 24 23   10 24 8 16   12 25 19   19 10 24 23

M A N O S _____ O N ! _____ S
3 12 7 24 1   22 18 8 8   4 15   13 24 7 15   19 10 16   5 25 18 15 1 19 10

O O _____ M A N S S ___ A ___ A S , _____ O
24 24 13   25 15 3 12 18 7 1   1 19 15 12 13 17 12 1 19   19 10 16

S _____ O O _____ M A __ N S ___ O N S __ A N ,
5 25 18 15 1   19 10 24 24 13   25 15 3 12 18 7 1   14 24 7 1 19 12 7 19

O _____ S _____ O O _____ M A __ N S _____ O
19 10 16   5 25 18 15 1 19 10 24 24 13   25 15 3 12 18 7 1   25 18 2 10 19 15 24

S . ___ O ___ A S ___ A _____ S , O
23 1   19 10 24 23   10 12 1 19   19 12 23 2 10 19   23 1   24

M A N O S , A N _____ A _____ S ___ N .
3 12 7 24 1   12 7 13   22 15   10 12 19 10   8 18 1 19 15 7 15 13

_____ A ___ O O _____ O ___ S , O M A N O S ,
2 18 20 15   15 12 25   19 24   24 23 25   22 24 25 13 1   24   3 12 7 24 1

A N ___ A ___ S ! ___ A ___ S ! ___ A
12 7 13   10 15 12 25   23 1   10 15 12 25   23 1   10 15 12 25

S ! ___ O _____ A _____ A _____ A N
23 1   17 24 25   22 15 15   12 25 15   17 12 18 19 10 17 23 8   12 7 13

O _____ A _____ O _____ O .
19 10 24 23   12 25 19   24 23 25   2 24 13

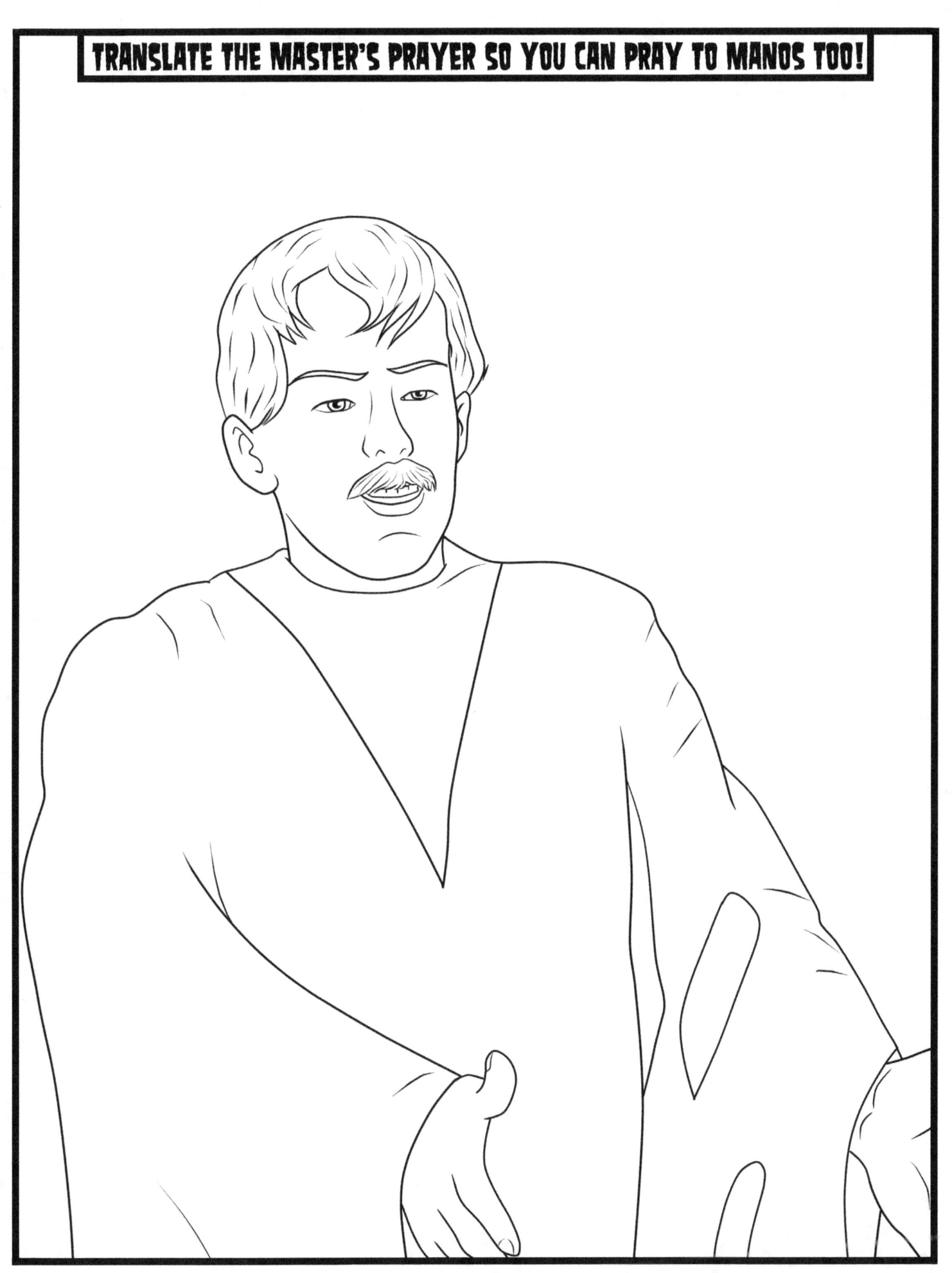

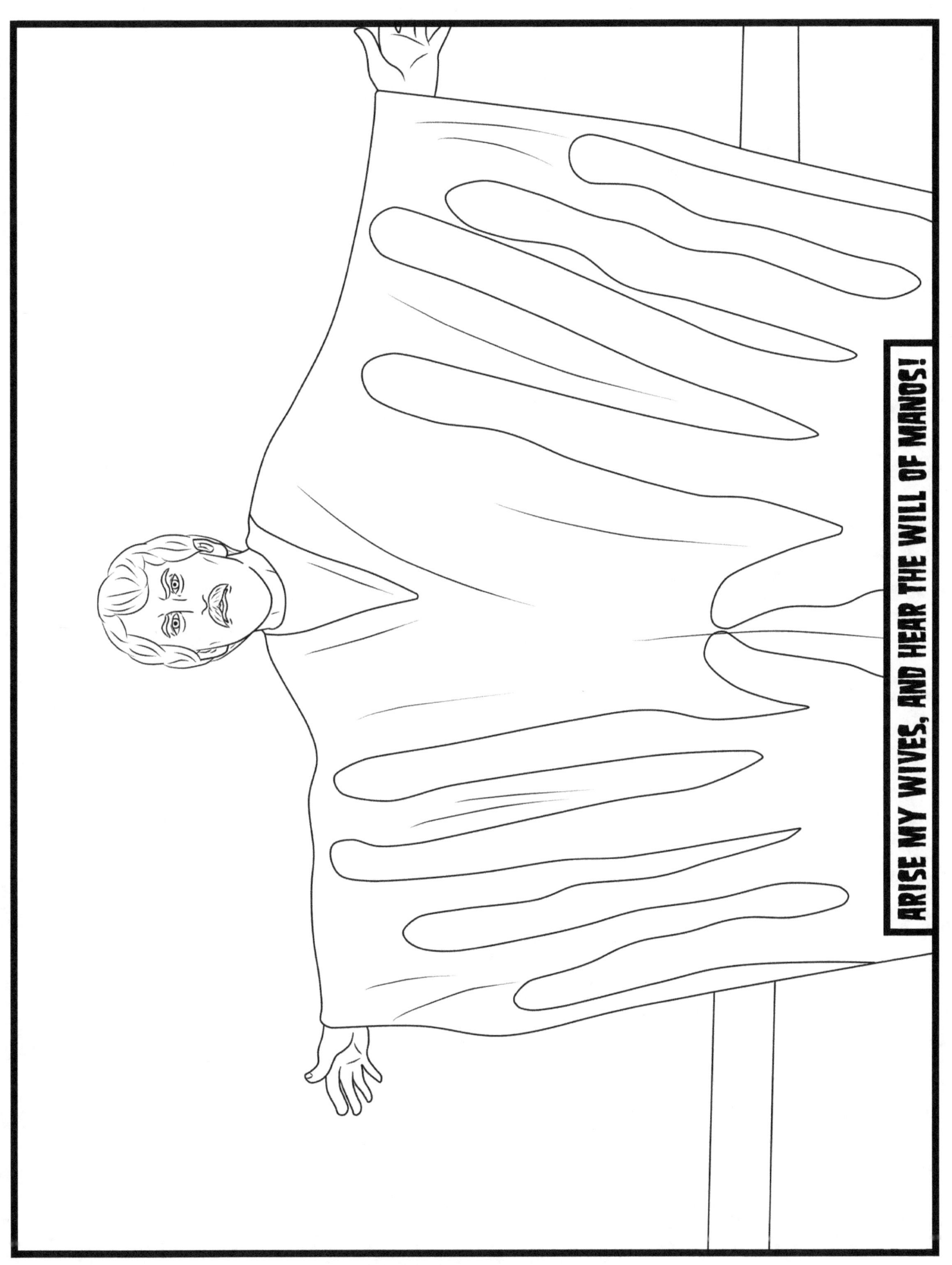

ARISE MY WIVES, AND HEAR THE WILL OF MANOS!

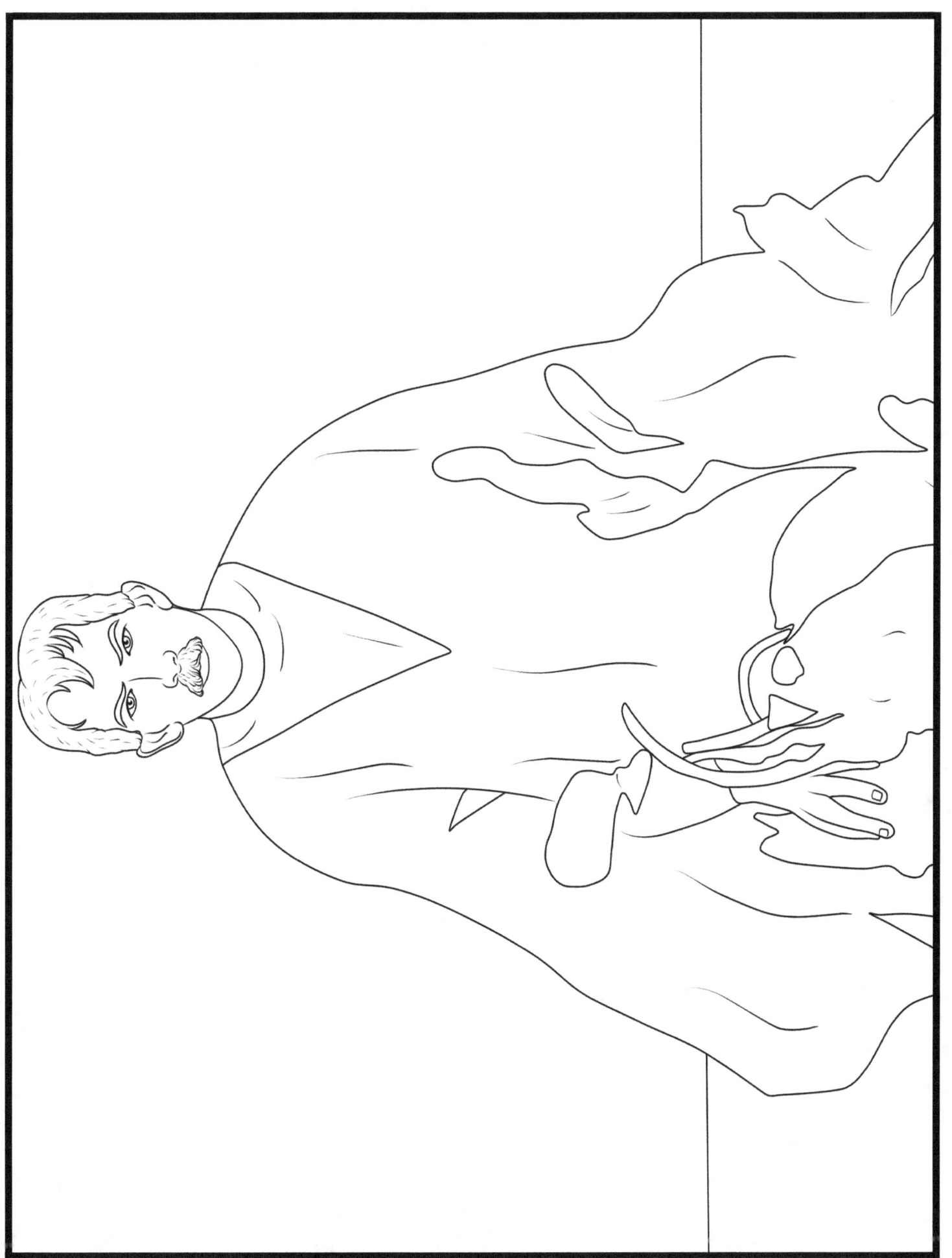

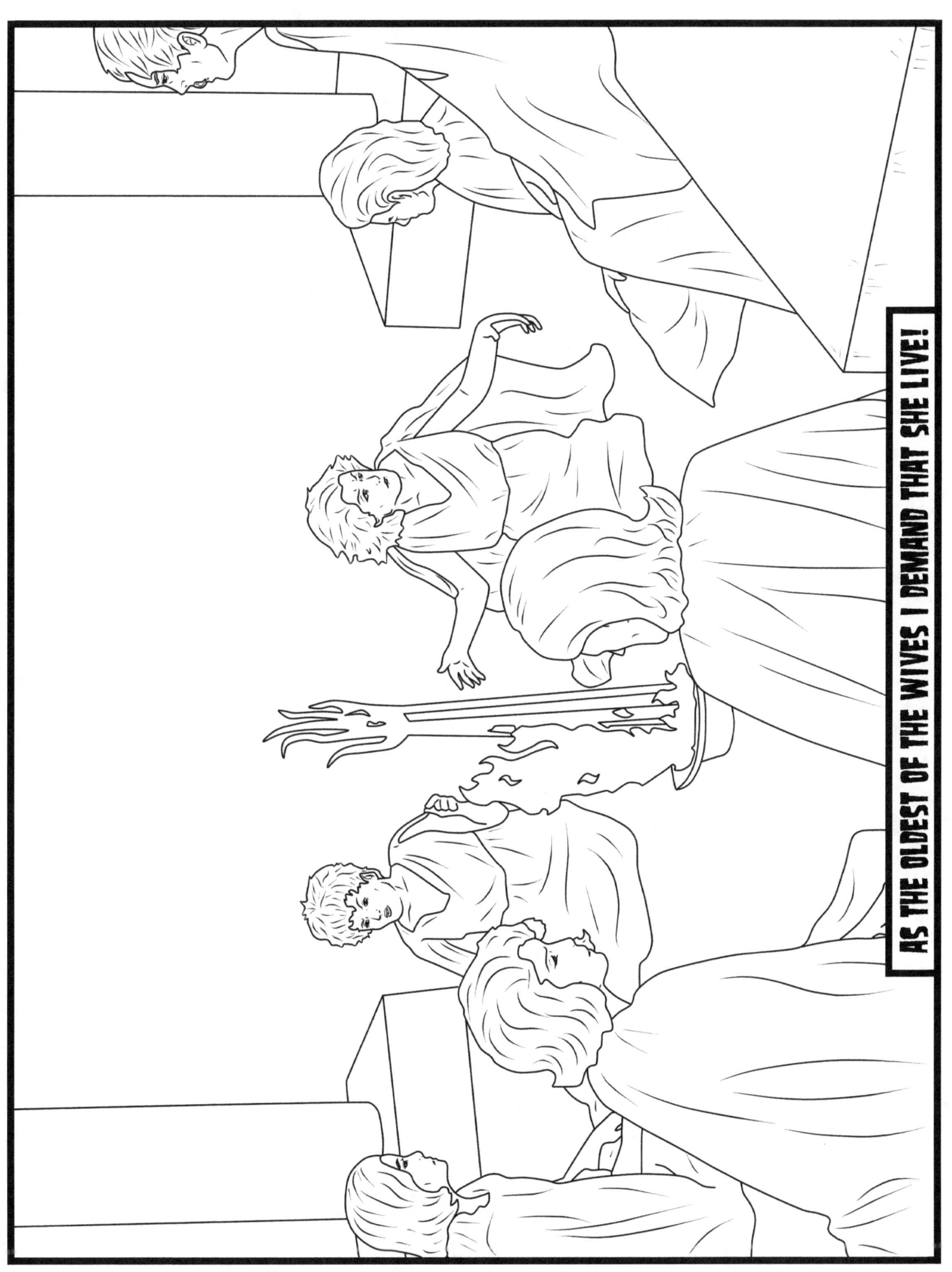

AS THE OLDEST OF THE WIVES I DEMAND THAT SHE LIVE!

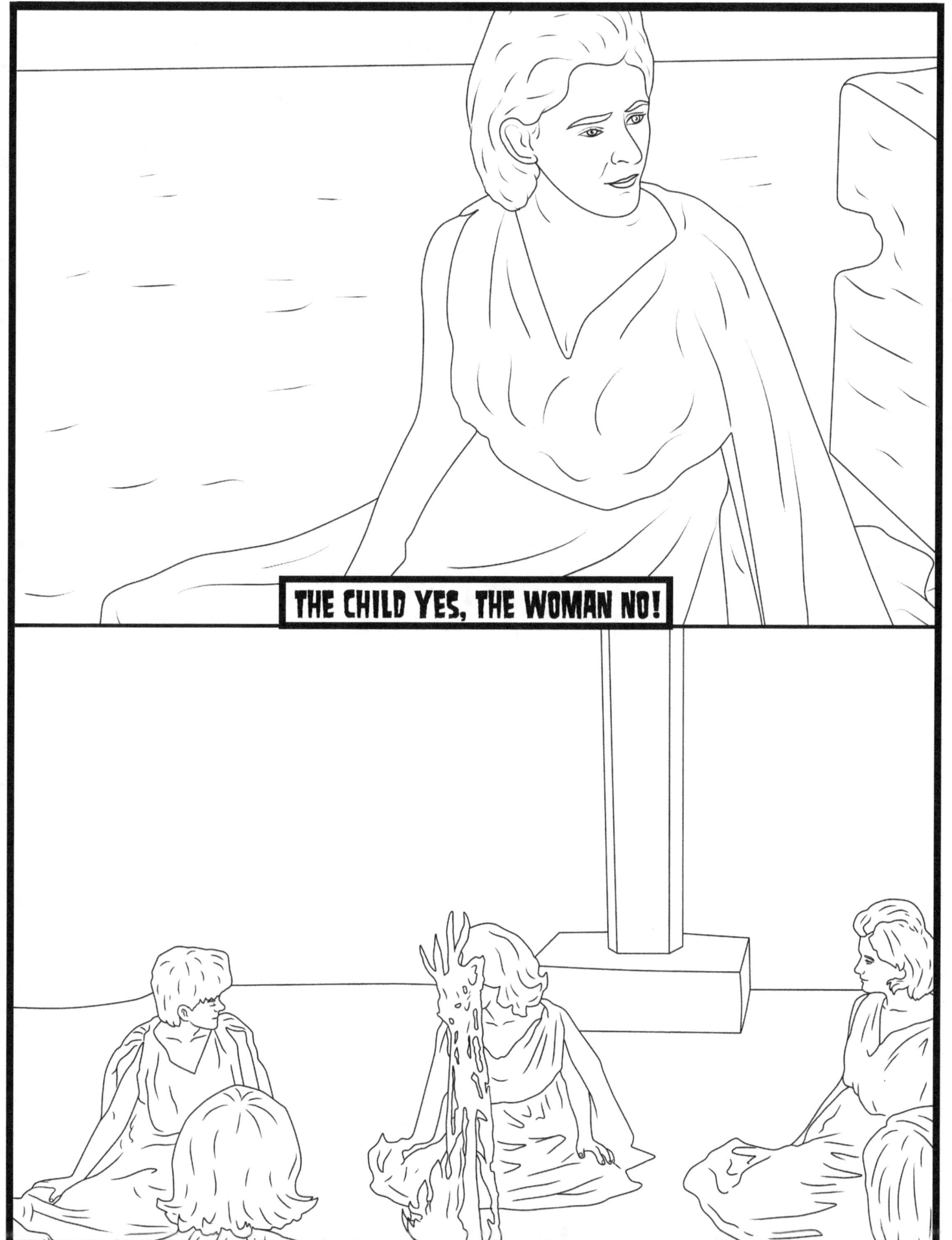

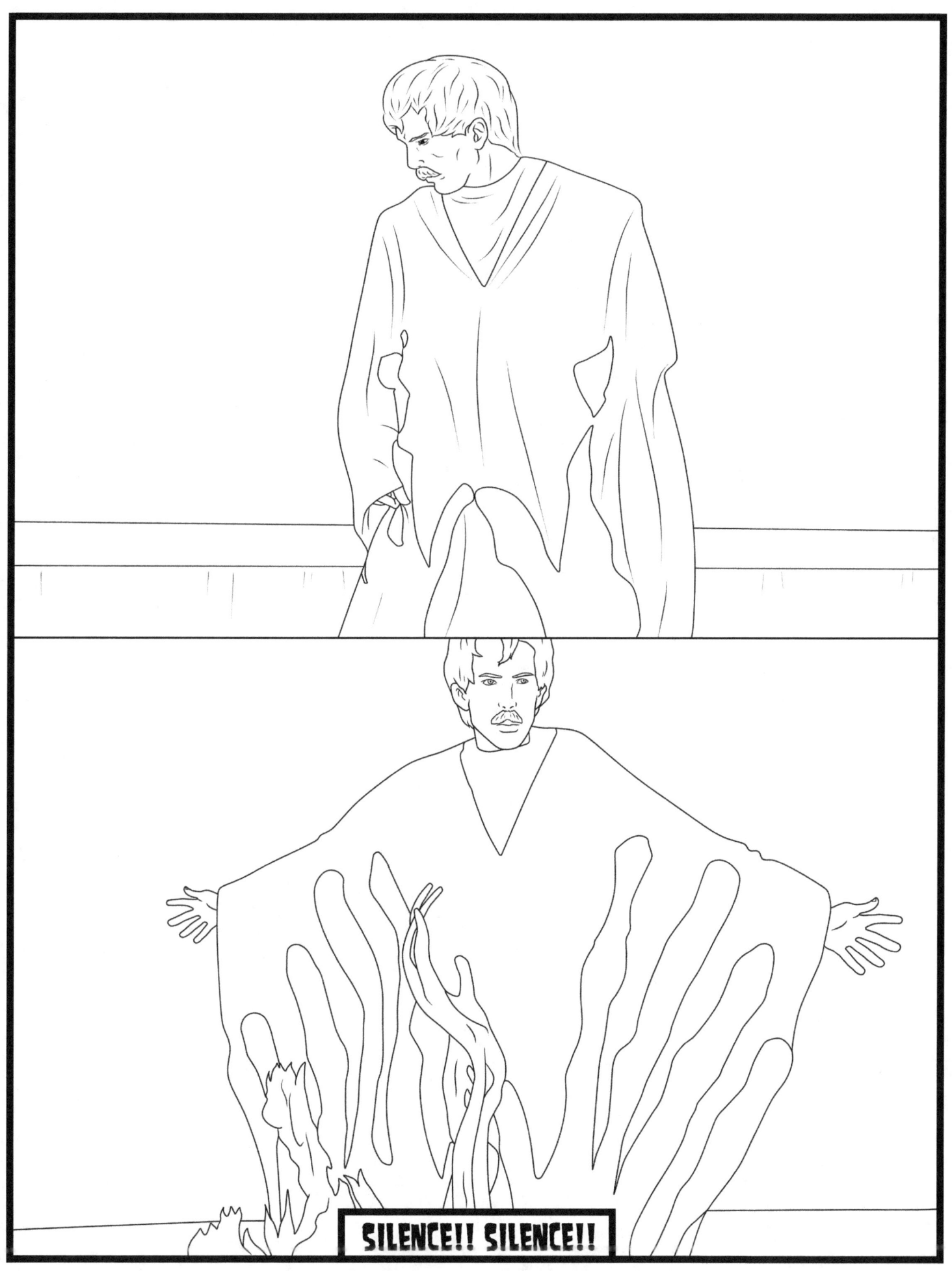

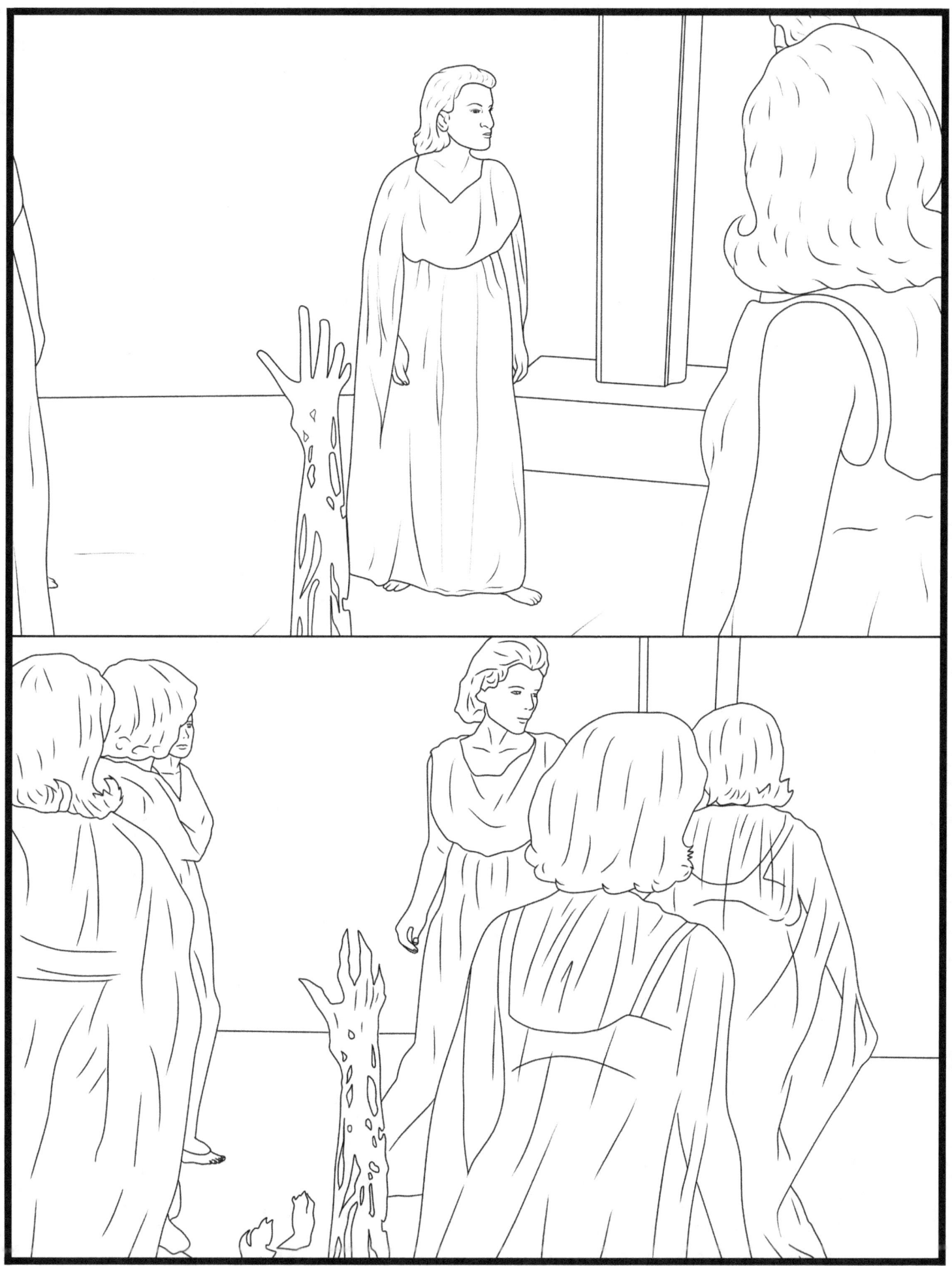

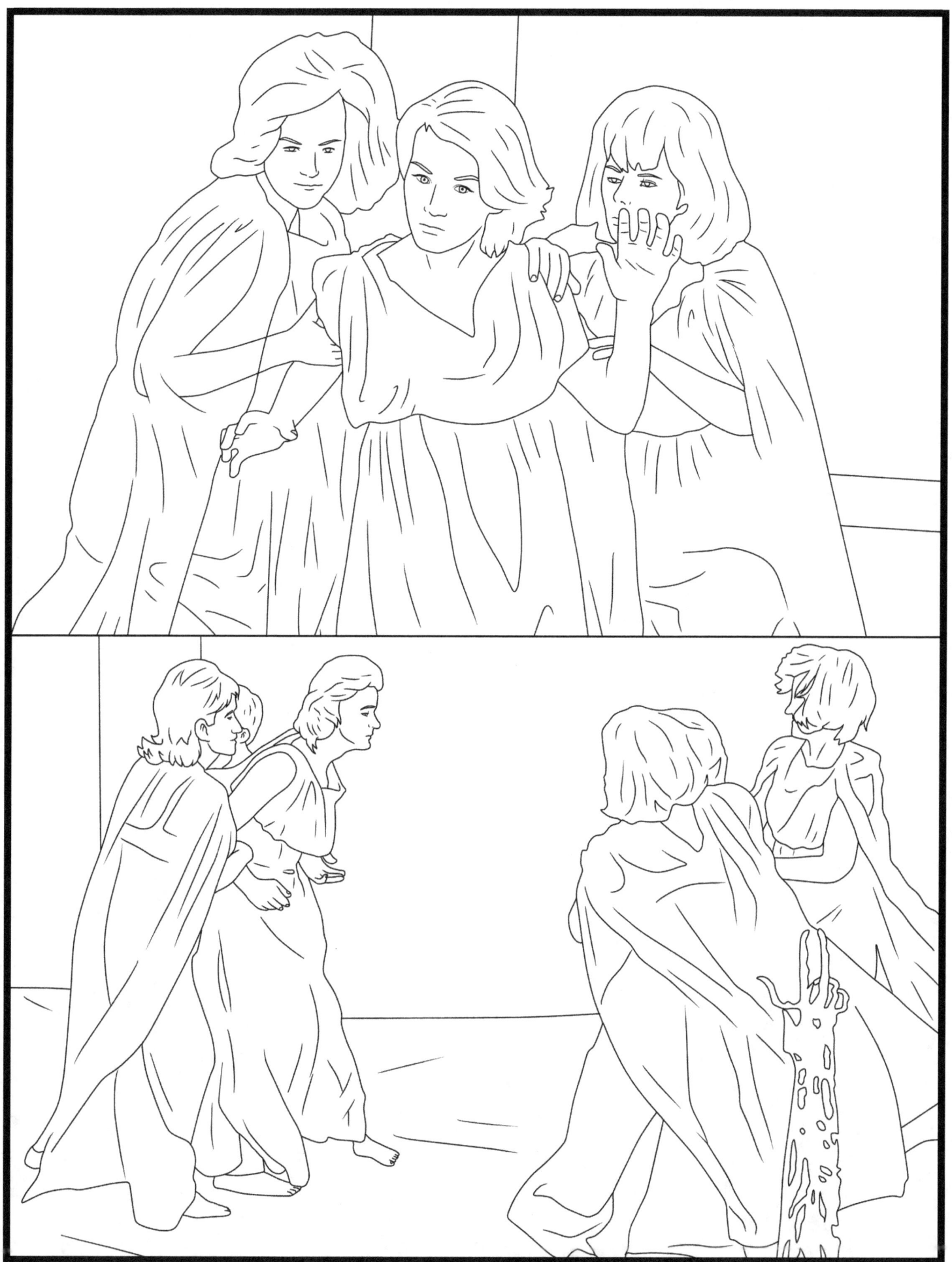

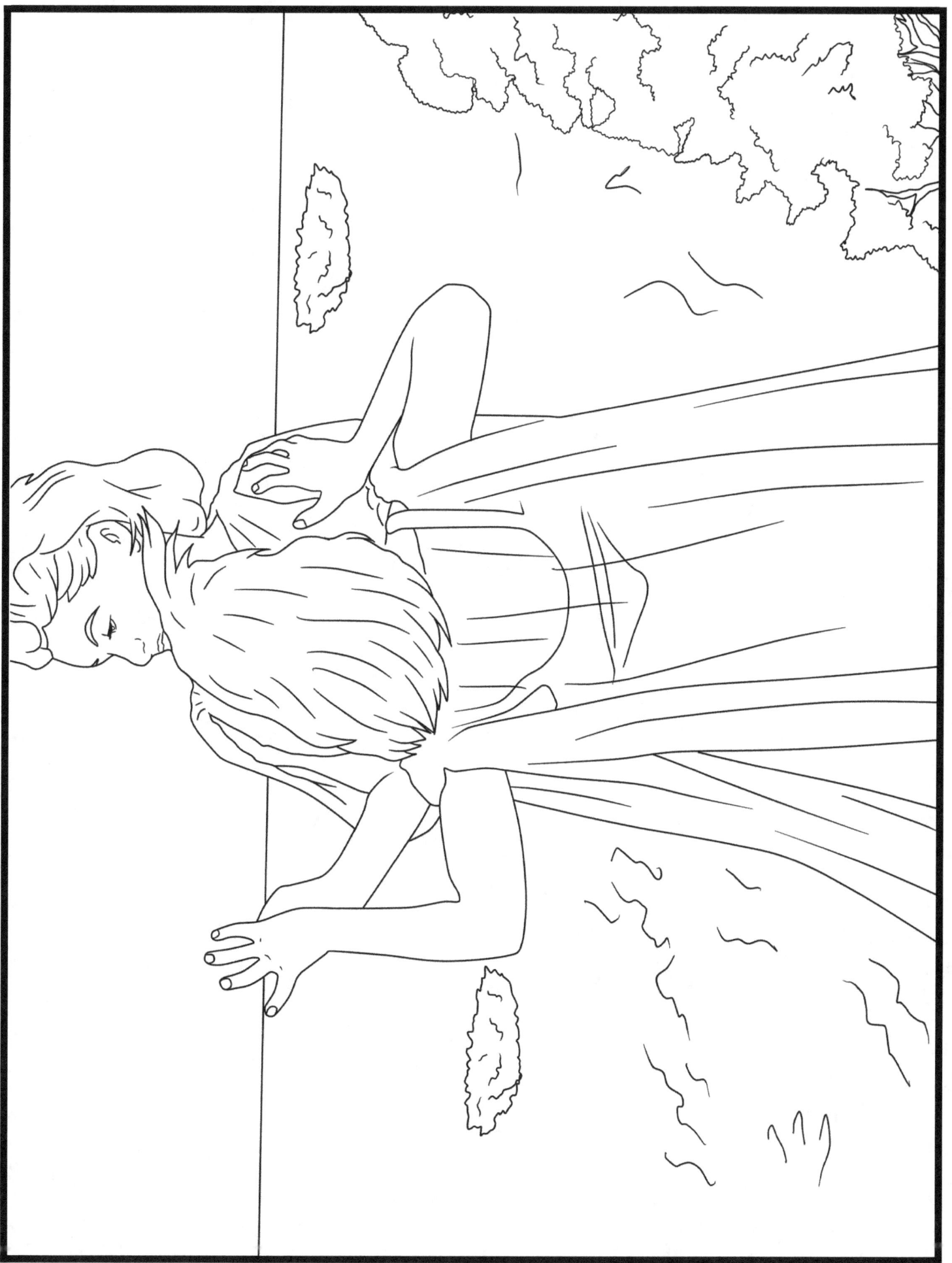

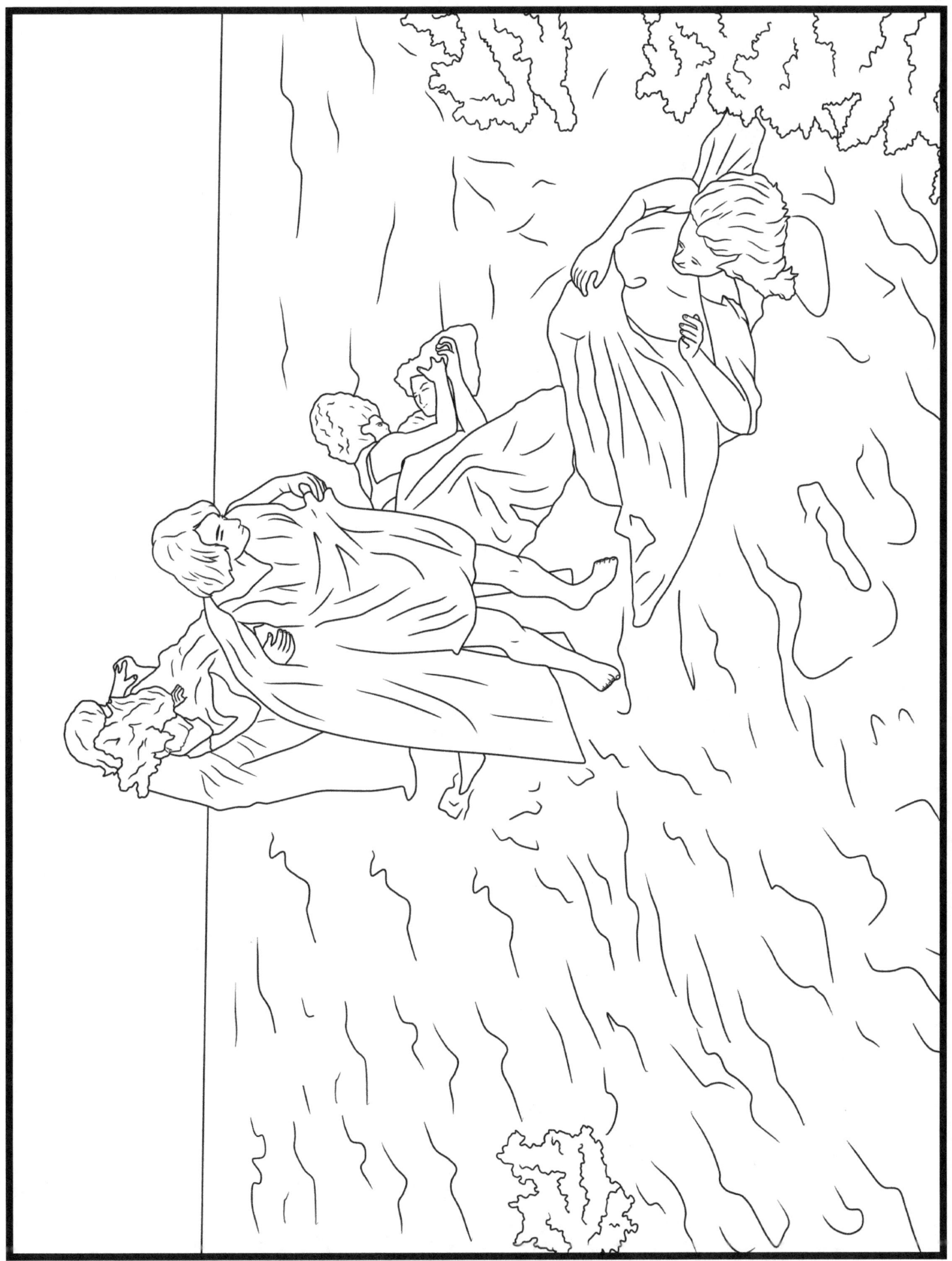

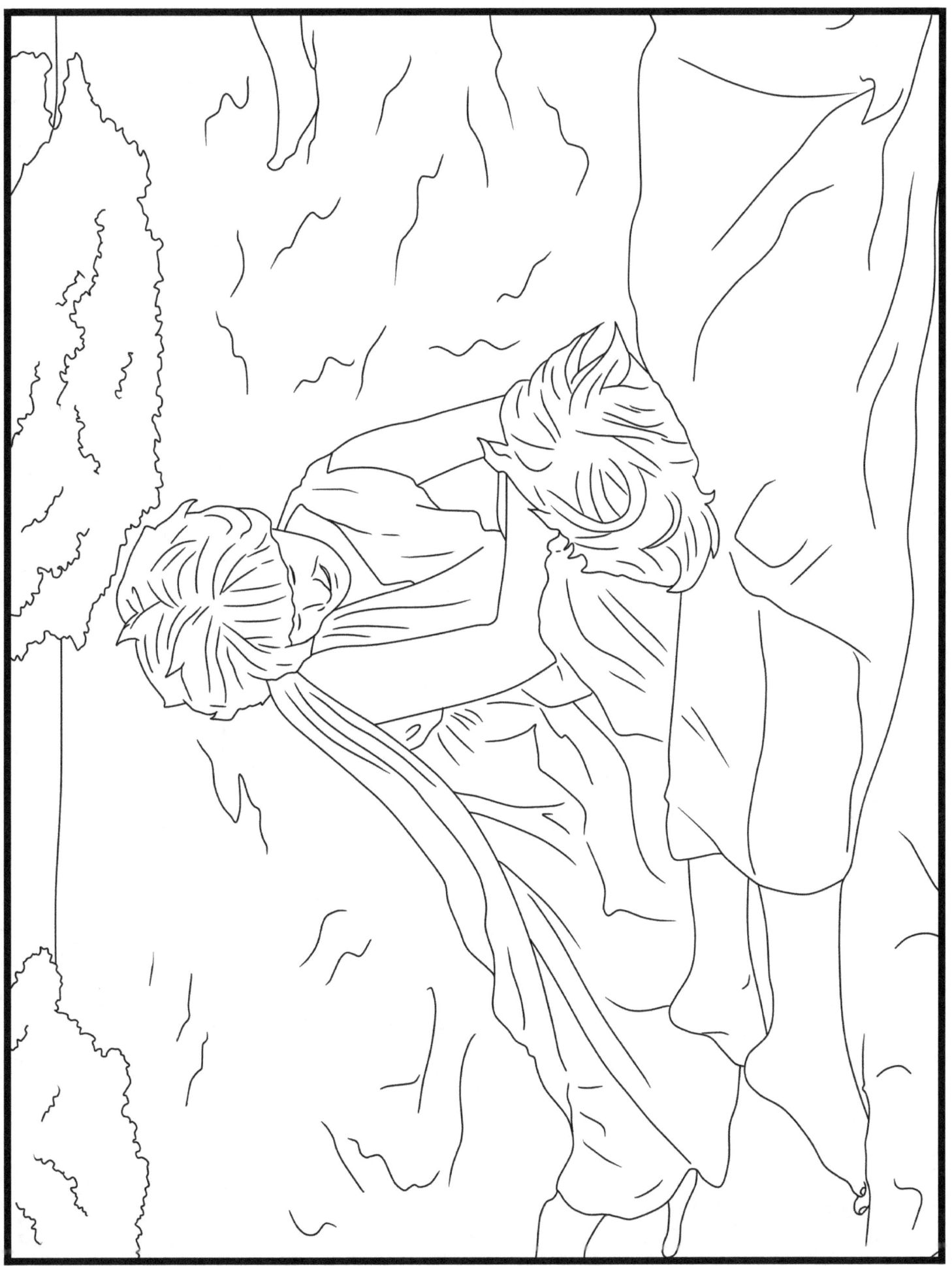

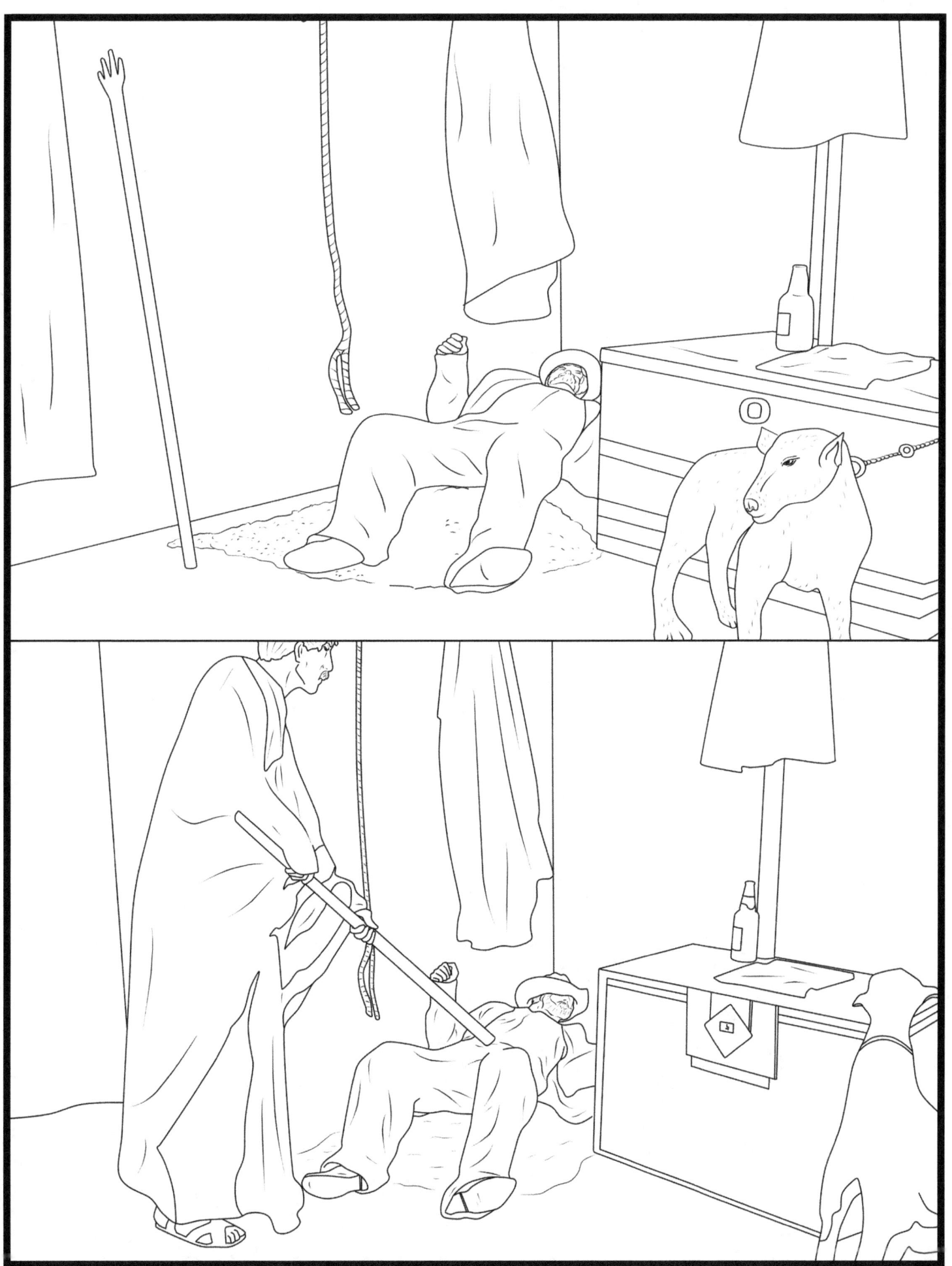

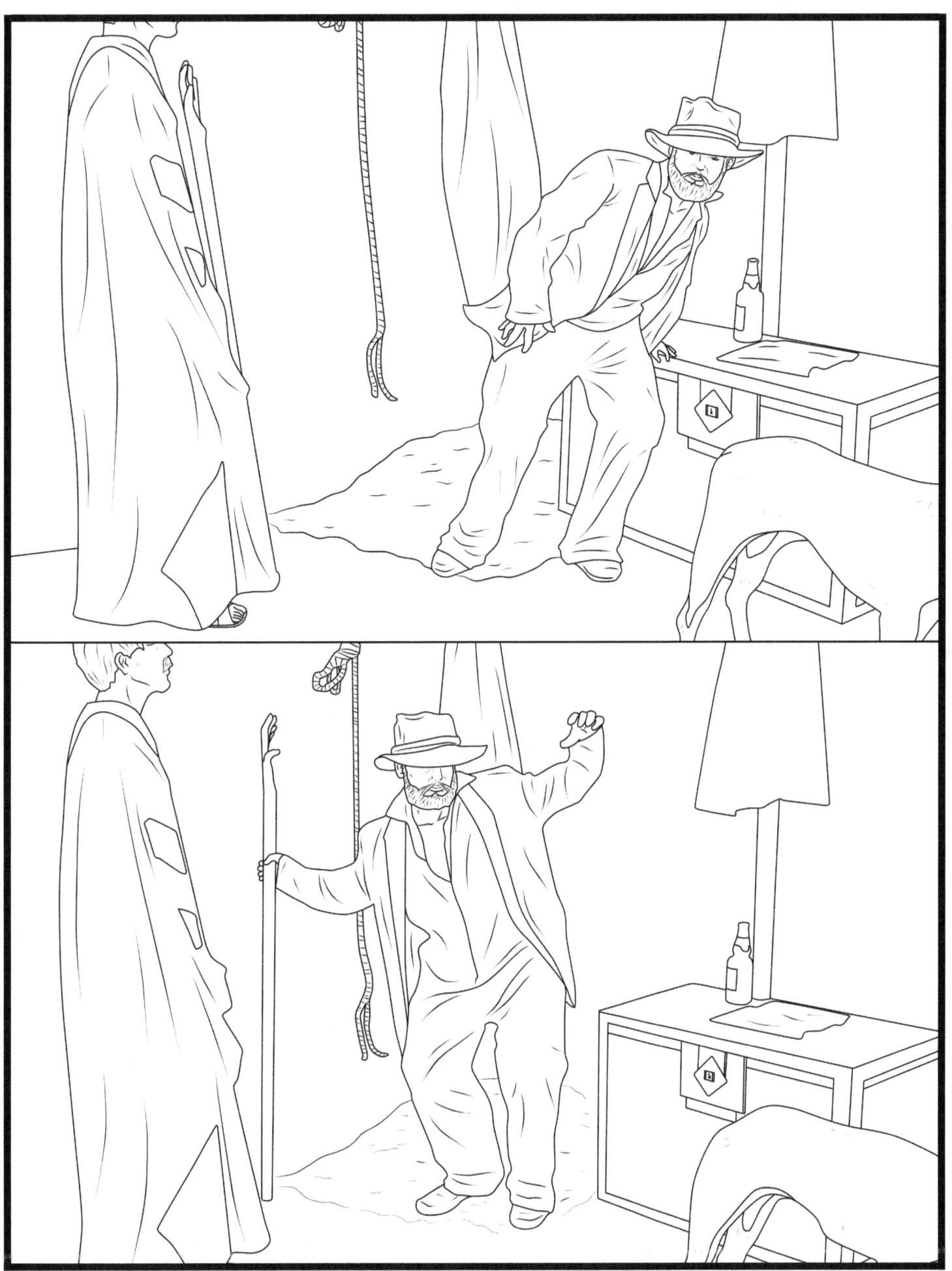

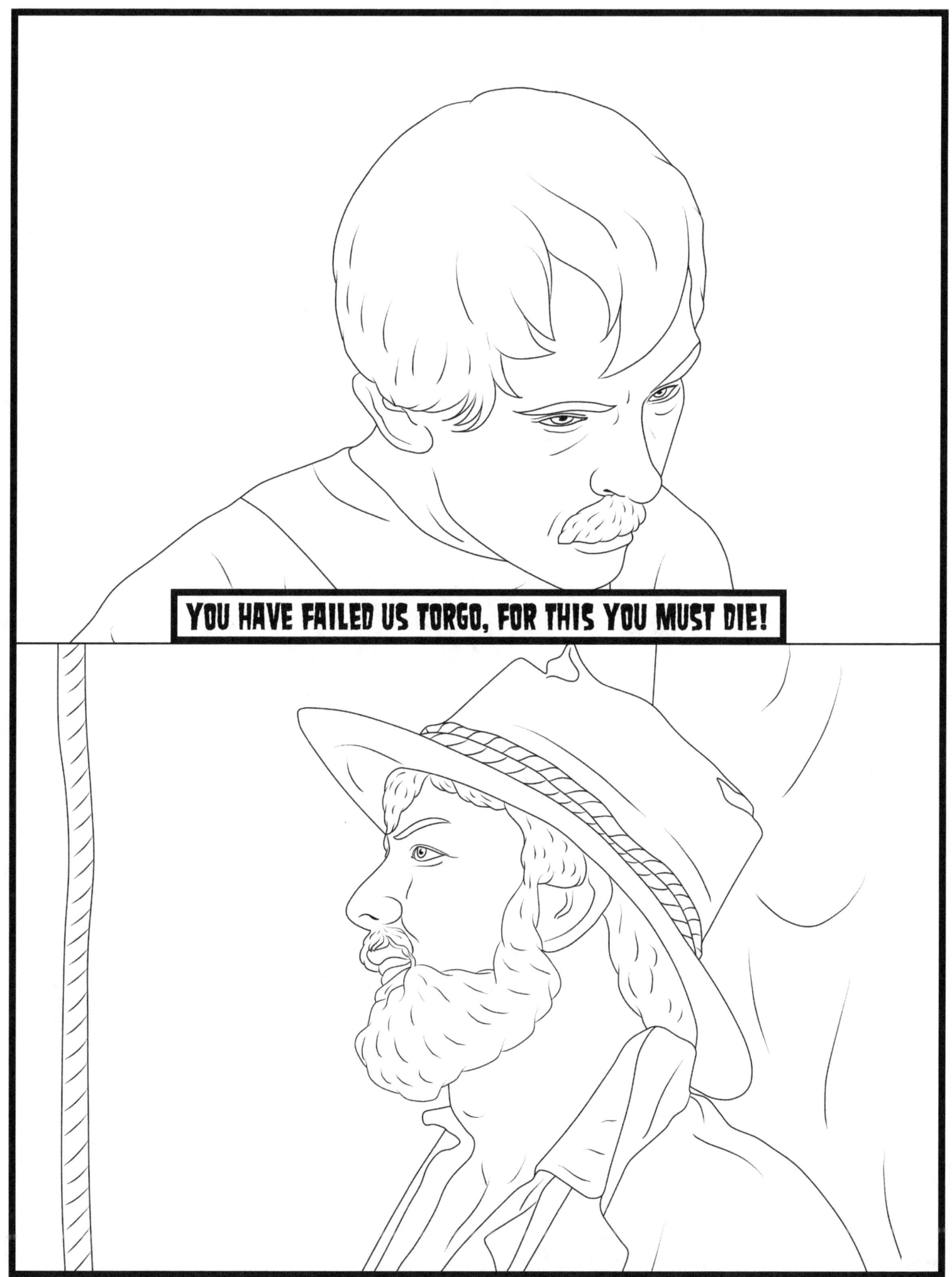

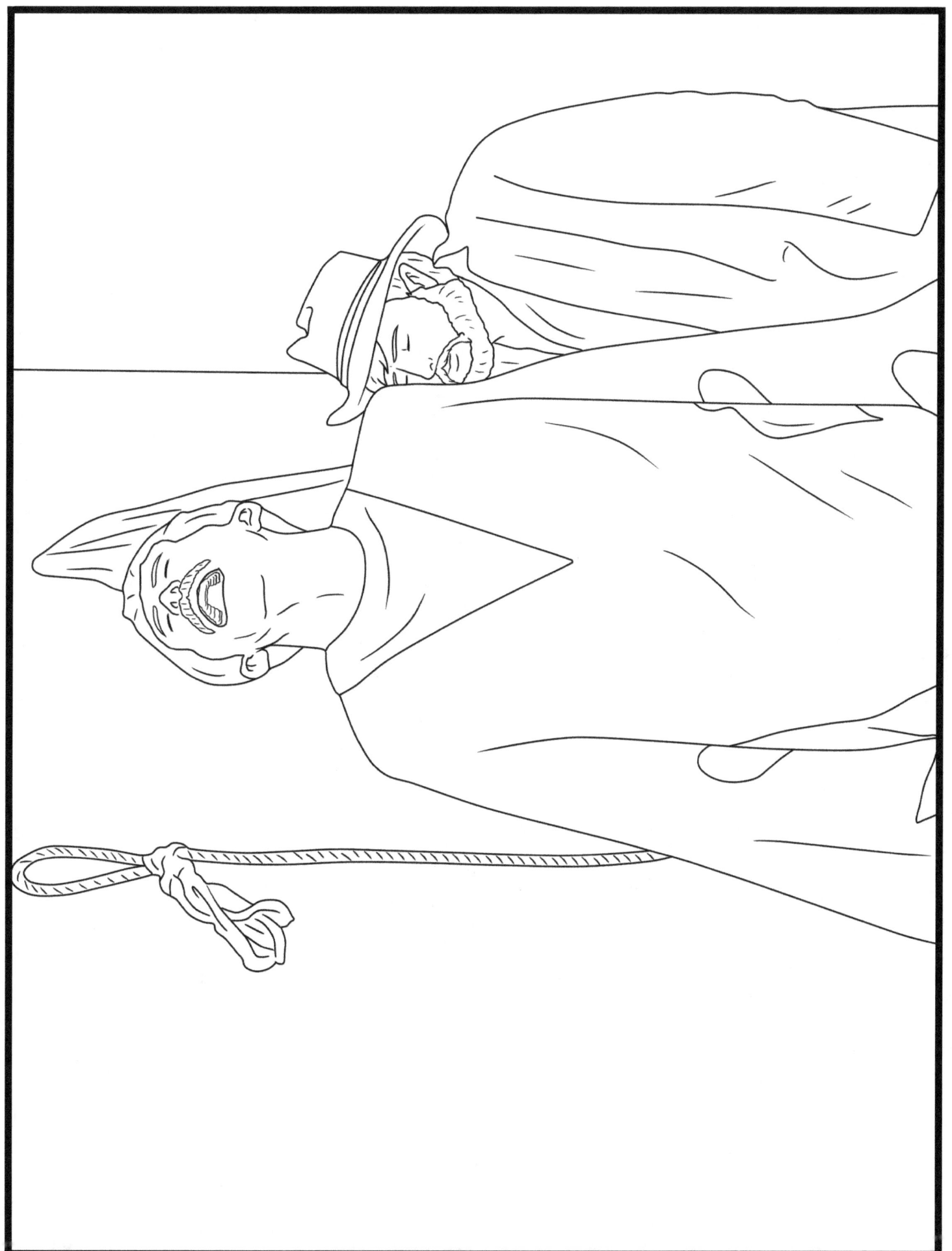

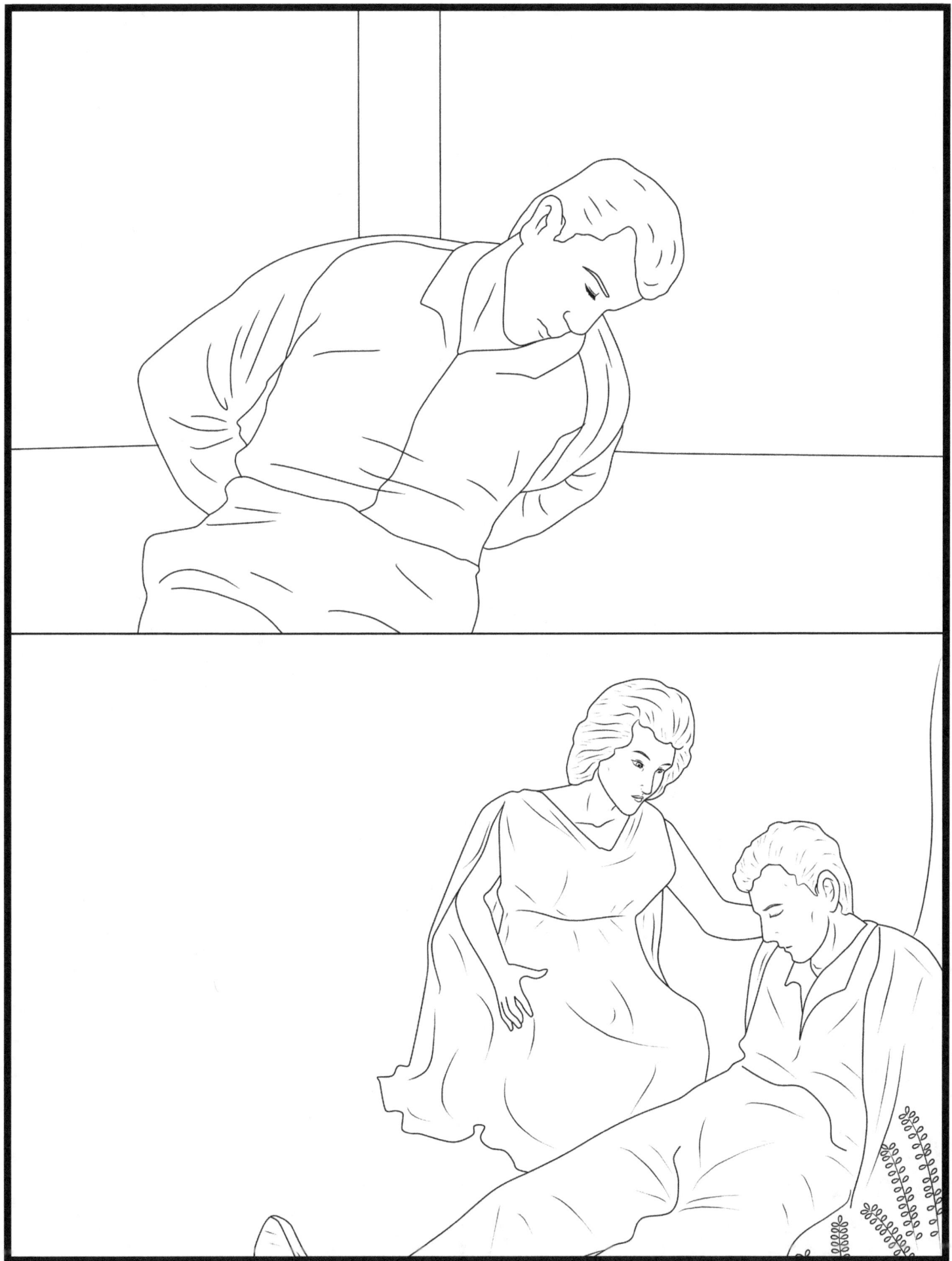

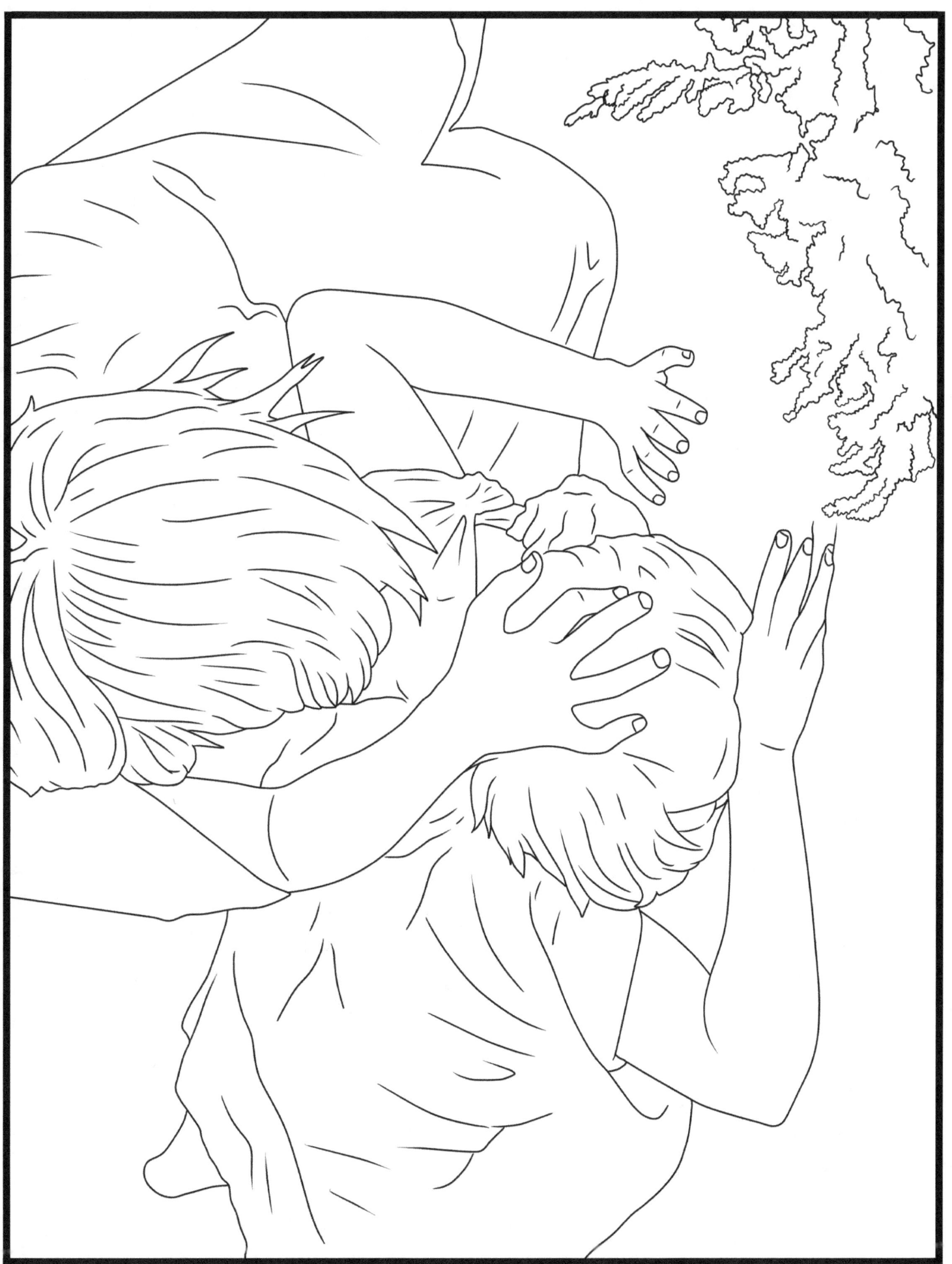

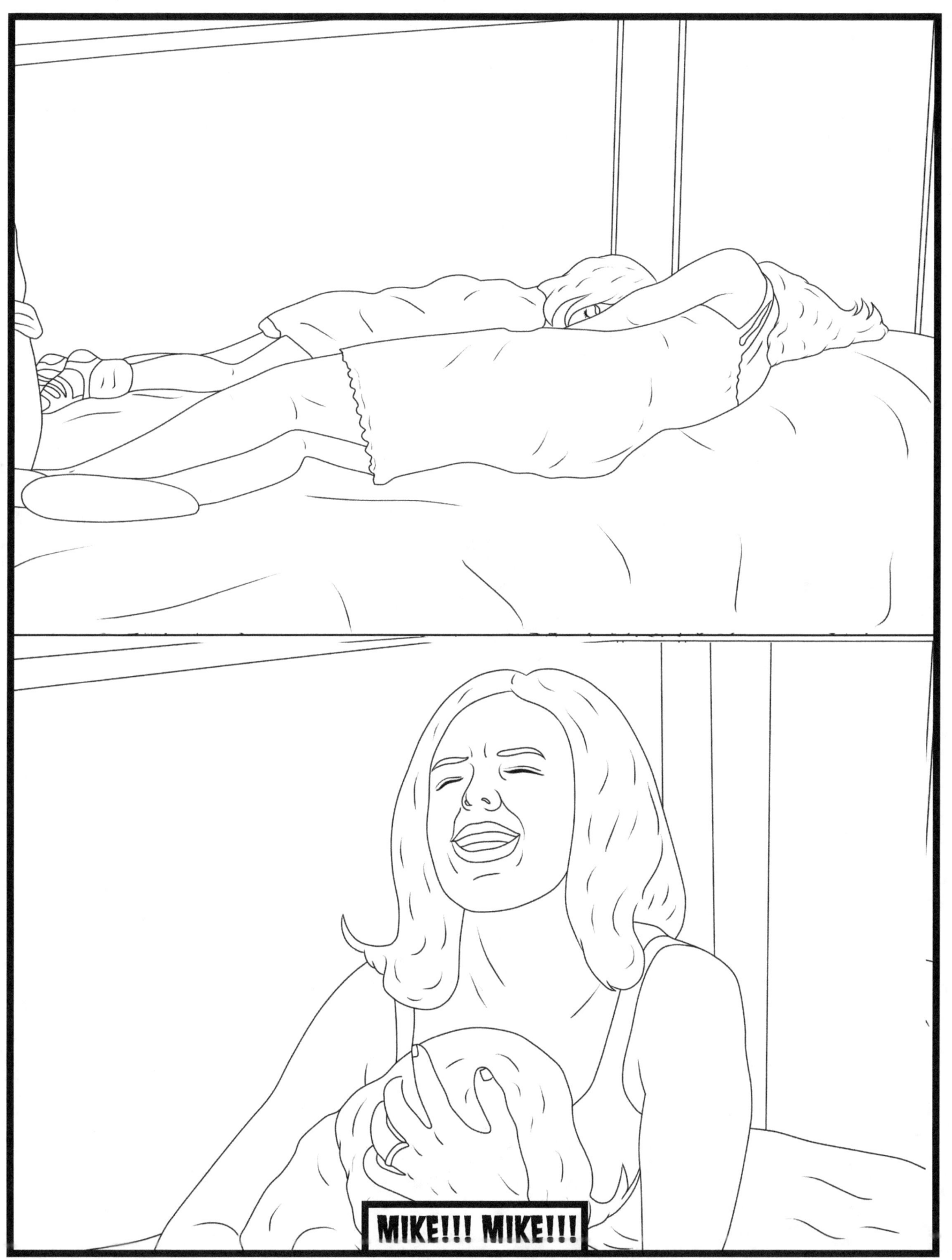

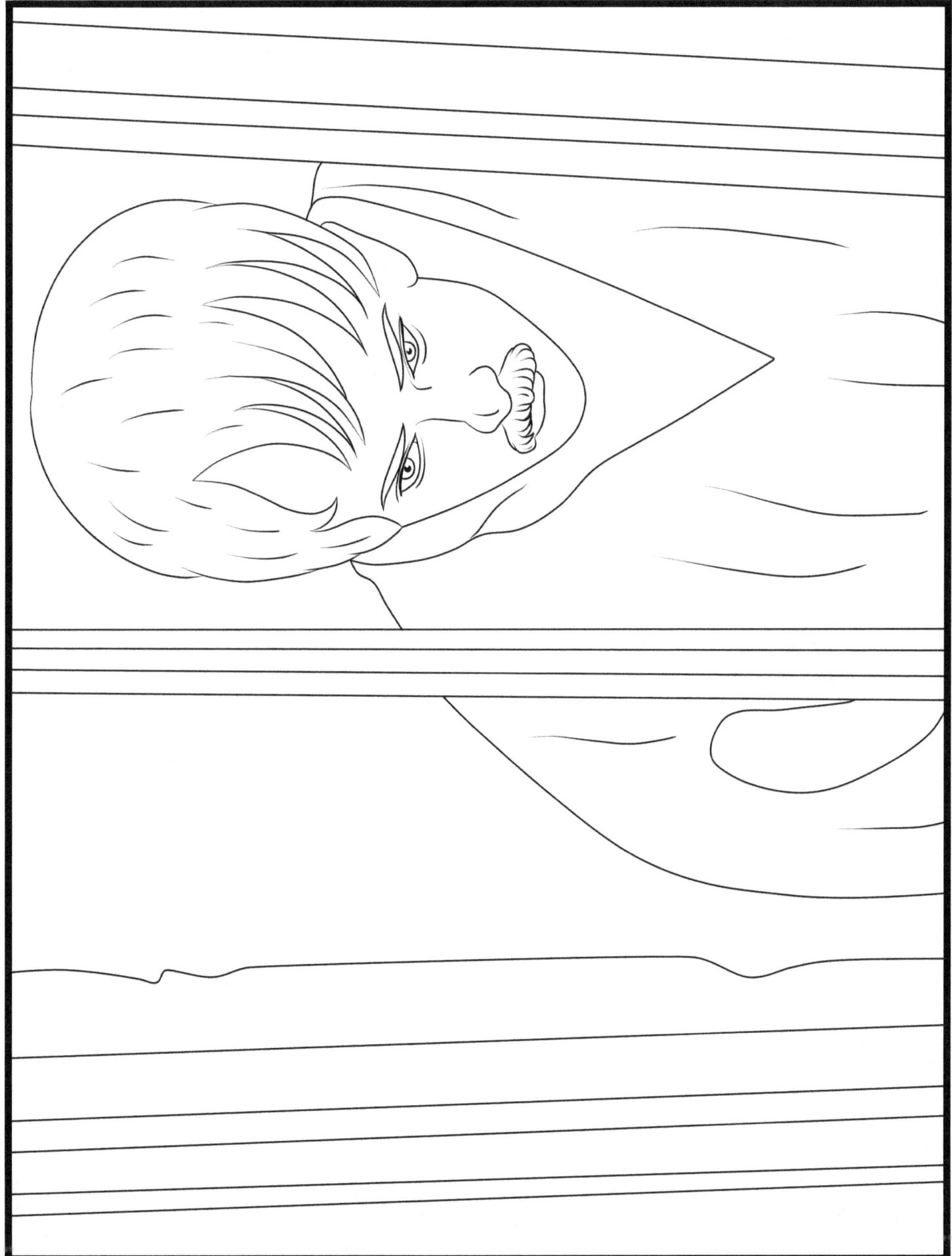

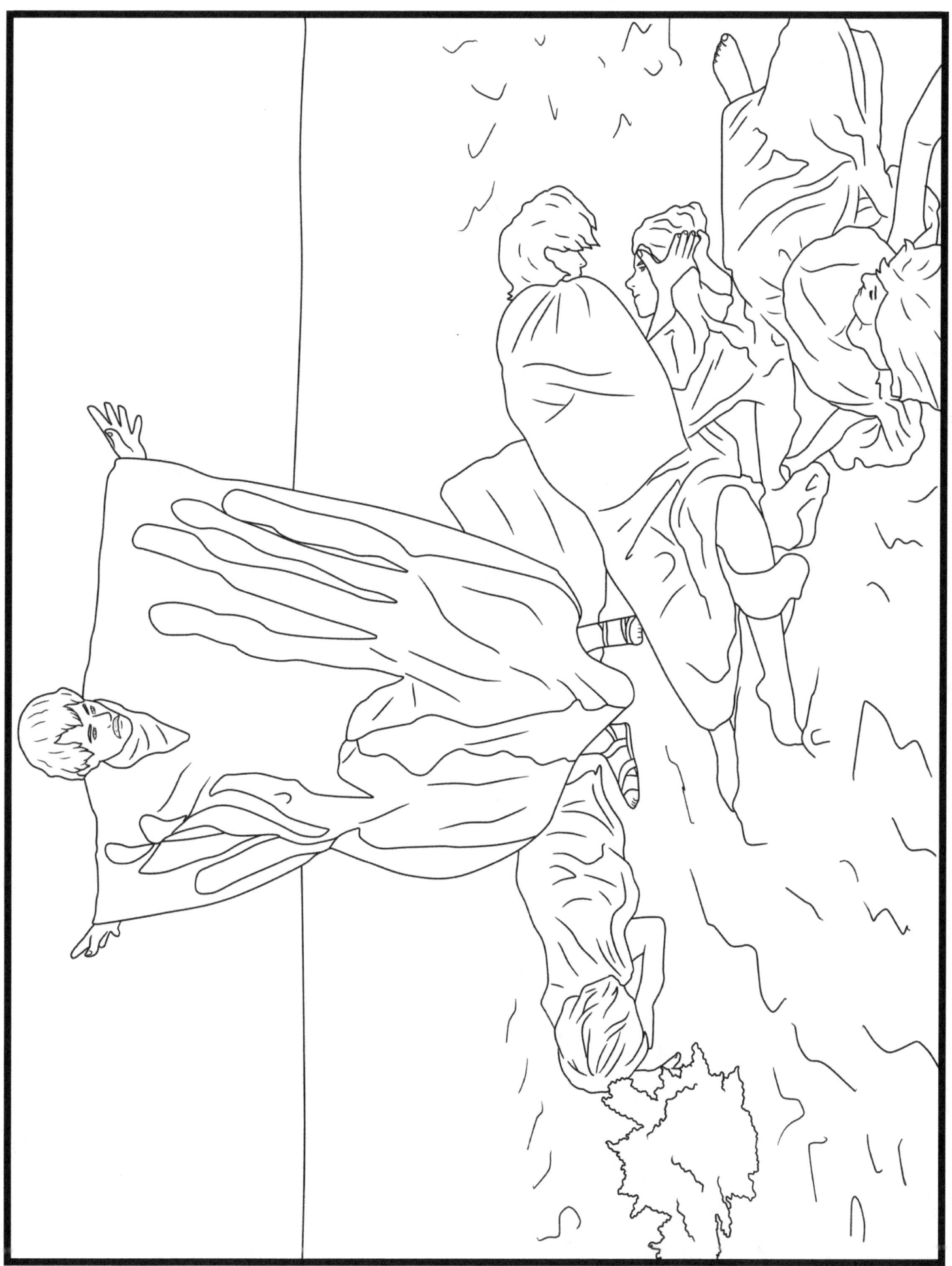

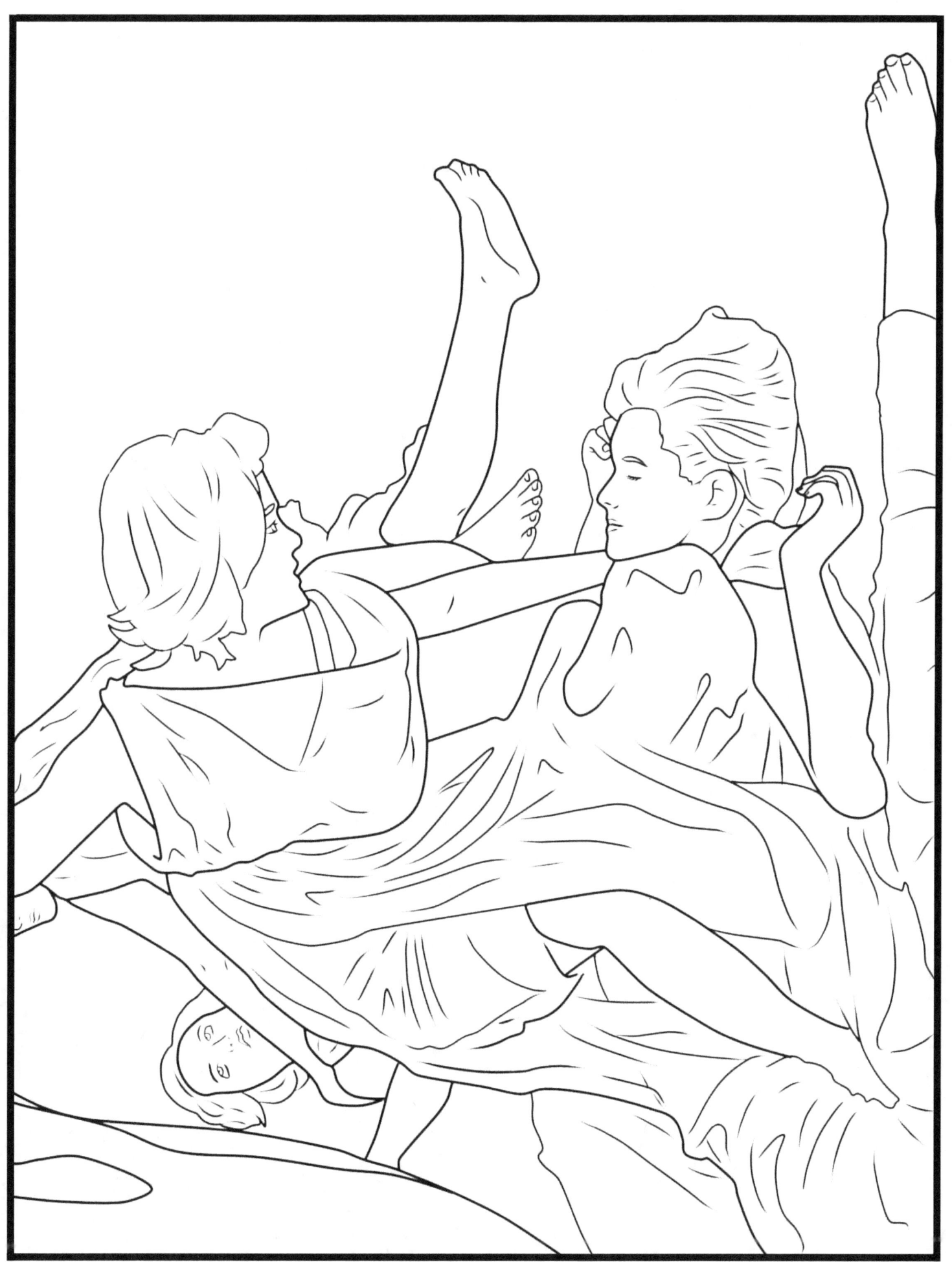

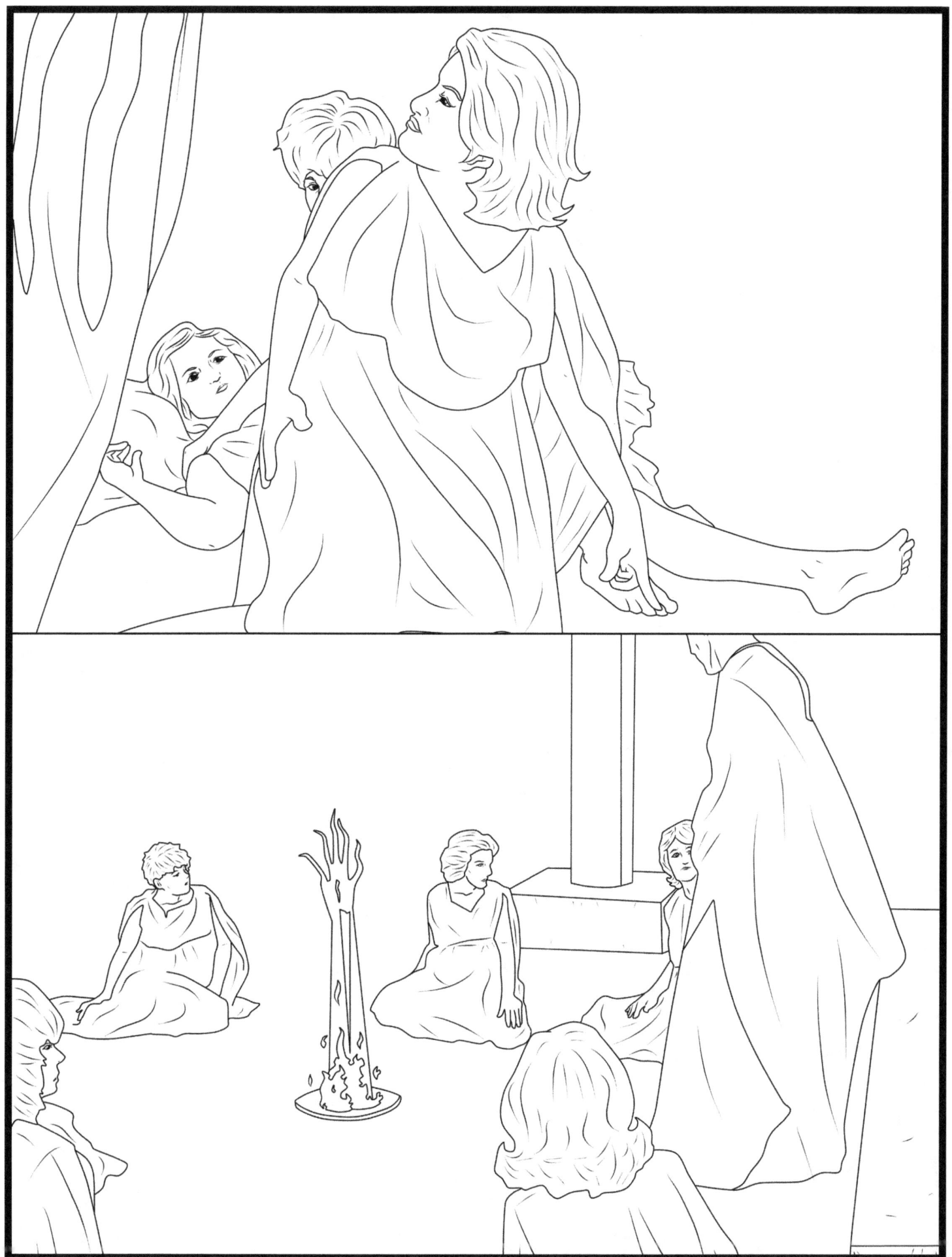

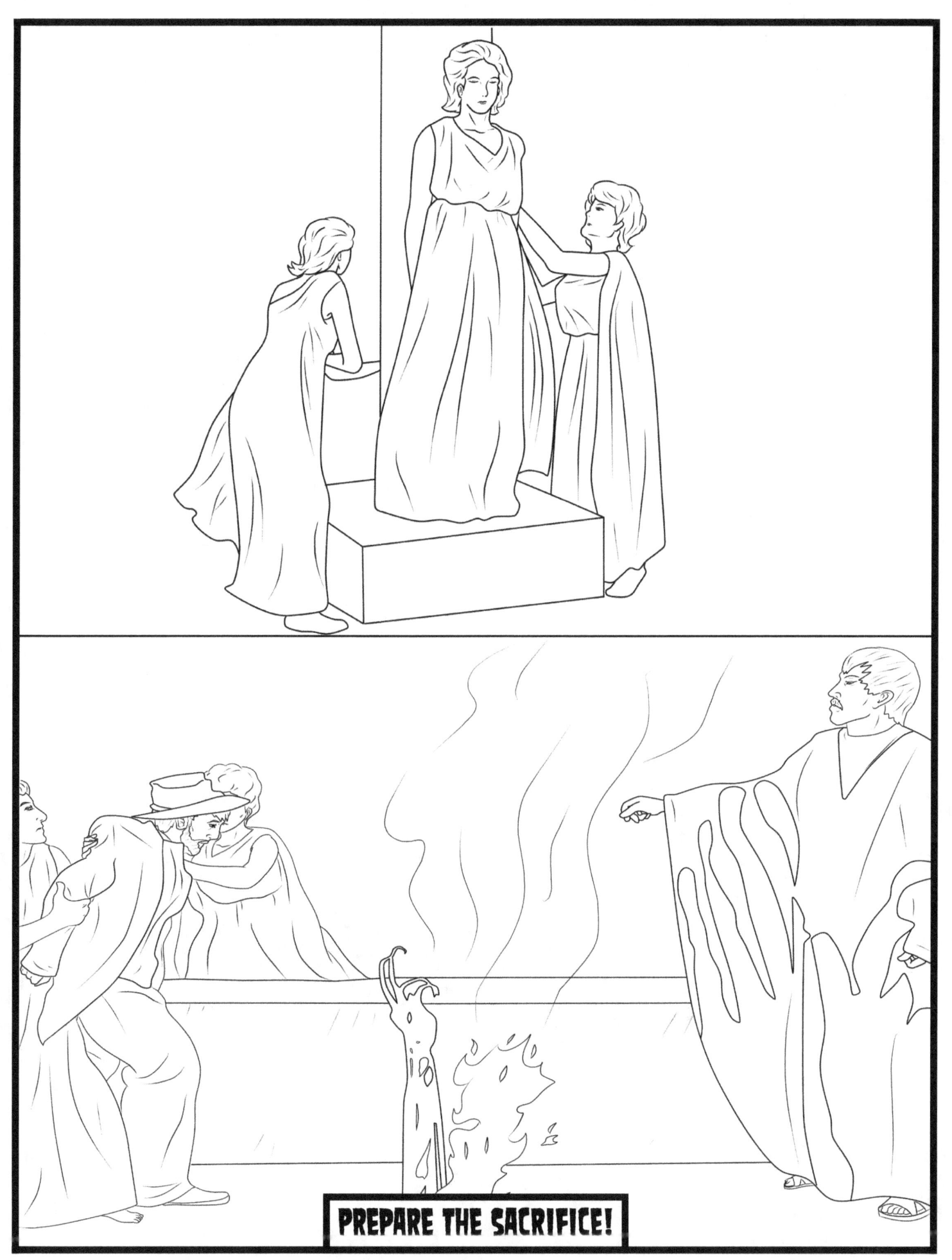

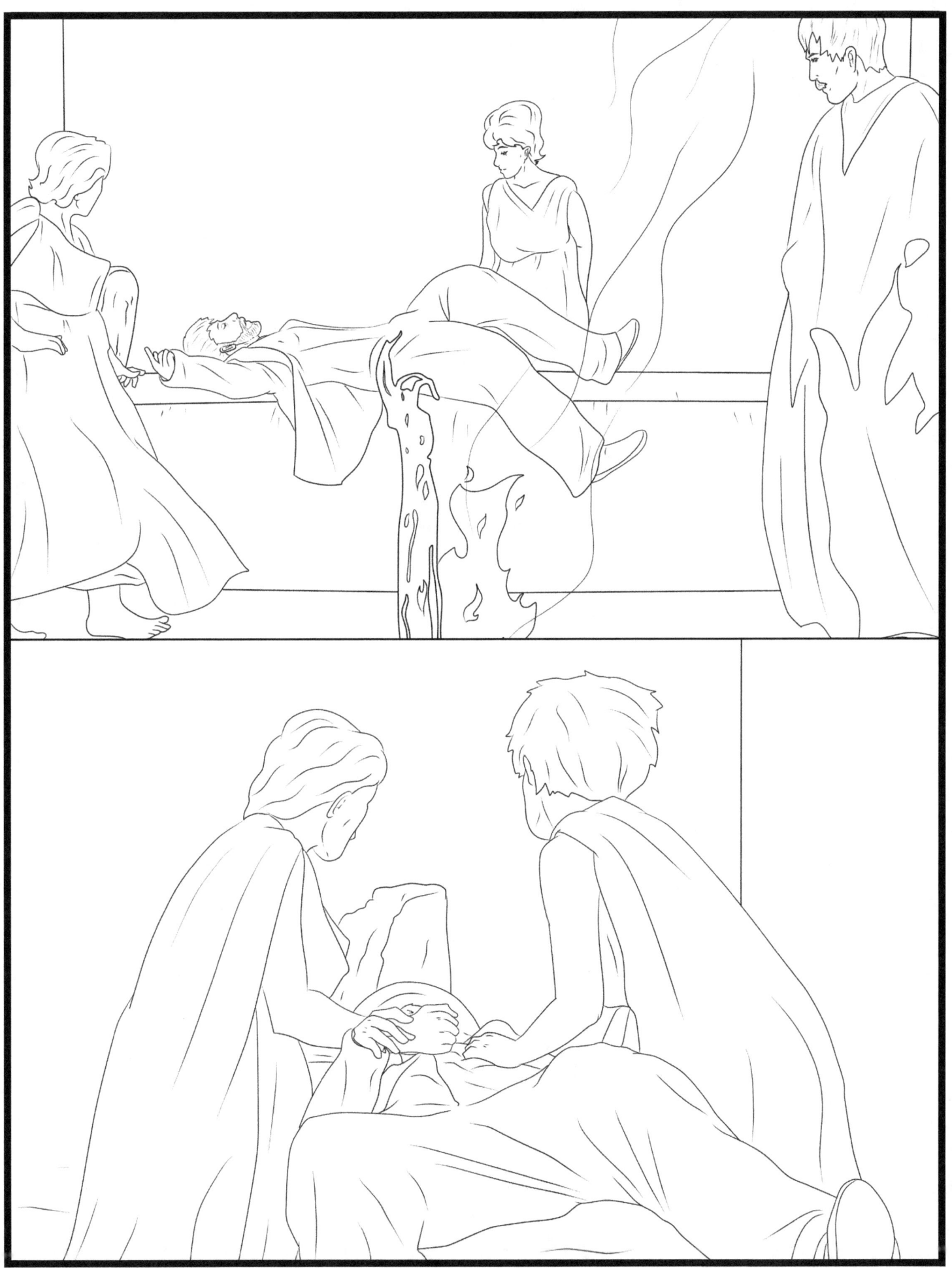

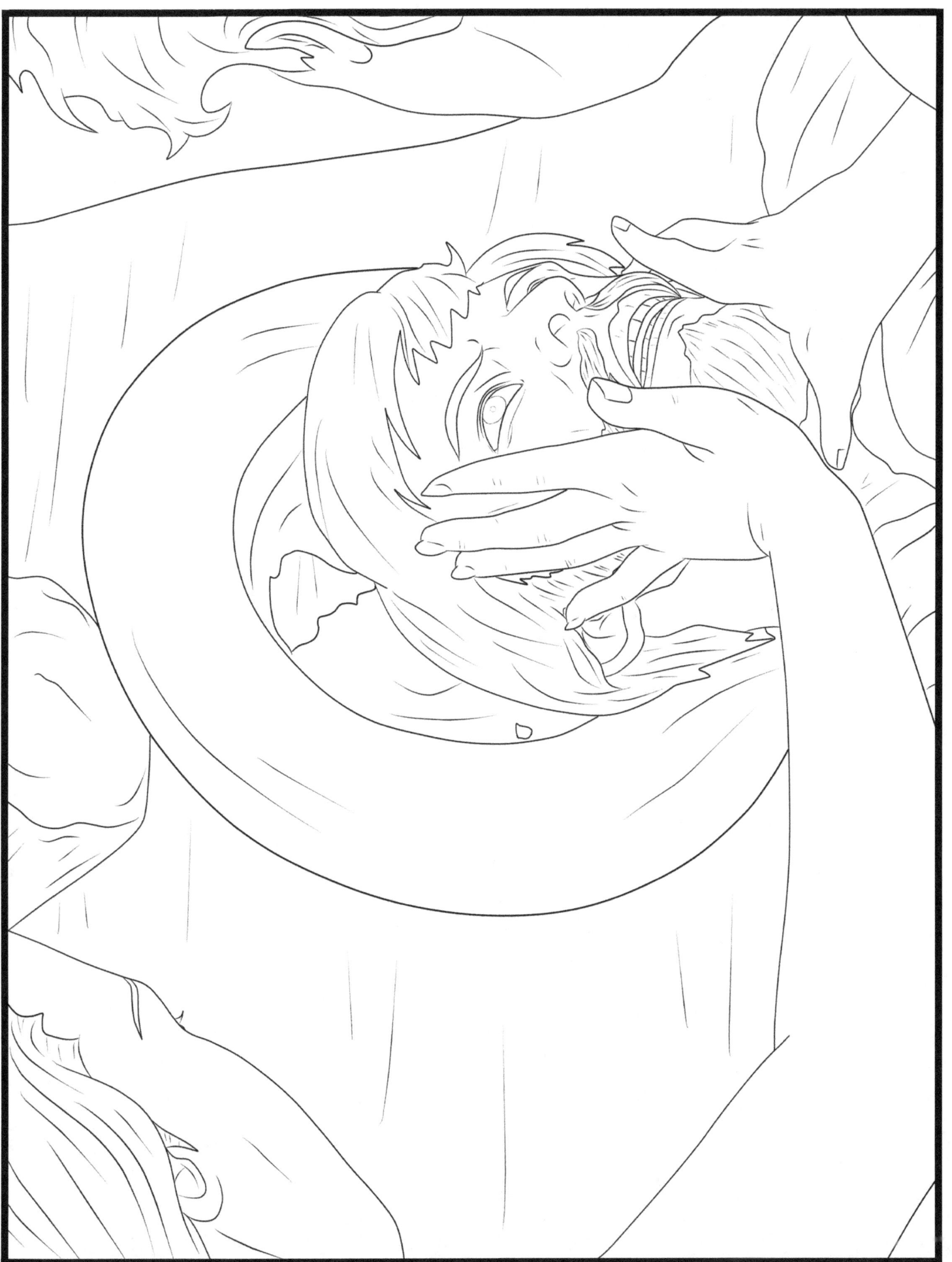

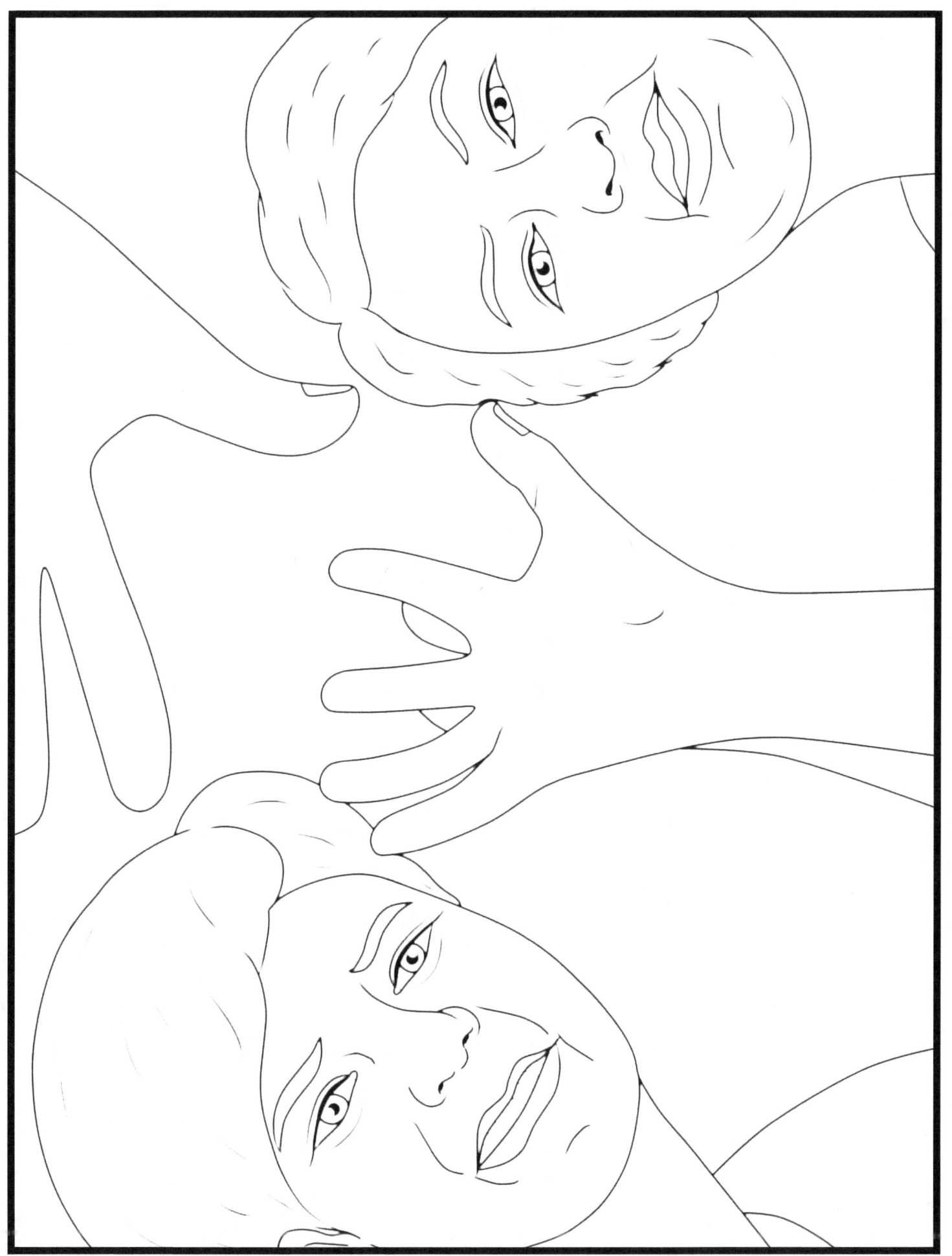

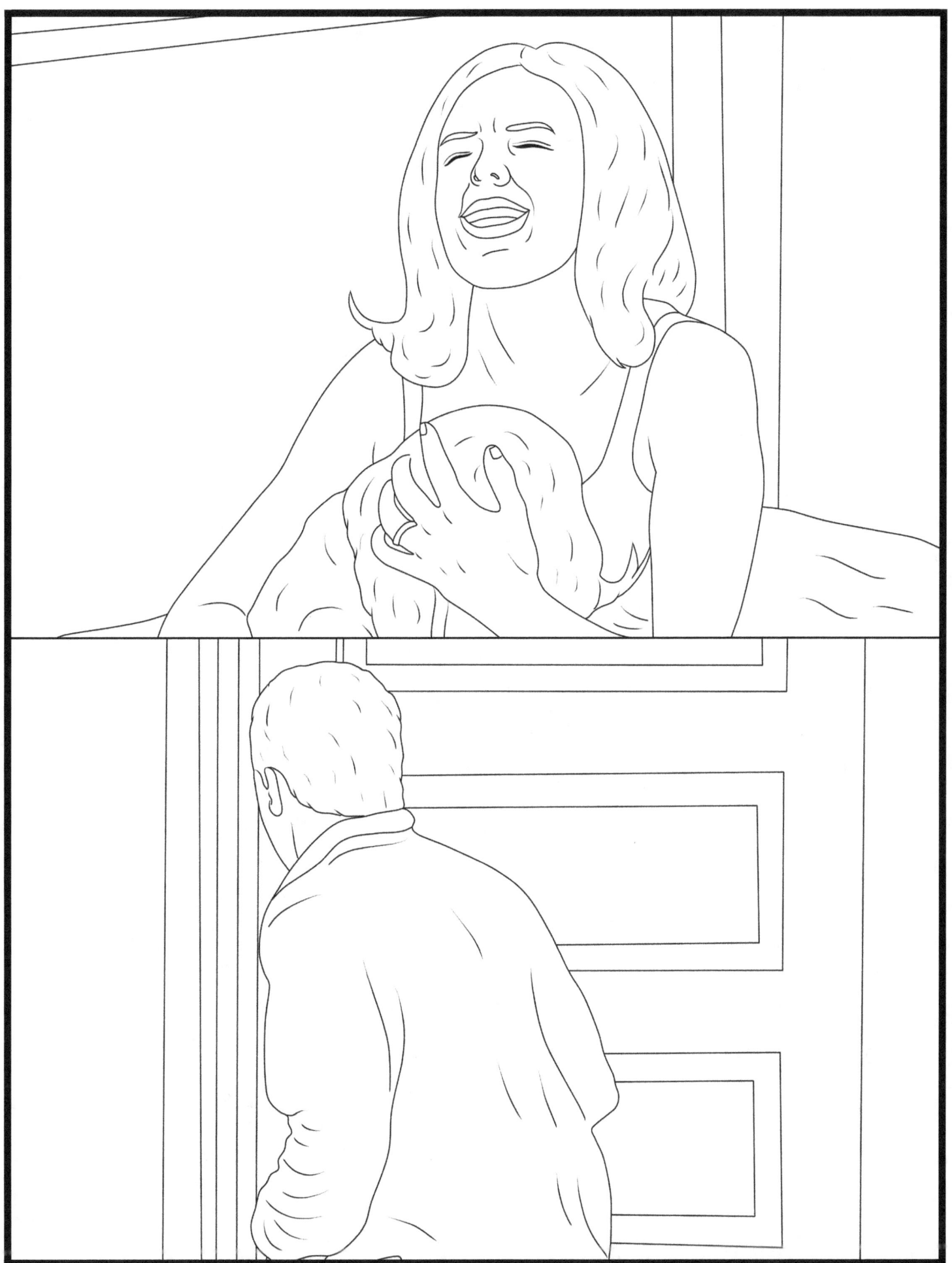

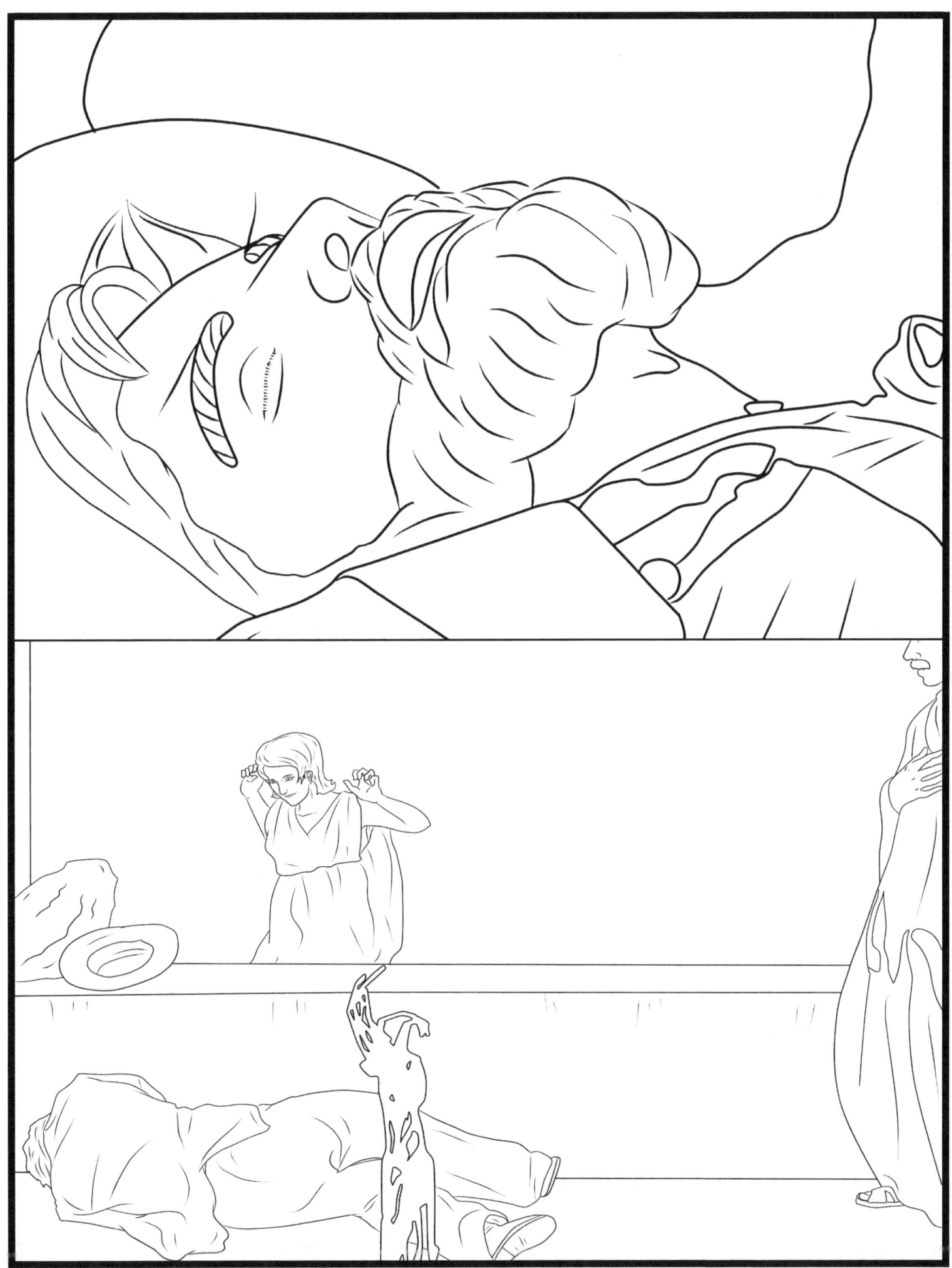

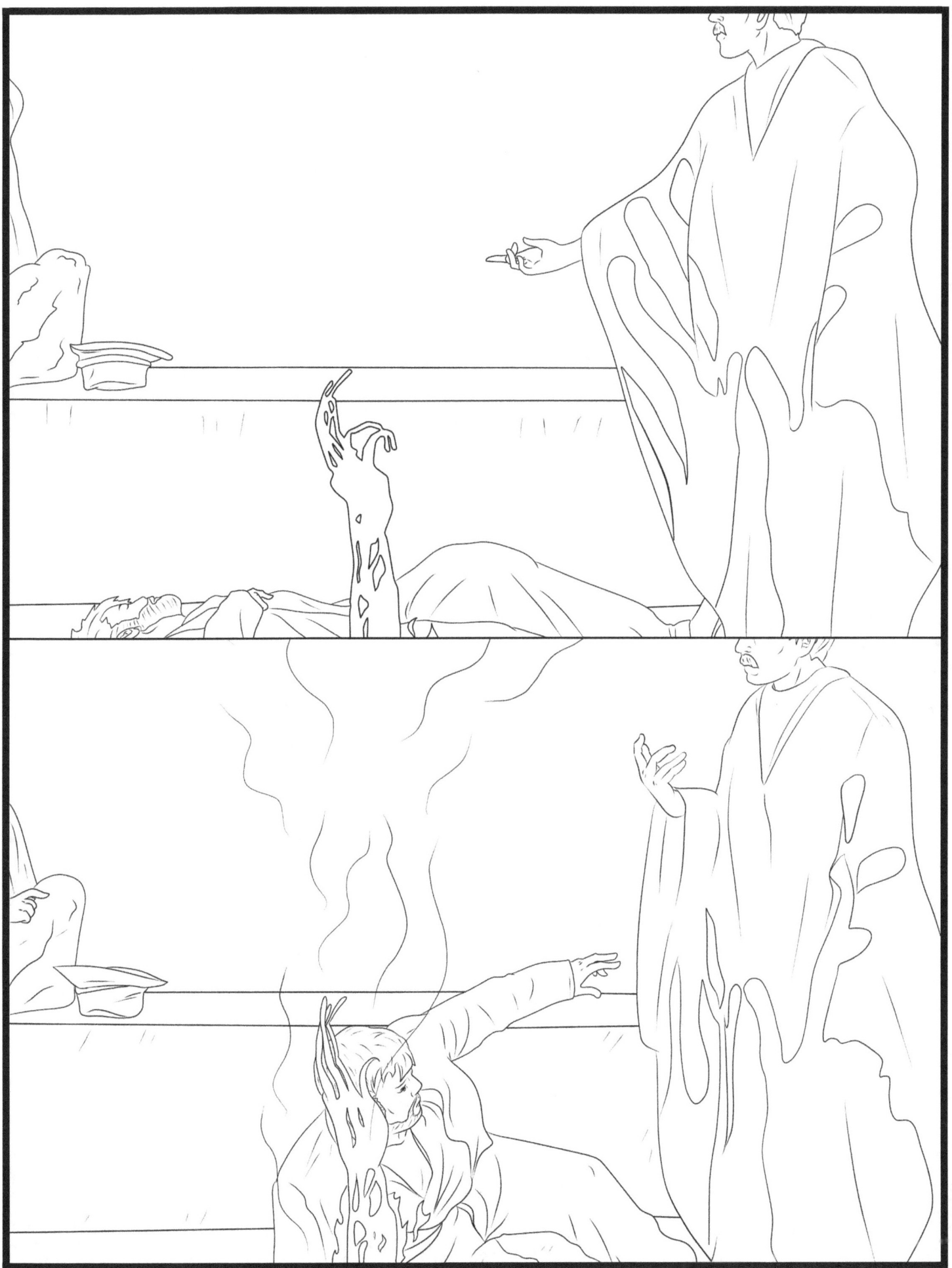

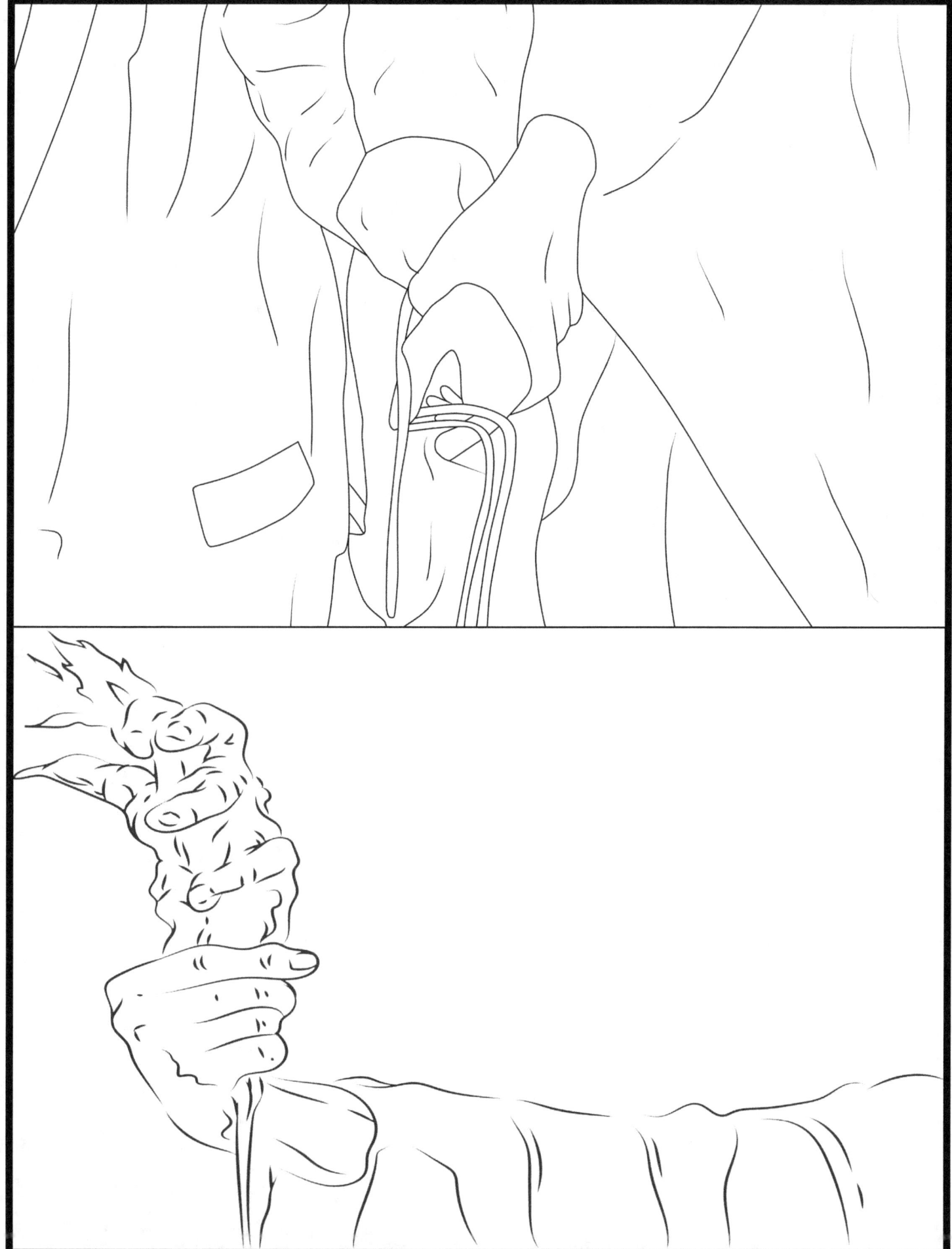

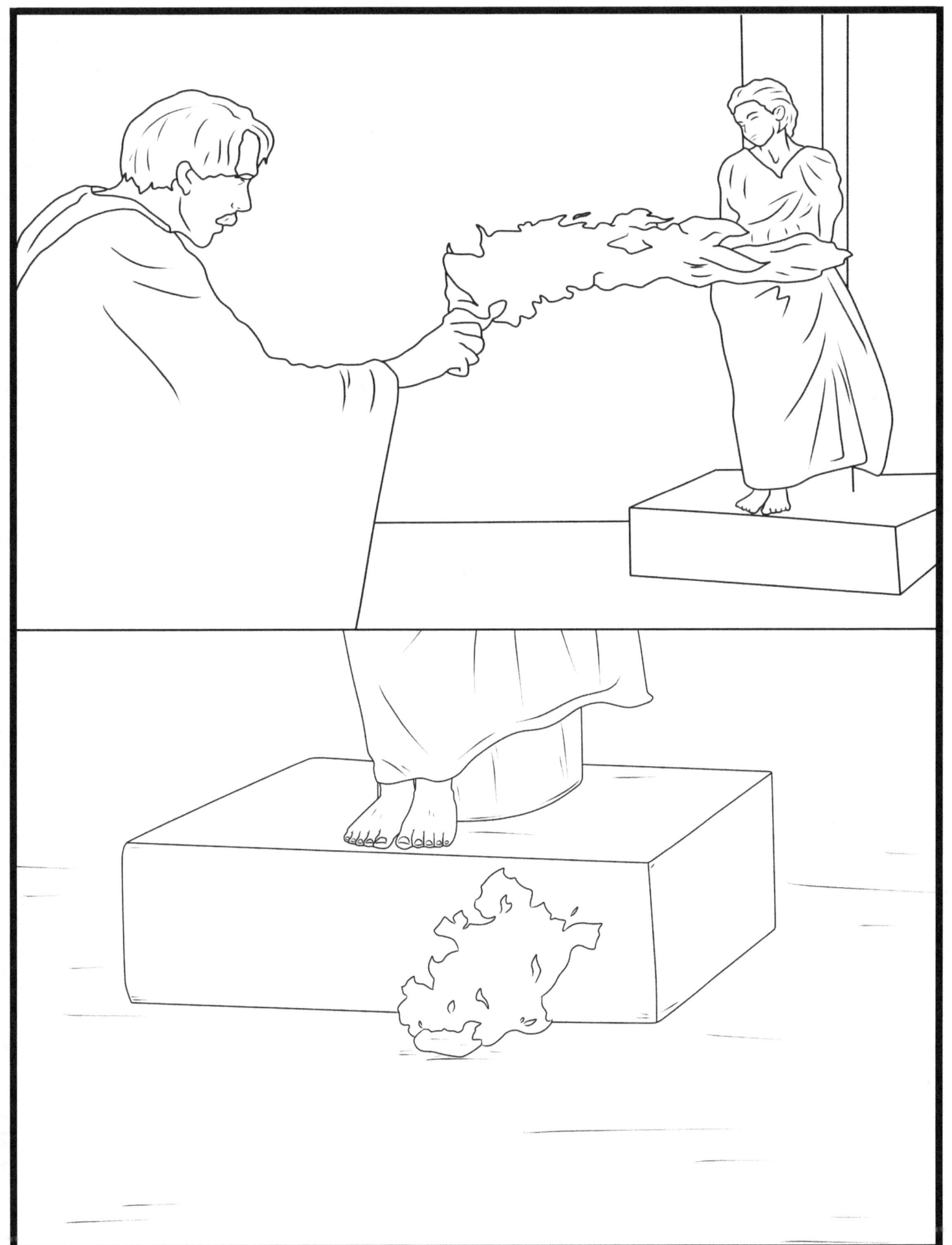

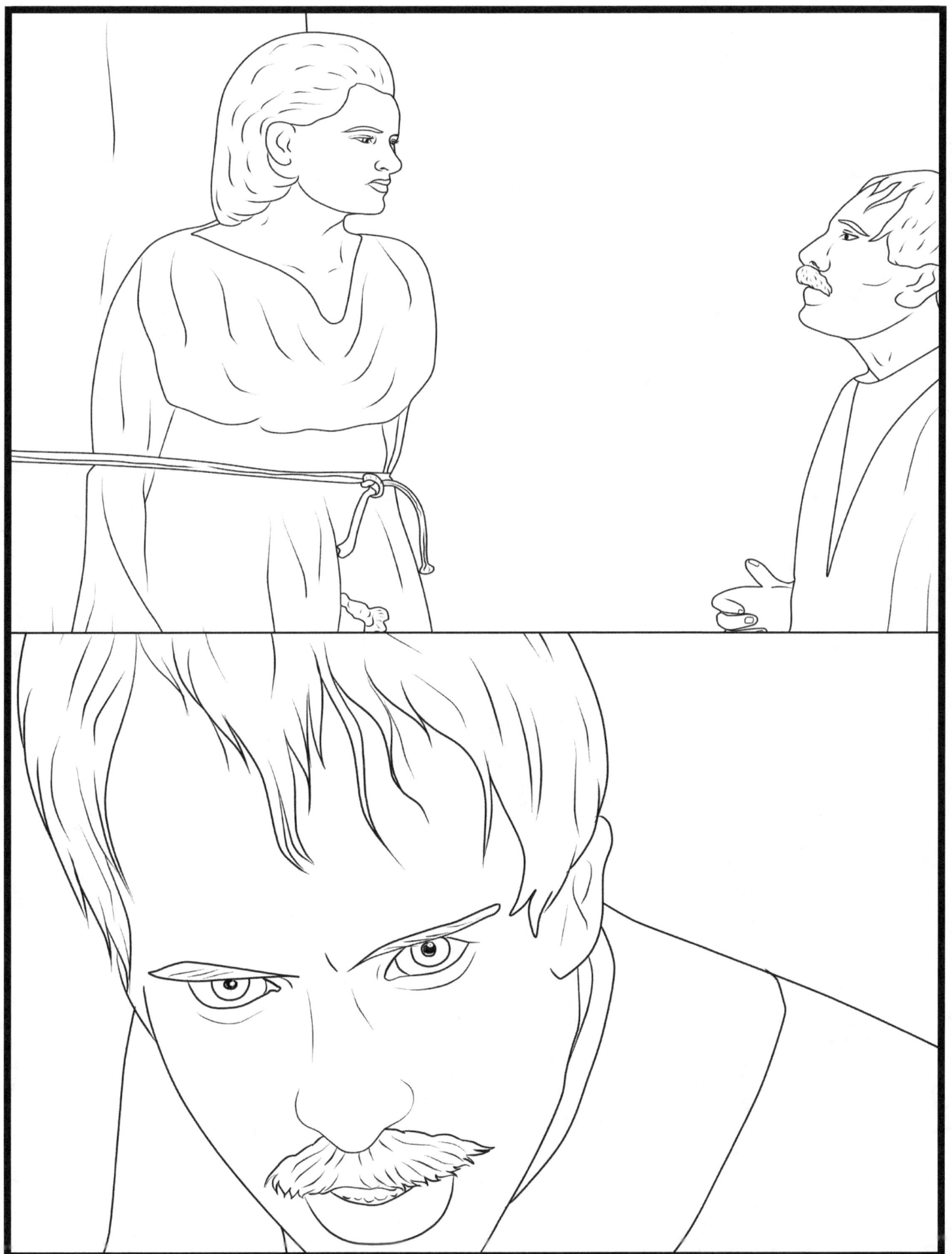

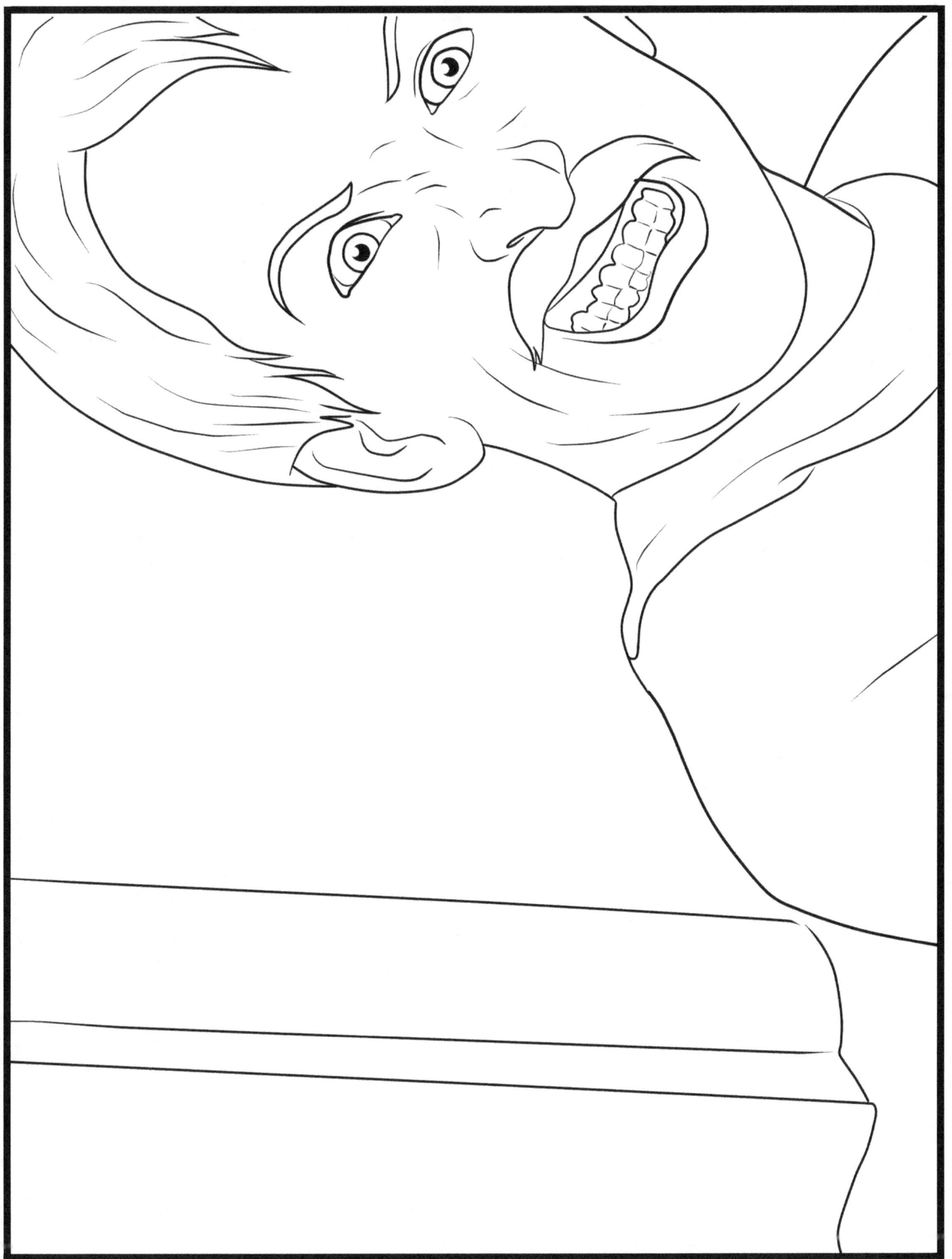

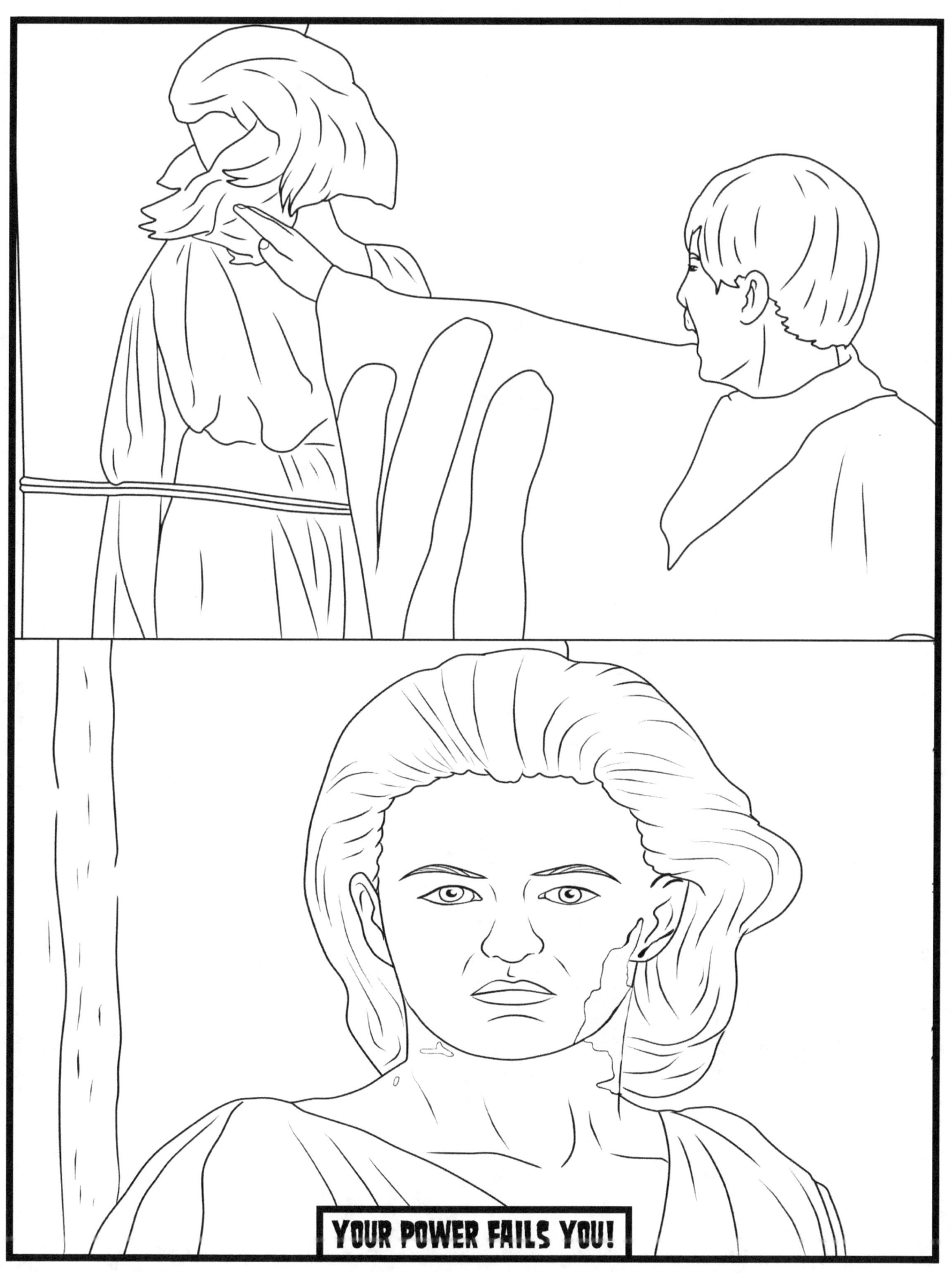

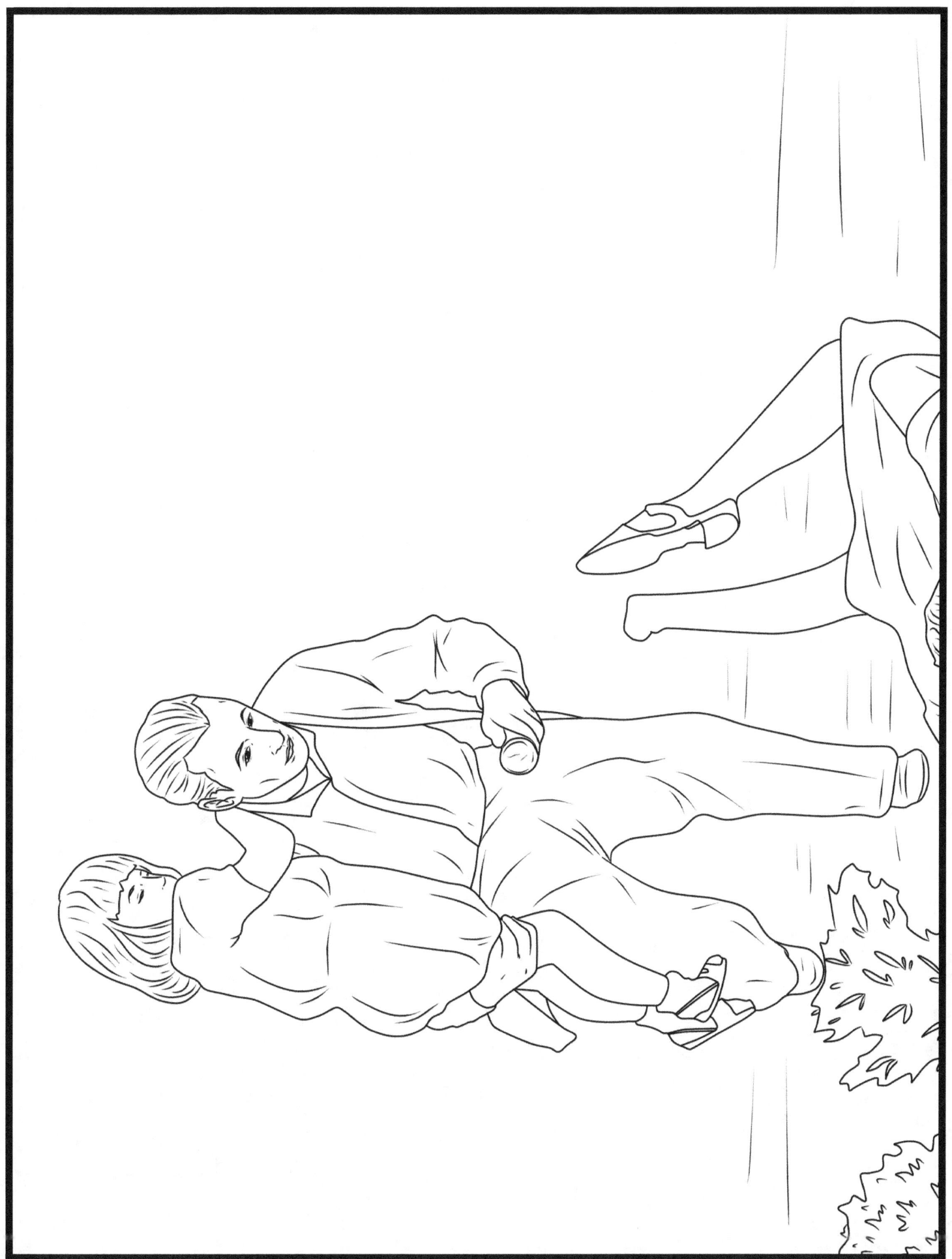

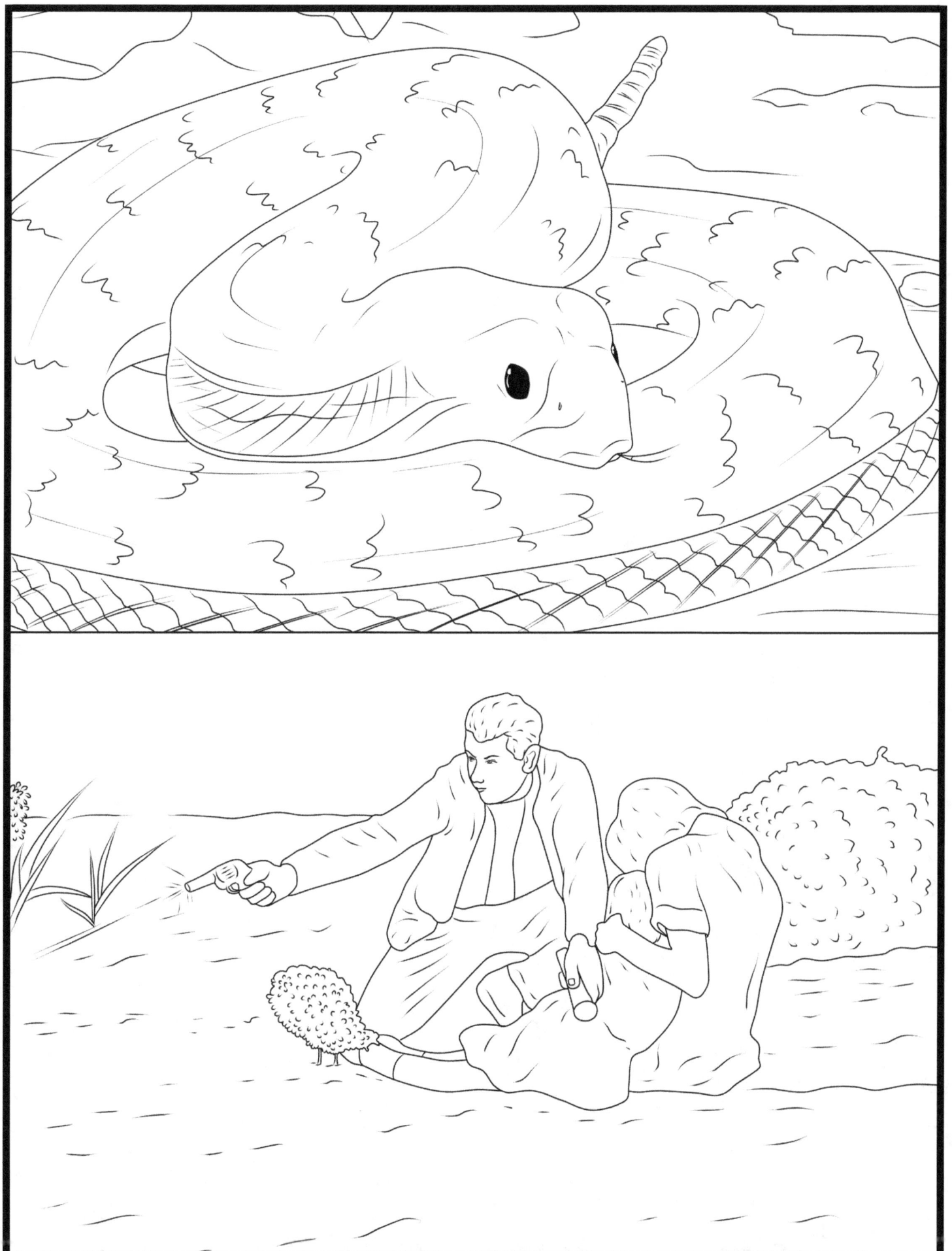

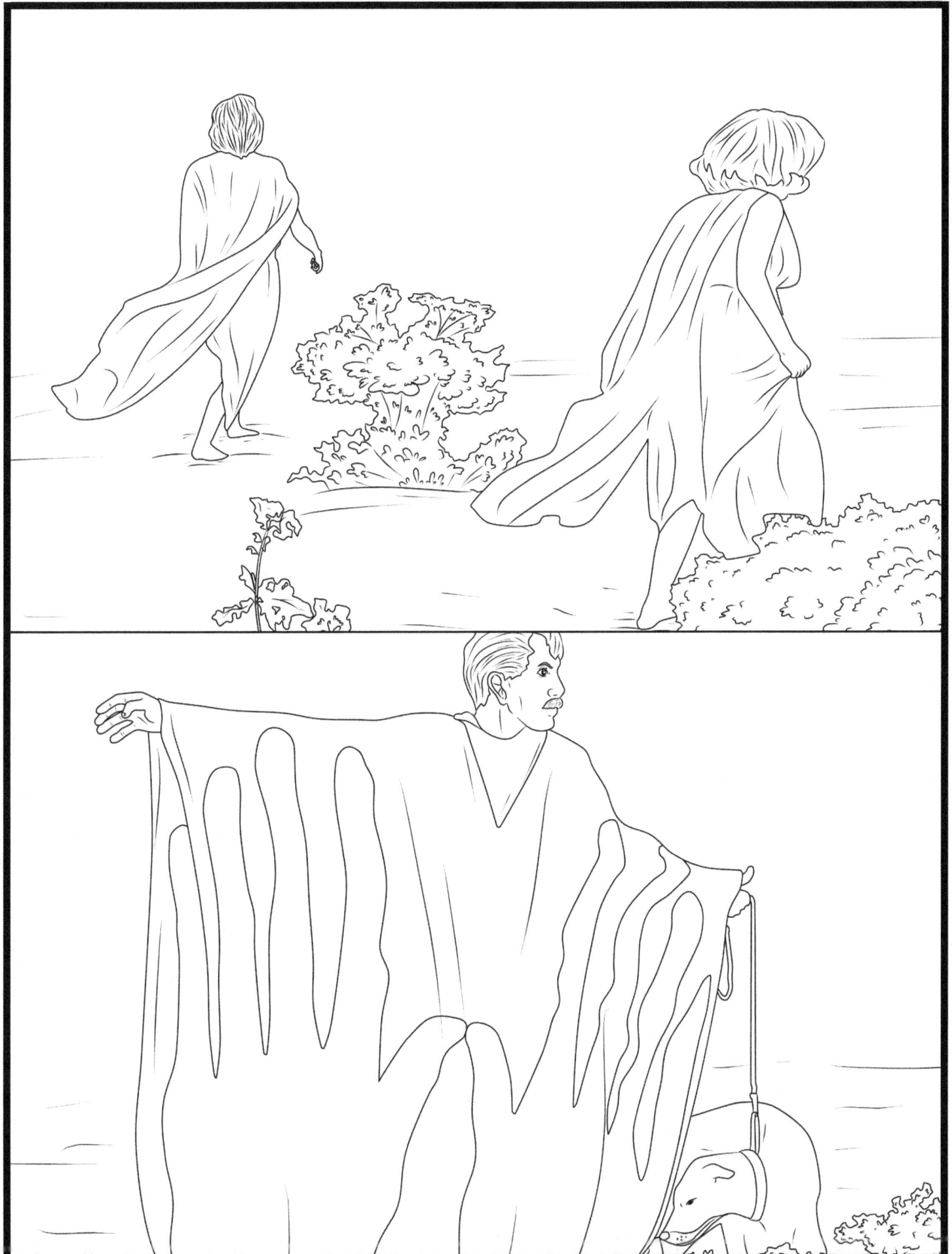

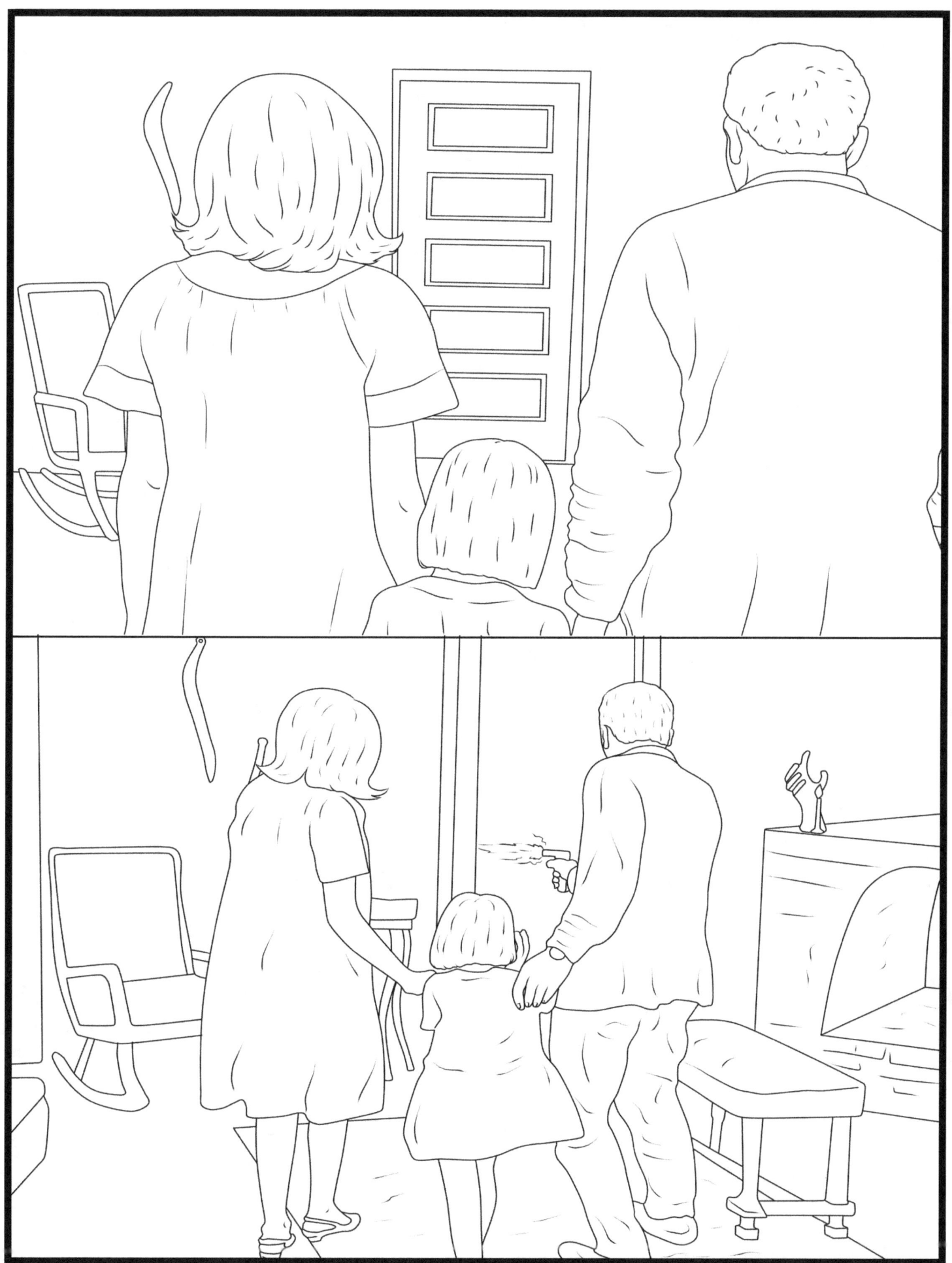

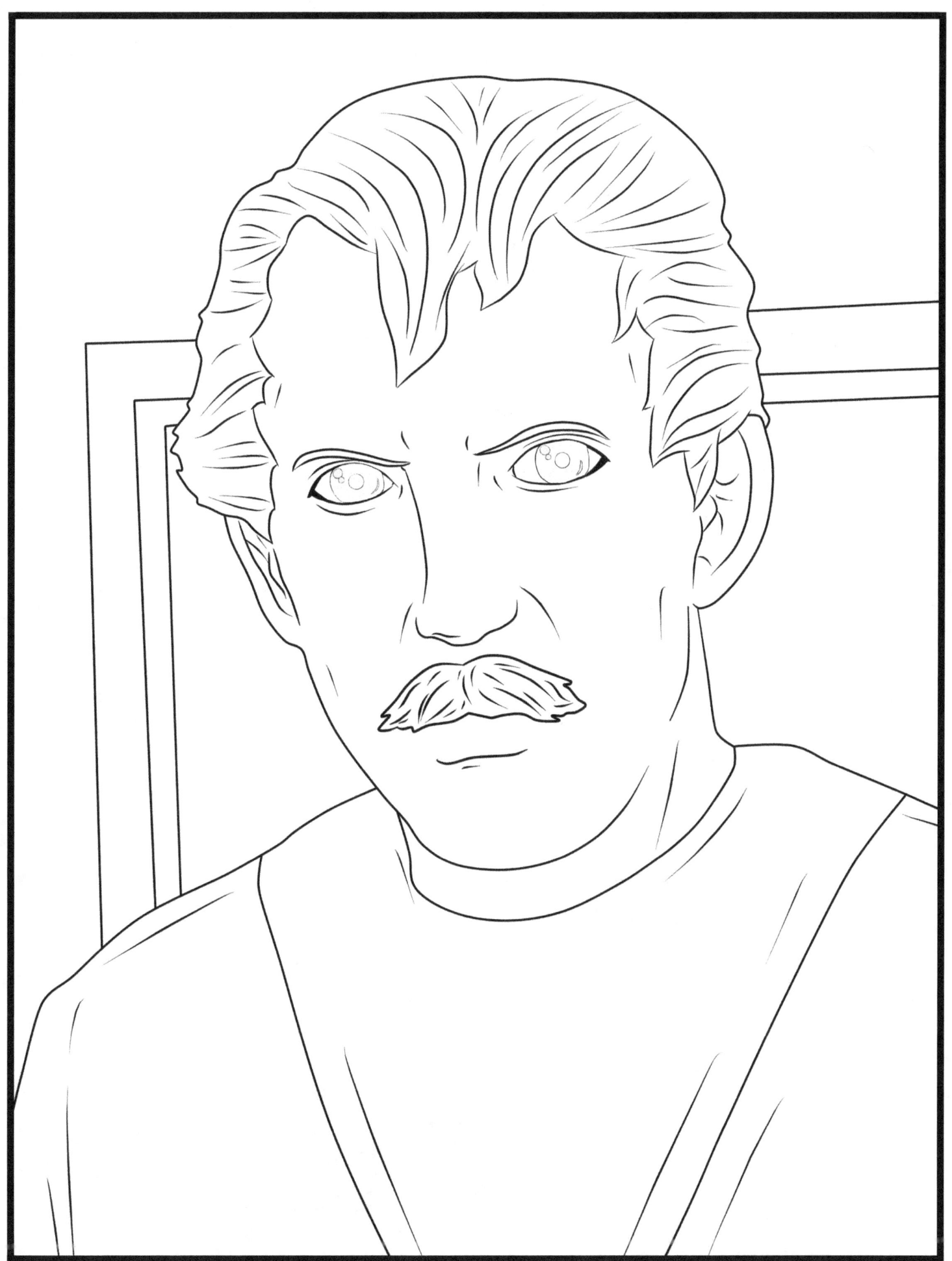

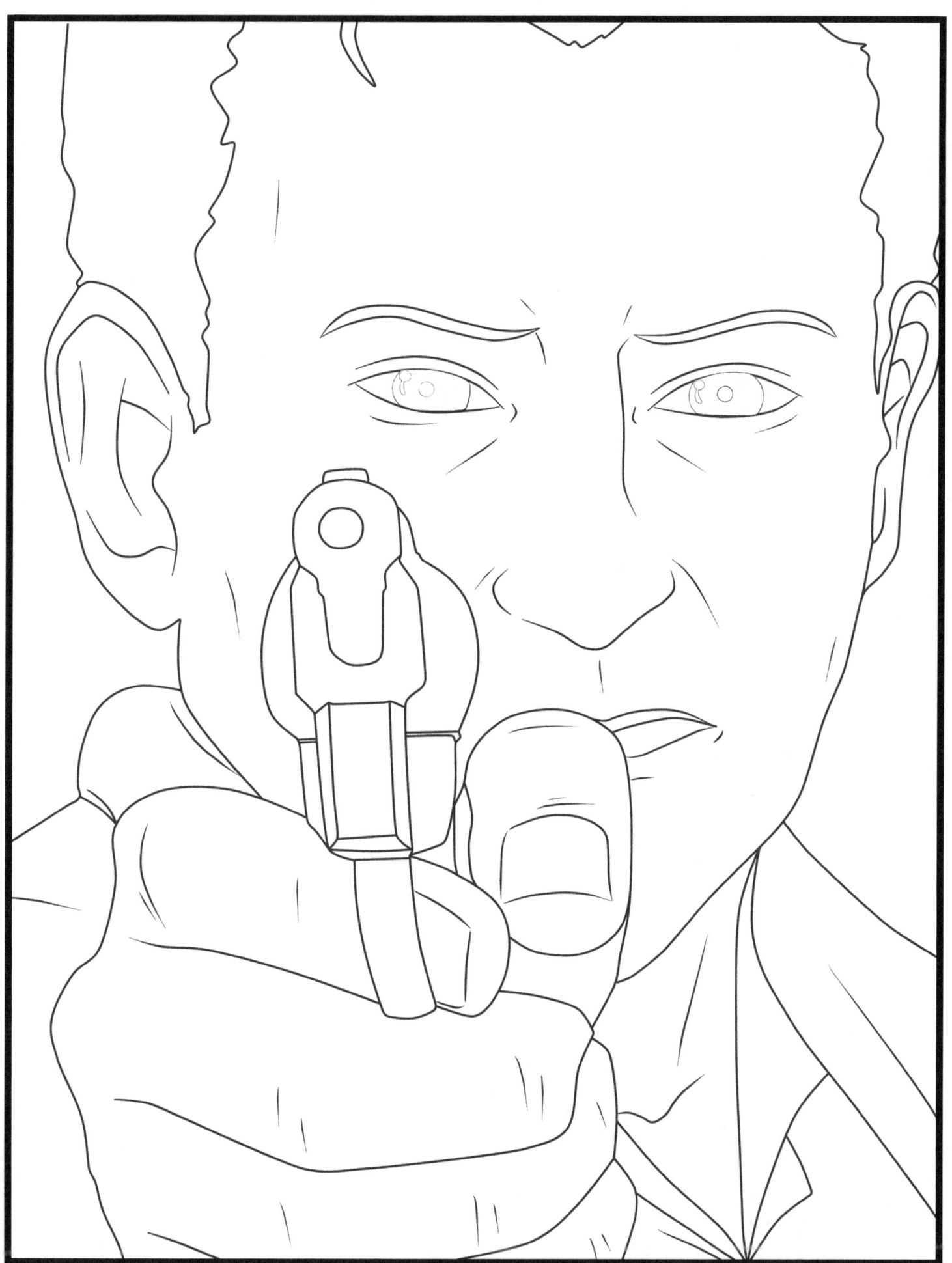

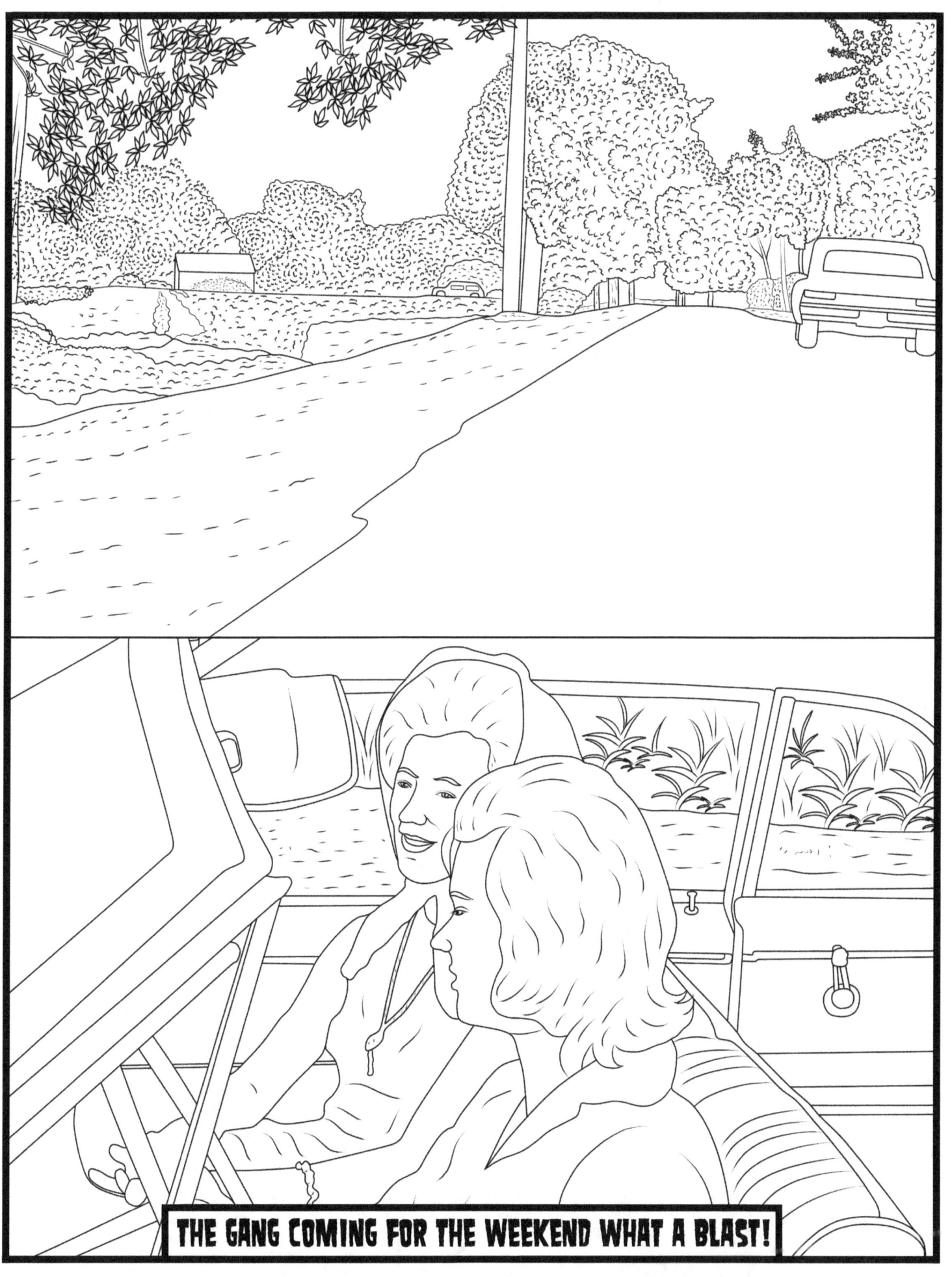

THE GANG COMING FOR THE WEEKEND WHAT A BLAST!

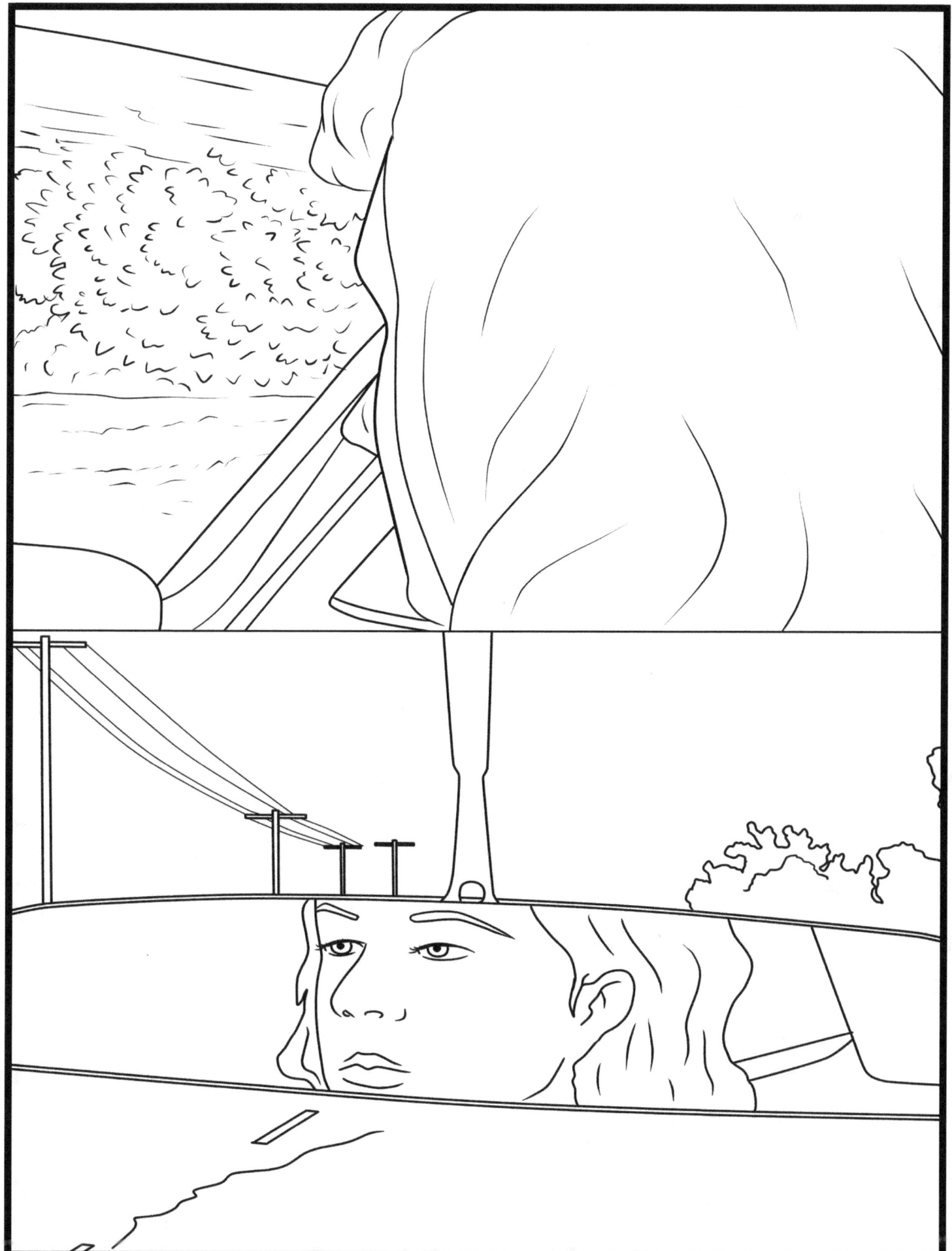

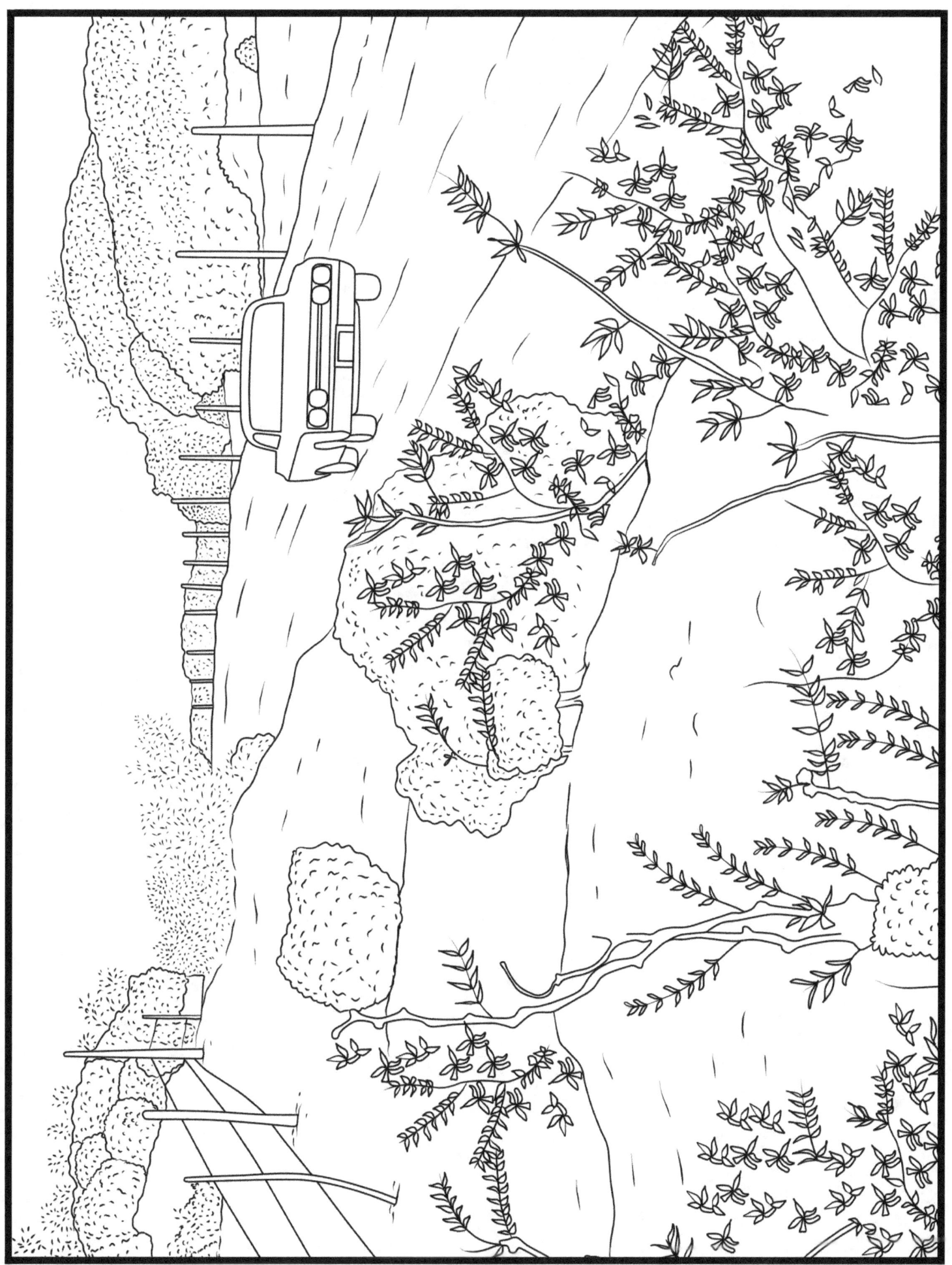

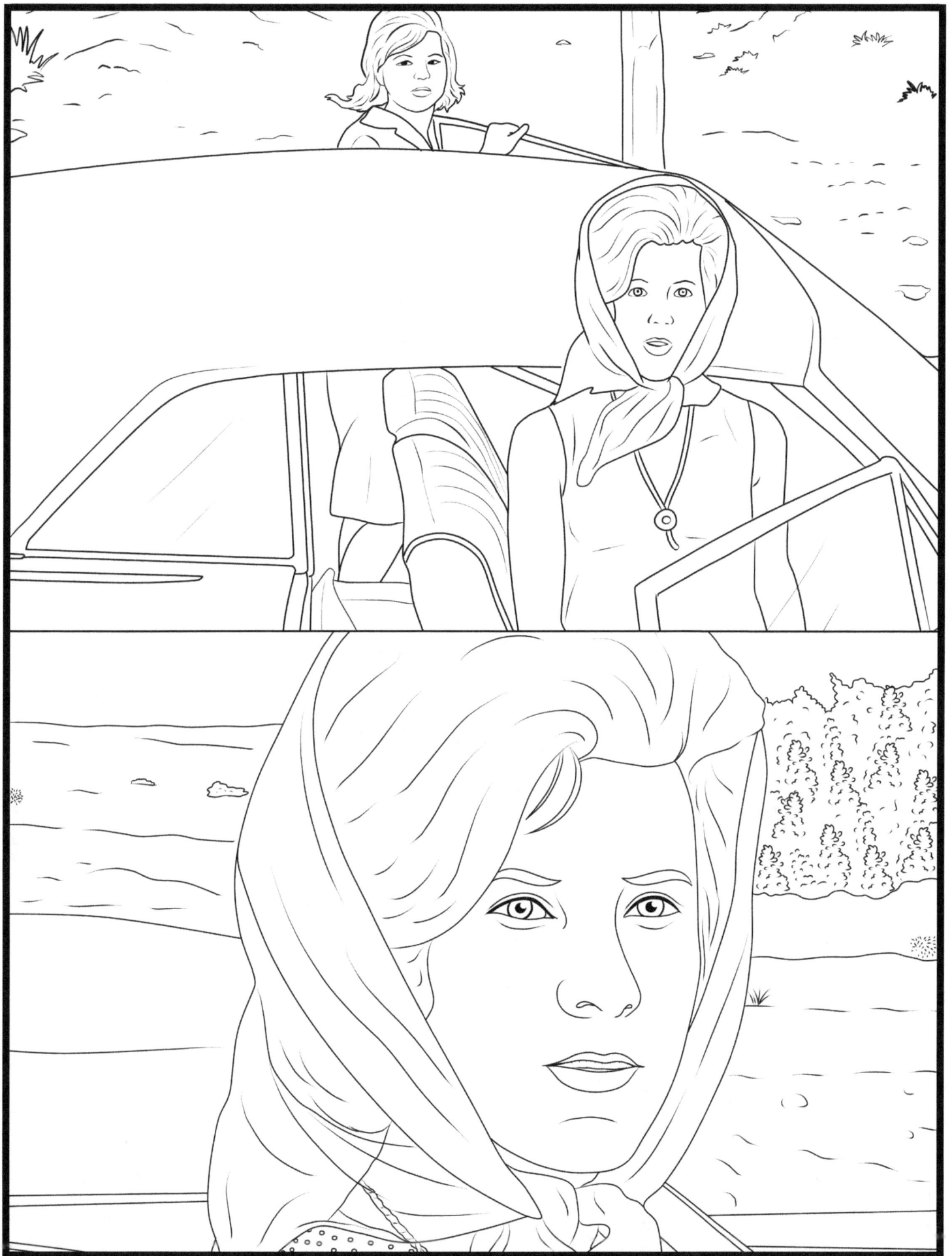

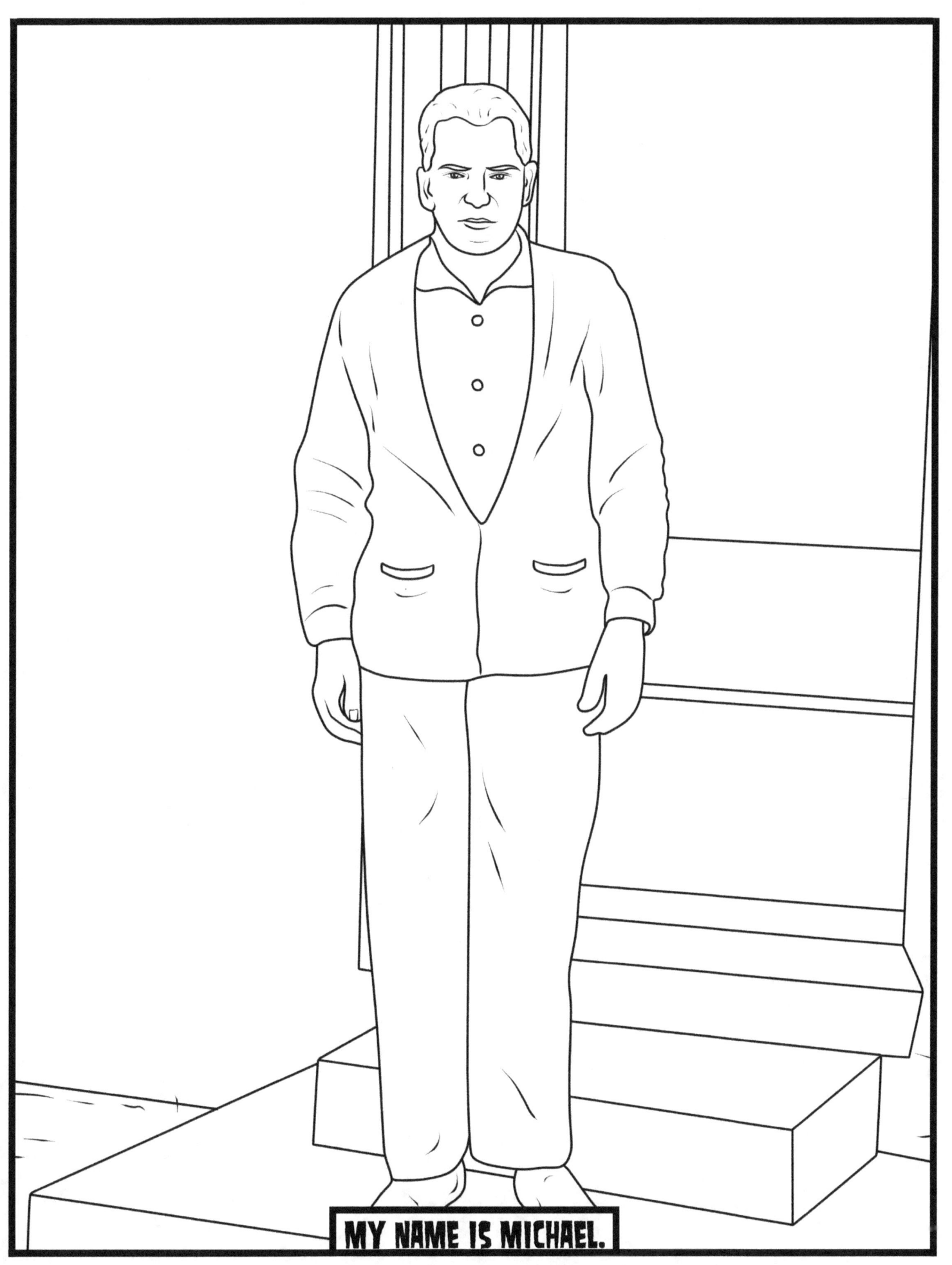

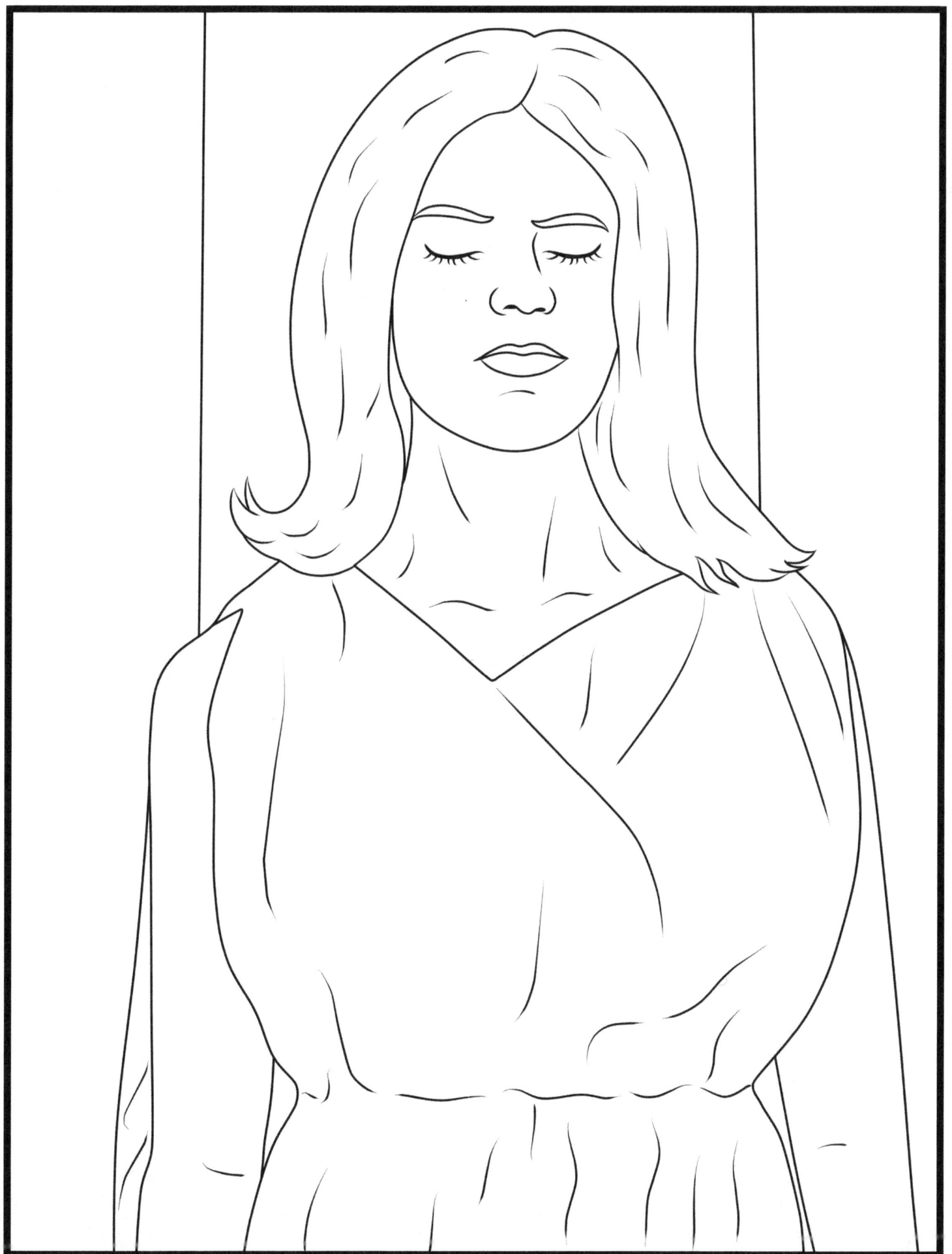

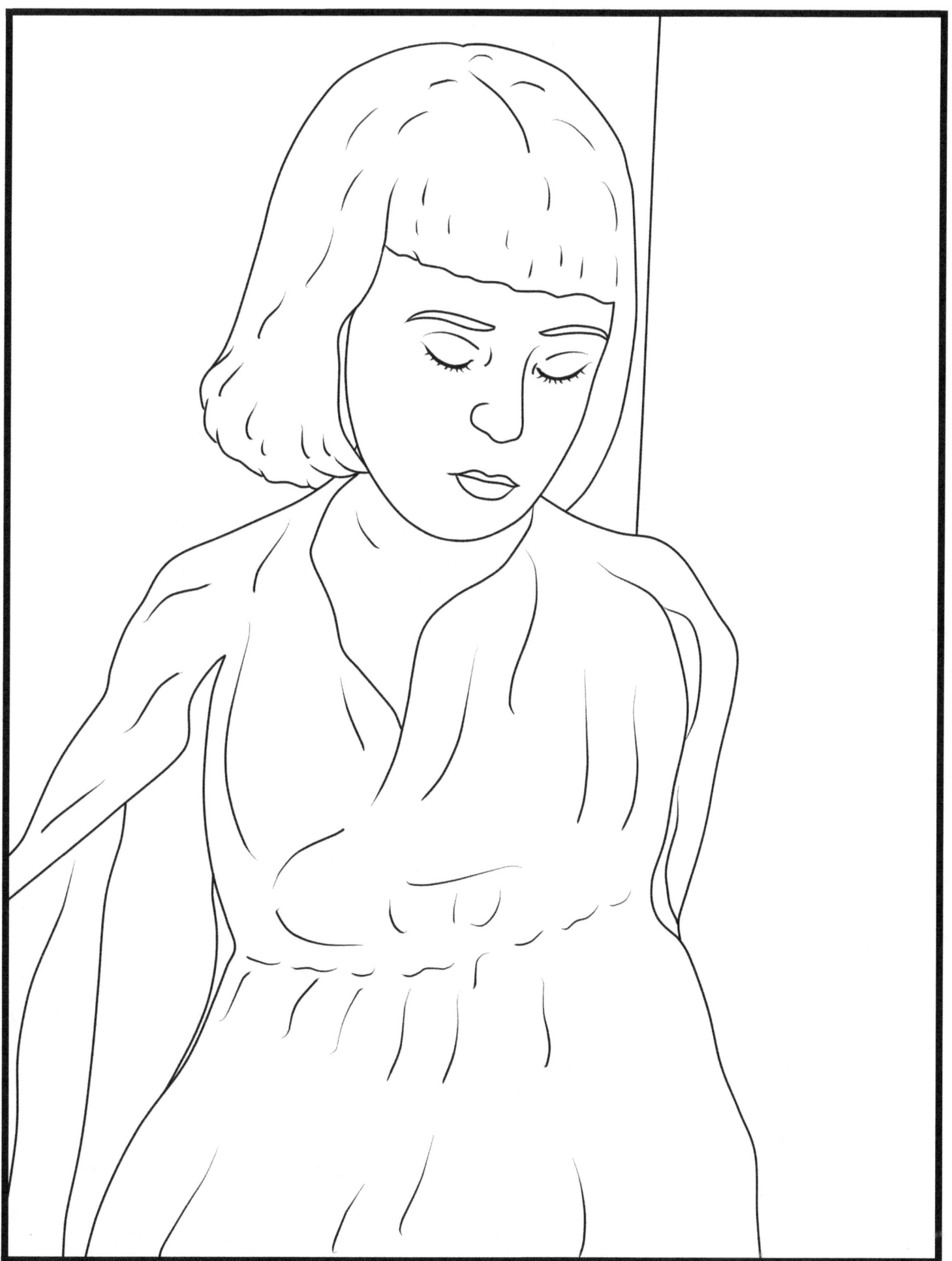

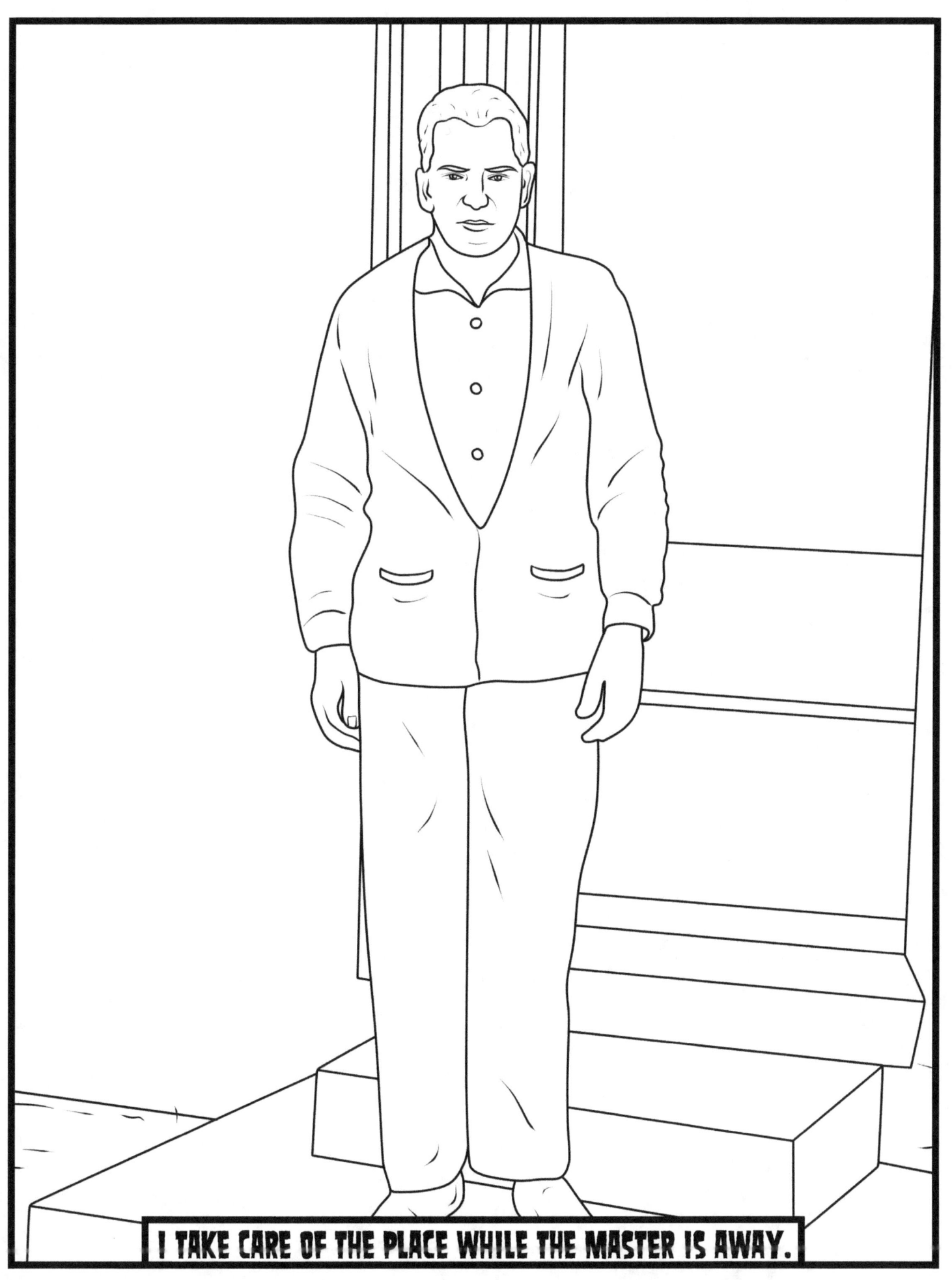

I TAKE CARE OF THE PLACE WHILE THE MASTER IS AWAY.

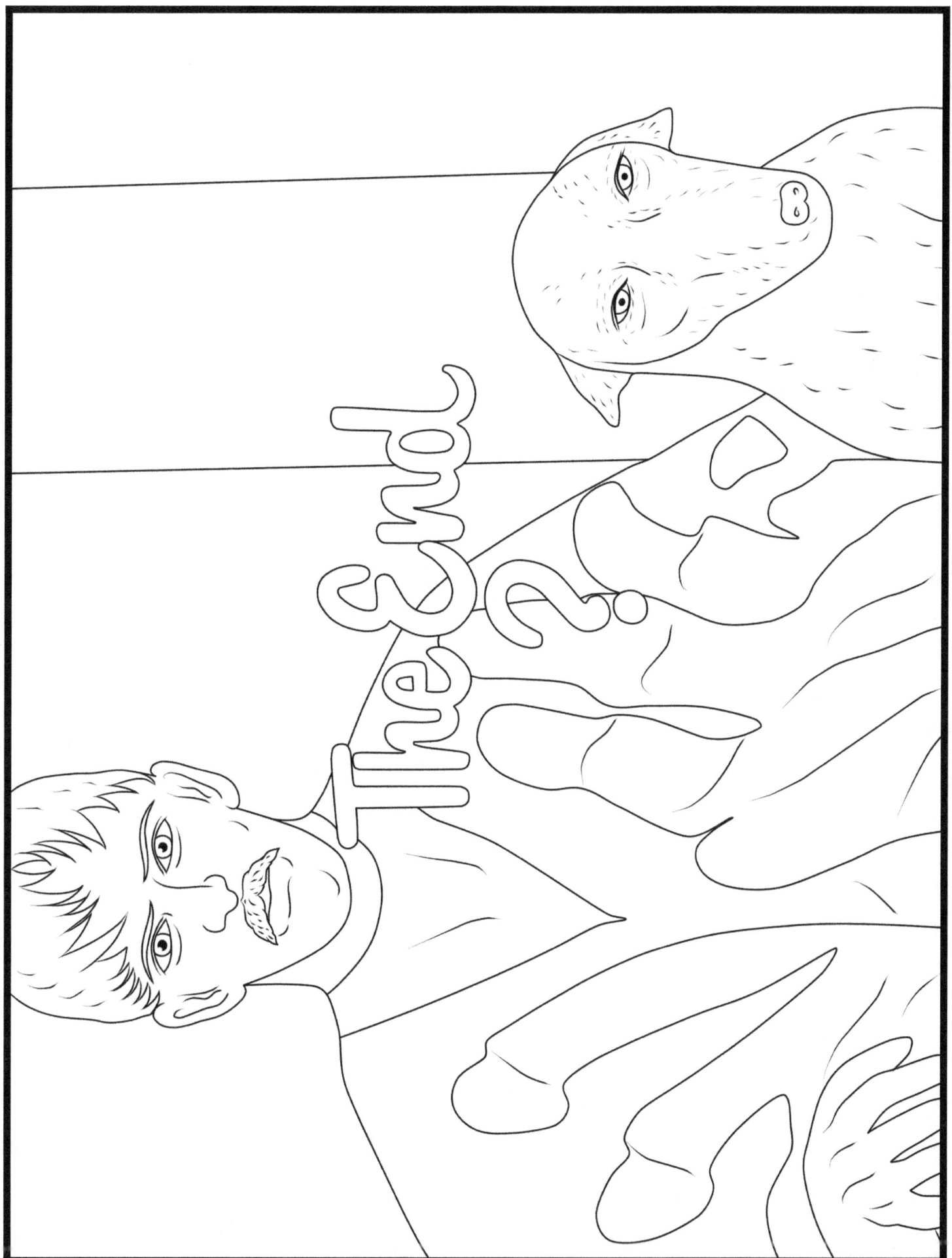

ABOUT THE AUTHOR

JORDAN COLTON IS AN AVID FAN OF HORROR & BAD MOVIES. MANOS THE HANDS OF FATE IS PROBABLY ONE OF THE BEST WORST MOVIES EVER MADE, AND DESERVED A QUALITY COLORING BOOK. HE CURRENTLY RESIDES IN UTAH WITH HIS CAT AND HORROR FILM COLLECTION.

YOU CAN LEARN MORE ABOUT HIS HORRID COLORING BOOKS AT:

WWW.HORRIDCOLORINGBOOKS.COM
USE THE PROMO CODE "TORGO" FOR FREE SHIPPING IN THE US

ALSO CHECK OUT HIS OTHER COLORING BOOKS:

VOLUME 1: THE NIGHT OF THE LIVING DEAD
VOLUME 2: THE KRAMPUS